Biographical Dictionary of Councilors of the Indies, 1717–1808

Biographical Dictionary of Councilors of the Indies, 1717–1808

Mark A. Burkholder

GREENWOOD PRESS
New York • Westport, Connecticut • London

Library of Congress Cataloging-in-Publication Data

Burkholder, Mark A., 1943-
Biographical dictionary of councilors of the Indies, 1717–1808.

Bibliography: p.
Includes index.
1. Judges—Latin America—Biography—Dictionaries.
2. Government attorneys—Latin America—Biography—
Dictionaries. 3. Spain. Consejo de Indias—Biography—
Dictionaries. I. Title.
KG81.B87 1986 347.8'014 [B] 86–401
348.0714 [B]
ISBN 0–313–24024–8 (lib. bdg. : alk. paper)

Library of Congress Catalog Card Number: 86–401
ISBN: 0–313–24024–8

First published in 1986

Greenwood Press, Inc.
88 Post Road West, Westport, Connecticut 06881

Printed in the United States of America

The paper used in this book complies with the Permanent Paper Standard issued by the National Information Standards Organization (Z39.48–1984).

10 9 8 7 6 5 4 3 2 1

For Kristen and Jennifer

CONTENTS

ACKNOWLEDGMENTS

This dictionary is based primarily on archival materials located in Spain. I am indebted to the National Endowment for the Humanities for providing the support that enabled me to spend 1984–85 working in a number of Spanish archives. I am grateful as well to the University of Missouri–St. Louis for awarding me sabbatical and research leaves and to the University of Illinois–University of Chicago Joint Center for Latin American Studies for a research fellowship enabling me to use their libraries during the summer of 1982. The Office of the Dean of Arts and Sciences at the University of Missouri–St. Louis graciously provided a word processor and dedicated operators who helped to complete this work in a timely manner.

Without the rich documentation available in Spain's archives, much of the material that the biographical entries present would have been impossible to gather. I thank the directors and staffs of the following repositories for allowing me to use their collections: the Archivo General de Indias (Seville), the Archivo General de Simancas (Simancas), the Archivo Histórico Nacional (Madrid), the Archivo de la Real Chancillería de Granada, the Archivo de la Real Chancillería de Valladolid, the Archivo Histórico Provincial y Universitario de Valladolid, the Archivo de la Universidad de Sevilla, the Archivo de la Universidad de Granada, the Archivo de la Universidad de Santo Tomás de Avila, the Archivo de la Universidad de Salamanca, the Archivo del Colegio de Santa Cruz (Valladolid), the Archivo Histórico de Protocolos (Madrid), and the Biblioteca Nacional (Madrid).

I thank my good friend D. S. Chandler for his help in collecting the material for a list of the members of the Council of the Indies. Suzanne Hiles and Lyman L. Johnson improved the introduction with their comments, and I thank them for their assistance. Finally, I thank my family for putting up with the absences that this project entailed. While I would like to foist blame on someone else for the errors and omissions this work unavoidably contains, I must claim sole responsibility.

INTRODUCTION

From the outset of his reign, Philip V took steps to improve the administration of his realms. The Council of the Indies was one of the Habsburg institutions affected by his actions, but the chaos arising from the War of the Spanish Succession delayed any definitive reform. After several earlier efforts proved unsatisfactory, he again reorganized the Council on January 20, 1717. The effort succeeded, and the Council entered a period of stability that continued until the Napoleonic invasion of Spain in 1808.

Once the supreme tribunal and administrative body for the affairs of the New World, the Council of the Indies saw its authority eroded in the seventeenth century. The creation of a Secretariat of State (or Ministry) of the Indies in 1714 vested in the hands of a single man much of the power and responsibility that had once resided with the Council. Nonetheless, the Council remained the supreme judicial tribunal for the Indies and retained important patronage responsibilities as well. Over the course of the eighteenth century, moreover, its importance increased. In a crucial decree issued in 1773, Charles III declared the Council of the Indies equal to the Council of Castile and the apex (*de término*) of a chain of promotion (*ascenso*) within the judicial bureaucracy. Thenceforth its members enjoyed rank, salaries, and prerogatives equal to those received by councilors and *fiscales* of Castile. Following the division of the former responsibilities of the Ministry of the Indies among five ministries in 1790, the Council of the Indies remained the only body whose sole focus was on the affairs of the New World. The expansion in the number of councilors from nine in 1717 to twenty-nine in 1808 reflected its increased importance.

This dictionary provides a basic reference work for students of the Spanish Empire by presenting biographical entries for the 172 men who were named to or served on the Council of the Indies from the reorganization of 1717 to the French invasion in 1808. The format parallels that employed in *Biographical Dictionary of Audiencia Ministers in the Americas, 1687–1821,*[1] and for those ministers who served on a New World court before advancing to the Council, the entries are in some cases almost identical. For these overlapping entries, however, the present work is preferred, for it incorporates archival material found since the earlier publication.

To provide a general framework for appreciating the common and unique characteristics of the men profiled in the dictionary, the introduction will consider the Council's growth in the eighteenth century, the regional origins, educational and family backgrounds, wives, and children of the ministers, the upward social mobility achieved through ministerial careers, the appointment process, periodization of appointments, and the way in which ministers ended their careers. The ministers of the robe (*ministros togados*), ministers of the cape and sword (*ministros de capa y espada*), crown attorneys (*fiscales*), and the presidents and governors will receive separate attention.

The analysis of appointments focuses on the 159 men who were named councilors (*ministros togados* and *ministros de capa y espada*) or *fiscales* of the Council for the first time. The term "ministers" is at times employed when the councilors and *fiscales* are combined. "*Letrado*" is employed when the analysis includes both *ministros togados* and *fiscales* and also when referring in general to men trained in the law. The following persons have entries but except when noted are not included in the analysis, for their initial appointment to the Council did not fall within the time period covered: Governor and Presidents Pez, Portocarrero, and Zúñiga y Guzmán; the *ministros togados* Alarcón, Ibáñez de Mendoza, Machado, Pérez de Araciel, Rojas y Ortega, Valcárcel Formento, and Zúñiga y Tovar; and the *ministros de capa y espada* Carnero, Silva y Meneses, and Ubilla.

When created in 1524, the Council had a president, four or five councilors, a crown attorney, and various subalterns. The first councilors were either *letrados* or clerics who probably had studied law. By the end of the sixteenth century, the number of councilors had increased and the staff had expanded. In 1600 a new body within the Council was created. Called the Cámara of the Indies, it was charged with overseeing patronage, and in particular with recommending candidates for many high-ranking civil and ecclesiastical posts in the Indies. Its first life was brief, however. It was abolished in 1609 and not reestablished until 1644.

In 1626 Philip IV began to appoint a different kind of councilor. These men, almost none of whom had any training in law, were called *ministros de capa y espada* to distinguish them from the *letrados* who were referred to as *oidores* or, in the more common eighteenth-century usage, *ministros togados*. However, while the backgrounds of the two types of councilors were substantially different, their responsibilities on the Council were identical except in one important regard. Since *ministros de capa y espada*, like most viceroys or captains general in the colonies, lacked training in law, the Crown prohibited them from voting on judicial matters. They could, however, participate in the Council's legislative, executive, and advisory functions, and were eligible for appointment to the Cámara of the Indies.

The sixteenth century was the apogee of the Council's existence. During the seventeenth century it found its powers gradually being eroded and the quality of its "ministers," in particular those *de capa y espada*, declining as a monarchy weakened by war and a depressed economy could not resist the pressures of its exhausted purse and penurious nobles anxious to benefit from royal largess. In 1683, the Marqués de Yscar purchased an appointment as a minister *de capa y espada* for 60,000 pesos.[2] A particularly shameless abuse of patronage was the appointment to the Council in 1695 of a nine-year-old boy, José María Francisco de la Cerda Manrique de Lara, Marqués de la Laguna and Conde de Paredes, as a minister *de capa y espada*.[3] This came about as a reward for the services of his father, a former councilor and viceroy of New Spain.

As the seventeenth century drew to a close the Council had a president or governor, eight regular (*número*) positions of *ministro togado*, and two positions *de capa y espada* as set forth in the organizational plan (*planta*) of July 17, 1691. Supernumerary appointees raised the number of ministers to nineteen by 1700.[4] The advent of Philip V and the attendant disruption caused by the War of the Spanish Succession, however, shattered the previous organizational stability and so aggravated the Crown's financial woes that it stooped to selling appointments to *letrado* positions on the Council.

On March 6, 1701, Philip abolished the Cámara of the Indies. Then, in a decree of September 27, 1706, he reduced the positions of *ministro togado* to four and those of *capa y espada* to two. In a dramatic but short-lived reversal of this reduction, by a decree of November 10, 1713, Philip expanded the number of ministers to twenty, ten *togado* and ten *de capa y espada*. Simultaneously he created three presidencies in place of the former single presidency or governorship, reduced the two *fiscalías* to one, and added two *abogados generales*. Within two years he reduced this unwieldy group by a decree of August 5, 1715, to a single president, eight *ministros togados*, two *ministros de capa y espada*, and two *fiscales*. The following April 29 he reestablished the Cámara, but almost immediately, on September 11, 1717, he abolished it again. Not until December 22, 1721, did the Cámara resume a stable and permanent existence.

In the midst of these various short-lived modifications to the Council made in the early and mid–1710s, Philip took one action that profoundly affected its future. As part of a major effort to organize government to provide greater efficiency through increased centralization and identification of individual responsibility, Philip created secretaries of state in 1714. Unlike the men who held the title under the Habsburgs, the new secretaries (or "ministers" as they were sometimes called) enjoyed extensive, formally delegated responsibility over their portfolios. In establishing a secretary of state for the Indies, Philip substantially reduced the Council's previous authority over the colonies. While it remained unchallenged in its judicial powers and continued to enjoy patronage responsibilities over judicial and ecclesiastical positions, the Council lost competence to the secretary of state in financial, military, commercial, and general administrative matters. The reduced size of the Council, decreed on January 20, 1717, reflected its diminished authority.

The decree of 1717 authorized a position of president or governor, six positions of *ministro togado*, two positions of *ministro de capa y espada*, and two *fiscales*. Although the Council's size would grow over time, subsequent changes were primarily responses to the increased business arising from an empire whose population and economy were expanding, particularly after about mid-century, rather than sporadic and aimless numerical adjustments. The 1717 decree was extremely important as it marked the return to organizational stability. Until the War of Independence following the French invasion of 1808, the Council functioned without major disruption.

Between 1717 and 1808, the Crown named eight presidents or governors, seventy-nine *ministros togados*, sixty *ministros de capa y espada*, and twenty-seven *fiscales* to the Council of the Indies who had not held these positions previously. Forty of the ministers were named to the Cámara by 1808. Because of overlap among the positions, a total of 162 men were involved. One hundred fifty-nine of these men held at least one position as a "minister"; they form the base for the analysis that follows. Ninety-nine of them were *letrados*; and sixty were *de capa y espada*. The remaining three, Pez y Malzarraga,* Zúñiga y Guzmán,* and Portocarrero Guzmán Luna,* held the office of governor or president of the Council and have been omitted from the group analysis although there are entries on them.

The *camaristas* were the elite group of the Council. The king named them to their positions without a recommendation by any official body. It appears on the basis of very sketchy evidence that the president or governor of the Council of the Indies and the secretary of state for the Indies and subsequently for Grace and Justice suggested possible *camaristas* to the king. The general guideline, which was followed faithfully from its reestablishment in 1721 until the death of Mangino Fernández de Lima* in 1806, was that the Cámara should include both *capa y espada* and *togado* ministers. Beyond this, the extent of experience as a Council member was often taken into account.

Given the importance of seniority for advancement in the Spanish bureaucracy, one might assume that the Crown would promote its most experienced Council ministers to the Cámara. In the cases of Goyeneche y Balanza* and Munive y Tello*, it certainly did. Thirty-seven years had elapsed for Goyeneche and thirty-five for Munive since their first appointments to the Council, although neither had been present on the Council continuously. Their cases, however, were unusual. No more than seven of the forty-six (six had original Council appointments before 1717 and are not included in the basic list of 159 men) *camaristas* named had over twenty years of service on the Council. At the other extreme, between 1725 and 1759, five *capa y espada* ministers were named directly to the Cámara without any previous experience on the Council. Leaving aside these twelve cases, the remaining thirty-four ministers had served on the Council from two to nineteen years when advanced to the Cámara. They averaged ten years of prior Council service.

Although only one *camarista* had been born in the Indies, twenty others had experience there. Indeed, after the 1773 decree creating equality between the Coun-

*An asterisk (*) after a name indicates that there is an entry on that person in this work.

cils of the Indies and Castile, only five of eighteen *camaristas* named had not served in the New World. Thus, in its last thirty-five years before 1808, the Cámara was heavily composed of "old hands" who had personal knowledge of the variety of experience desired in men named to posts in the New World.

The fact that the Cámara of the Indies in the eighteenth century had both ministers *de capa y espada* and *letrados* distinguished it from the Cámara of Castile. Aside from the presiding officer, who might be *de capa y espada*, the Cámara of Castile was made up of *letrados*. A large proportion of these *letrados* were men who had been affiliated with the prestigious *colegios mayores* located at the universities of Salamanca, Alcalá de Henares, and Valladolid. Already in the seventeenth century alumni of the *colegios mayores* had established themselves as the cream of the *letrado* bureaucracy. While the *colegios* came under attack in the latter third of the eighteenth century, their alumni continued to be well represented on the Cámara of Castile. Thirty-one of the sixty-four *camaristas* who served on that Cámara from 1717 to 1808 had belonged to a *colegio mayor*. In contrast, only ten of the forty-six *camaristas* of the Indies had been *colegiales*. Excluding the nineteen *capa y espada* ministers from the total increases the percentage to thirty-seven, still significantly lower than the 48 percent for the Cámara of Castile.

Given the different composition of the two cámaras, one would expect a higher percentage of *colegiales* to be named to the Council of Castile than to the Council of the Indies. This, in fact, was the case. Forty-two percent (ninety-five) of the *ministros togados* named to the Council of Castile had been *colegiales* in contrast to thirty-four percent (twenty-seven men) for the Council of the Indies.

The Crown named men to the Council of the Indies in one of two ways. One was to appoint a minister after a *consulta* or formal personnel recommendation by either the Cámara of Castile until the middle of the eighteenth century (the last confirmed case occurred in 1744) or, later, by the Cámara of the Indies. The other way was to make the appointment by royal decree without a preceding *consulta*. The difference between the two methods had significant implications for patronage. When a cámara was involved, there was invariably a concern that the men proposed meet appropriate professional qualifications. On the other hand, the king could name someone by decree without explicit consideration of such qualifications. If counseled by a knowledgeable adviser, the king could make excellent appointments without a cámara's advice. However, an examination of appointments to courts throughout Spain and the Indies during the eighteenth century indicates that when men of questionable credentials were named, their apppointment was more apt to have come via decree than *consulta*.

Although the Cámara of Castile routinely recommended men without legal training for provincial positions in Spain, neither it nor the Cámara of the Indies made recommendations for *ministros de capa y espada*. Uniformly these men were named by decree. In contrast, thirty-nine of seventy-nine appointments of new *ministros togados* from 1717 to 1808 took place after a cámara had made a recommendation.

The first twenty-four appointments of *ministros togados* took place during the years from 1717 to 1744 in which the Cámara of Castile was involved in staffing the

Council of the Indies. Twelve of the appointments were made following a *consulta*. In six of these cases, the candidate ranked first by the Cámara was appointed; in the remaining six cases the men named were not even among the candidates proposed for the position. Nine other appointments were made by decree, and circumstantial evidence suggests the remaining three were as well.

Between 1752 and 1773, when a decree declaring the Councils of Castile and the Indies equal was issued, all sixteen *ministros togados* named to the Council of the Indies were appointed by decree. Neither cámara was involved in any of the advancements.

Following the 1773 decree of equality, thirty-nine men were promoted to the Council of the Indies. From the decree to 1788, seventeen of the twenty-one appointments came after a *consulta* by the Cámara of the Indies. Then followed a decade and a half in which eight of eleven appointments were made by decree and at least one of the remaining three appointees was not recommended for the position by any *camarista*. The final seven appointments were made by *consulta*. In at least six cases the Cámara's first choice was named.

Except in rare circumstances, ministers on the Council of the Indies, whether *togado*, *de capa y espada*, or *fiscales*, received identical salaries. Beginning in 1763 *camaristas* received additional compensation for their labors. The men named when the Council was reorganized in 1717 received 3,600 *escudos* a year. This remained the standard annual salary for several years. Beginning with the appointment of Mutiloa y Lodosa* on November 20, 1725, however, ministers began to receive 4,000 *escudos* or 40,000 *reales de vellón*. This amount remained in effect until a general upward revision of salaries for all judicial tribunals in Spain on January 12, 1763. By a decree of that date, members of the Council would henceforth receive 48,000 *reales de vellón* and *camaristas* would receive 50,000 *reales*. The sums were high if compared to salaries of the *oidores* of Spain's audiencias who received only 18,000 *reales* but noticeably less than the 55,000 *reales* earned by councilors of Castile and the 66,000 *reales* paid to *camaristas* of Castile. This disparity in salaries remained until the decree of equality in 1773. Henceforth, members of the Council and Cámara of the Indies received the same amount enjoyed by their counterparts on the Council of Castile.

Although ministers received substantial salaries, their expenses were considerable as well. In addition to travel expenses from one post to another, advancement routinely brought the necessity to pay the *media anata*, or half of the first year's salary of the new position. Although the terms of payment were made easier in 1774 when men were given four years to pay and ultimately only the increase in salary was taxed, repeated advancements could be a financial burden. Thus ministers appreciated the opportunity to earn extra compensation. For example, Gutiérrez de Piñeres,* Escobedo Ocaña y Alarcón,* and Jacot Ortiz Rojano Ruiz de la Escalera* served successively as the legal adviser to the tribunal of the *comisaria general de cruzada* for an additional 9,000 *reales de vellón* a year.

By the same decree that increased salaries for ministers in 1763, Charles III established a pension fund for the widows, surviving minor children, and unmarried daughters of ministers. A contributory fund into which ministers paid one month's salary annually, the *monte pío* was set up to provide 10,000 *reales* in annual pension to a minister's survivors. After the equality decree of 1773 the figure increased to 12,000 *reales* for the survivors of councilors and *fiscales* and 14,000 *reales* for those of *camaristas*. The introduction of the pension fund eliminated the previous ad hoc system of widows pleading poverty in order to secure assistance from the Crown.

The regional, family, and educational backgrounds of the ministers of the Council of the Indies varied. The councilors and *fiscales* of the Indies came from every major region of peninsular Spain, the Canary Islands, the Americas, and even from Sicily and Oran. For the 146 men for whom place of birth is known, the breakdown can be seen in the following table.

Regional Origins of Ministers, 1717–1808

Region of Birth		Number of Ministers	Percentage
Kingdom of Galicia		7	5
Kingdom of León		20	14
Basque Provinces		8	5
Kingdom of Navarre		6	4
Old Castile		18	12
New Castile		24	16
Kingdom of Extremadura		4	3
Kingdoms of Andalusia		32	22
Kingdom of Murcia		5	3
Kingdom of Aragon		8	5
Canary Islands		6	4
Americas		6	4
Other		2	2
	Total	146	99
	Unknown	13	
	Grand Total	159	

The table reveals that four regions of Spain—the Kingdom of León, Old Castile, New Castile, and Andalusia—together accounted for well over two-thirds (71 percent) of the 132 appointees born on the peninsula. Since the 1787 census reveals that these four regions accounted for only 51 percent of the total population of peninsular Spain, their native sons clearly enjoyed disproportionate representation on the Council. The city of Madrid alone provided ten members of the Council, while four more men came from other parts of the same province. This overrepresentation came about to a large extent at the expense of the Crown of Aragon. Despite its having 23 percent of peninsular Spain's population in 1787, only 5 percent (eight ministers) came from this area. Thus Castile's historic discrimination against natives of the Crown of Aragon in New World affairs continued throughout the eighteenth century on the Council itself.

The presence of men from the Canary Islands on the Council of the Indies distinguished it from the Council of Castile. From 1621 to 1808 only one *canariano*, Maldonado Sánchez Romero,* was named to Castile's senior tribunal. Appointed in 1760 after service on the Council of the Indies, his advancement was one of a number given to Council ministers before 1773. Besides Maldonado, five other *canarianos* served on the Council of the Indies. Four of them had prior service in the New World. Given the long-existing trade relationship of the Canaries to the Indies, it is not surprising that men from the islands followed careers that involved American service.

The appointment of creoles, Spaniards born in the New World, to the Council of the Indies also warrants attention. Although as many or more creoles were named than men from several major regions of Spain, their relative underrepresentation demands emphasis. Given that the population of the American colonies was greater than that of Spain by several million persons at the close of the colonial era and the white population was probably larger than that of the Crown of Aragon throughout the eighteenth century, Americans were grossly underrepresented on the Council demographically. Moreover, from 1717 to 1773 only one, Munive, was named. The absence from the Council of Mexicans, who came from the most populous and wealthy region in the empire, is particularly striking. Although Galisteo* was from adjacent Guatemala, the remaining five men were from Panama southward. Four of the six men, moreover, had followed careers in Spain itself rather than being advanced after significant employment in the colonies. Only the two Peruvians, Munive and Orrantia,* had proceeded to the Council after substantial service in the New World.

The dearth of Americans on the Council of the Indies was not compensated for by their presence on the Council of Castile. Only seven were named for the years from 1621 to 1808, and only two of them were after 1717. Both men advanced after careers on Spanish courts. Thus the discrimination Americans faced in pursuing high positions in the colonies, especially after the middle of the eighteenth century, was even more exaggerated in Spain.

Information on family backgrounds of the councilors is incomplete. Even in those cases in which the names of parents and grandparents are known, knowledge of their occupations is frequently unavailable. This is particularly true if they did not occupy civil or military positions. Almost unique is the case of López Quintana,* for which documents reveal his family had lived for generations by raising cattle, or Fernández Sarmiento y Ballón,* whose father had commercial interests in Mexico.

Some councilors, of course, were sons, often but not invariably younger sons, of titled nobles with entailed estates. Acedo y Ximénez, for example, was the younger son of the Conde de Echauz. Carvajal y Lancaster* was the younger son of the Duque de Linares and a grandson of the Duque de Abrantes. Titled fathers of fifteen councilors can be identified. Since there are two sets of brothers (Casados* and Yopulo y Espadaforas*), there are only thirteen titled fathers. In ten other cases a brother of a councilor held a noble title other than one inherited from his father. Some of these titles were new creations, as in the case of Moñino's* brother the

Conde de Floridablanca; others were received through marriage, as in the case of Mon y Velarde's* brother the Conde del Pinar.

Another thirteen fathers were knights of one of Spain's military orders. Since knighthood followed an extended genealogical examination, receiving it confirmed unblemished ancestry and conferred lifetime nobility, in those cases in which the recipient was not already an acknowledged noble. In the cases of Santos de San Pedro* and Romay Armada y Sotomayor,* grandfathers have been identified as knights when the fathers were not. The total figures for titled or knighted fathers, however, yield only twenty-six cases or twenty-eight ministers. Thus the vast majority, approximately four ministers out of five, could not claim illustrious ancestry, although all would certainly have made a case for noble status if pressed to do so.

Eleven ministers had fathers who had served on either an audiencia in Spain, or, in the case of López Lisperguer,* in the Indies, the House of Trade, or a Spanish council. Four councilors—the two Casados, Rojas y Contreras,* and Sola y Fuente*—had fathers who had been councilors of the Indies. The fathers of Borrull y Ramón* and Girón Venegas de Córdoba* were councilors of Castile, and Mata Linares y Vázquez's* father was a *camarista* of Castile. Sixteen ministers had brothers who served in high *letrado* positions as well. The ministers with the most notable *letrado* brothers were Moñino, whose brother the Conde de Floridablanca was one of the dominant secretaries of state during the reign of Charles III; Mon, who had two brothers who reached the Council of Castile; and Remírez de Baquedano,* who had brothers who reached the Council of Orders and the Cámara of Castile.

The limited number of immediate relatives on the courts and councils reveals few *letrado* dynasties represented on the Council of the Indies. The available evidence shows only five grandfathers who served on councils and only two others who served on audiencias. Of these seven cases, only Cerdán y Pontero,* Girón, and Mata had both fathers and grandfathers who held council or audiencia positions.

In some cases it was an uncle rather than or in addition to a father, grandfather, or brother who was well placed. Aparici Alvarez y Pérez's* father was a treasury official, but his uncle Francisco Aparici was an *oidor* of the Audiencia of Barcelona. While Bazán y Melo's* father was not a *letrado*, his paternal grandfather and an uncle were councilors of Castile. Contreras y Zúñiga* had one uncle who reached the Council of Castile and another who became a *camarista* of Castile. Mon had not only a brother and an uncle on the Council of Castile but another brother who became a *camarista* of Castile.

Some fathers, of course, held high non-*letrado* positions in Spain and the Indies. The service of Mendoza's father, the Marqués de Villa García, as viceroy of Peru, however, was unique. No comparable service by another minister's father who was not also a councilor has been uncovered. On the other hand, a number of fathers served in a variety of lesser posts, both civil and military. The fathers of both Banfi y Parrilla* and Laysequilla y Palacios y Aguilar were provincial administrators in Spain. Villalengua y Marfil's father was a notary in Vélez-Málaga while García León y Pizarro's* was an army colonel. Soto's* father was a treasury official in Jaén.

Although the backgrounds of the *capa y espada* ministers were so varied that no generalization would be appropriate, one can suggest that the families of the *letrados* on the Council, even if of modest means, were well enough off to enable the future minister to receive a formal education. Unlike *capa y espada* ministers who often entered their first position at the age of about sixteen years, *letrados* normally did not complete their professional training until their mid-twenties. And, unless they were scholarship students, the many years of education could entail substantial expenses.

The ninety-nine *letrados* named to the Council mastered Latin as youths and then proceeded to one or more universities where they studied either canon or civil law or both. Normally they were about twenty years old when awarded the baccalaureate degree. Following the baccalaureate, they chose one of two paths. Either they pursued an advanced degree in civil or canon law or they took a practicum or clerking experience for four years with an established attorney. Men who aspired to a university chair as a stepping stone to an audiencia position normally followed the former route. Those who planned to practice law tended to select the latter. Combining the two approaches, however, was not uncommon.

Although historians have paid more attention to the university and especially *colegio mayor* experience of *letrados*, the practicum or years of clerking was also important. This not only provided helpful practical experience for the future lawyers but also at times gave them personal connections that could later advance their careers. Occasionally, in fact, the onetime students might even help their mentor advance. Castaño,* for example, clerked with Gálvez y Gallardo.* Hernández de Alva Alonso* worked with the future *camarista* of Castile Santiago Ignacio de Espinosa. Patiño* was mentor to Castro,* González de Mena y Villegas,* and the future governor of the Council of Castile Manuel Ventura de Figueroa.

Whether he continued at a university or clerked, an aspiring *letrado* generally received approval to practice law from the Council of Castile, a chancellery, or an audiencia at the age of about twenty-five years. Men who had clerked and lacked an earned licentiate degree had to pass an examination. Those with a licentiate from Salamanca, Alcalá, or Valladolid were simply "incorporated" or approved on the basis of their advanced degrees alone. The widespread attribution and use of the title "*licenciado*" by lawyers after they had been approved to practice law even if they had earned only a baccalaureate degree reveals public acceptance that the two approaches conveyed comparable status.

The *letrados* studied, graduated, or incorporated one or more degrees at a number of universities. From 1717 to the 1773 equality decree, at least 47 percent of the *letrados* named (twenty-five of fifty-three) had been affiliated with two or more universities. Following the decree the figure declined to at least 39 percent (eighteen of forty-six). More important than the frequency of multiple affiliation was that before the equality decree only six of fifty-three of the *letrados* lacked an affiliation with one of Spain's preeminent universities: Salamanca, Valladolid, or Alcalá de Henares. The dominant presence of alumni from Spain's three most prominent universities diminished considerably after 1773. Of the forty-six *letrados* named after the equality decree, nineteen had no ties to any of them. Indeed, while over half (twenty-seven of fifty-three) of the men named before the decree had ties to Salamanca, by far the most frequently attended university, subsequently the number dwindled to less than a quarter of the appointees (eleven of forty-six). In contrast, the University of Granada increased the number of its alumni named to the Council from four to nine, making it the third most represented school behind Valladolid with twelve and Salamanca with eleven.

The reduced representation of Salamanca, Valladolid, and Alcalá alumni corresponds in broad terms with a discernible geographic shift in *letrados*' place of birth from the center and northwest of Spain toward the south. While the Kingdom of León and Old and New Castile together had accounted for nearly half of the *letrados* named from 1717 to 1773, after the decree of equality these regions provided only a third of the appointees. The difference was largely made up by an increase from the historic Kingdoms of Andalusia. Accounting for only ten of fifty-three men in the first period, Andalusians numbered fifteen among forty-six men after the decree of equality.

Only rarely did any *letrado* initiate his career with an audiencia appointment while still in his mid-twenties. Commonly men spent years associated with a university and competing for or holding academic chairs, practicing law, or serving in minor advisory or administrative positions. A number of men combined these occupations.

The elite among the *letrados* were those men who belonged to one of the six *colegios mayores*. Men might remain *colegiales* for many years, generally competing for and often winning academic chairs before moving directly into an audiencia position, the most common initial appointment that ultimately led to an appointment to the Council. Well before the eighteenth century this was an accepted pattern as former *colegiales* who had achieved positions of eminence were expected to benefit their younger brethren. Thus the presence of *colegiales* on the cámaras of the Indies and Castile was the best security for those still in residence at the universities.

From 1717 to the time of the equality decree, twenty of fifty-three *letrados* named to the Council had been *colegiales*. The proportion dropped after the 1773 decree to eight of the forty-six appointees. This decline is not surprising since the reform of the *colegios mayores* in 1771 had reduced substantially the number of *colegiales* available for careers in the *letrado* bureaucracy. As late as 1807, however, a former *colegial* reached the Cámara.

An overwhelming majority of men who served on the Council married at least once and most took their vows before reaching the Council. At least 109 (68 percent) of the ministers married, and complete information would undoubtedly increase this number. Only twelve ministers definitely died as bachelors, although circumstantial evidence suggests seven others did so as well.

Within a segment of society in which the extended family was the most important unit, the choice of a wife had implications that transcended the decision of the couple itself. Romantic considerations might have been present in some cases, but social suitability and economic resources were more important. The Crown considered misalliance disruptive for society as a whole and took steps in 1776 to try to prevent it with legislation that required parental consent for minors to marry. All ministers were required to secure permission to marry from the governor or president of the Council of the Indies or Castile. The creation of the *monte pío* for widows and orphans of ministers in 1763, however, had already provided a powerful incentive for securing royal permission for marriages since the absence of a license to marry and the accompanying registration of the wife with the *monte* deprived the wife and future children of rights to a pension. Ministers fully appreciated the importance of pension rights, and Requena y Herrera,* for example, sought and obtained a special dispensation that entitled his proposed second wife to a pension although he was over sixty years of age at the time of the wedding.

Most ministers married before their appointments to the Council. Cerdán, for example, married in Chile in 1779, twenty-four years before his appointment to the Council. Similarly, Requena married his first wife in Guayaquil, Ecuador, in 1772, twenty-six years before he advanced to the Council. Soler Ruiz* had married in 1751, over thirty years before becoming a councilor. In contrast, a few men married after reaching the Council or, indeed, in several cases as a condition for their appointments. Pedro Casado, the Yopulo brothers, and Romay all received their positions as dowries.

The length of time between marriage and an appointment to the Council later in life could have important consequences for the social position and future careers of a minister's children. It is reasonable to assume that the younger a minister's children were at the time of his appointment the more able he was to benefit them through the status, income, and personal contacts enjoyed while serving on an important and influential body.

Very few wives worked outside the home prior to or after their marriages. Those who did, however, were a special group whose employment served them and their husbands well. These were the ladies-in-waiting (*camaristas*) of a queen or princess. Isabel Piscatori, *camarista* of Queen Isabel Farnese, the wife of Philip V, married three successive ministers of the Council and brought each his appointment as her dowry. Later in the century, four *camaristas* of Princess and then Queen María Luisa, wife of Charles IV, married men who were or would become ministers of the Council. Only two of the eight men, Romay and Cistué y Coll,* were *letrados*. Of all the men, Cistué was the only one already on the council at the time he married.

The social standing of the wives is difficult to ascertain. Available evidence reveals only thirteen were daughters of titled nobles. At least five of these wives were creoles, three of them the Chilean daughters of the Marqués de Villapalma. Thus only ten different families were represented. In two cases, moreover, the matches were the consequences of the husband's high position rather than his status at birth. While a councilor, José de Gálvez married in 1775 the daughter of the Conde de la Puebla de los Valles. His two previous marriages, contracted while a young lawyer, were less distinguished. Also while a councilor, Moñino married the daughter of the Marqués de Casa Pontejos in 1786. Although his position was elevated, the fact that his brother the Conde de Floridablanca was at the time the first minister of Charles III undoubtedly added to Moñino's attractions.

At least eight wives of Council members were themselves the daughters of audiencia or council ministers. Three were daughters of councilors of Castile and three others had fathers who served on the councils of the Indies, Exchequer, and Orders respectively. The remaining two were the daughters of audiencia ministers in Mexico and the Philippines. Nine other wives had brothers who served in Spanish or American audiencias or on a council. Thus there are glimpses of bureaucratic inbreeding, but not enough to prevent the constant entry into the high bureaucracy of men whose families had no history of *letrado* service.

At least seventy-four men (46 percent) named to the Council of the Indies had high-placed, titled, or knighted relatives or wives. This figure is deceptively high, however, for thirty-nine of the seventy-four ministers qualified for inclusion in one of the categories only. Expressed differently, just thirty-five of the 159 ministers (21 percent) could be considered solidly tied to Spain's social and governmental elites by virtue of their family or in-laws' backgrounds. The difference is immense between Soto, the son of a struggling low-ranking provincial treasury official, and Rojas y Contreras, the son of a councilor of the Indies, a knight of Calatrava who married the daughter of a titled noble, the grandson of a knight of Santiago, the brother of a governor of the Council of Castile and knight of Calatrava, a minister *de capa y espada* of the Council of the Exchequer and knight of Calatrava, and a third knight of Calatrava. The backgrounds of Carvajal, Cerdán, and Remírez reveal similar distance from men like Soto. They, however, are the exceptional cases that enable one to appreciate the distance between the average minister's family background and ties and those of the social elite.

To summarize, scarcely over 20 percent of the Council's ministers were solid members of the elite from birth. The vast majority of ministers had reached the Council primarily as a result of their own efforts and personal contacts. Rather than benefiting from their ancestors' records and connections, they themselves became the eminent relatives whose accomplishments their children, grandchildren, and nephews would cite with pride.

The conclusion that most ministers reached the Council because of their own abilities rather than accrued family merit underscores the upward social mobility taking place in eighteenth-century Spain. With the notorious exception of Manuel Godoy, no one in late-eighteenth-century Spain rose higher than José de Gálvez, Marqués de Sonora. Antonio de Porlier,* Marqués de Bajamar, and Francisco Leandro de Viana y Zavala,* Conde de Tepa, also exemplified advancement on the basis of talent rather than distinguished family background. These three men received titles and membership in the Order of Charles III in recognition of their service to the Crown.

The extent to which Council ministers advanced socially is best seen in the lives of their children, grandchildren, and nephews. A minister's early career, the time of his marriage, and the ages of his children when he reached the Council profoundly affected how much he could benefit them by his high position. Unfortunately the data for examining this important topic are very incomplete, in part because the disruption associated with the French invasion, the War of Independence, and Ferdinand VII's return added an overt political dimension to government employment that altered previous social and career patterns. Nonetheless, the evidence available suggests that throughout the eighteenth century new bureaucratic dynasties emerged and some previously established ones continued to perpetuate themselves.

Eight ministers had sons named to American audiencias. Seven of them, all *letrados*, had initiated a family tradition of service on the courts. Four other ministers, three of them first-generation *letrados*, had sons who served on Spanish courts, with one reaching the Council of Castile. In addition, four other ministers had sons-in-law who had careers on the courts. One of them, Palacios,* also had a grandson who served on a Spanish audiencia. The granddaughter of Manuel Jacinto de Salcedo,* in turn, married Machado Fiesco,* thus maintaining the family's association with the Council of the Indies. The nephews of five ministers reached American audiences and a sixth nephew served on the Chancellery of Granada. All six uncles were first-generation *letrados*.

The Spanish Crown rewarded high-ranking bureaucrats who rendered notable service in a number of ways. Depending on the circumstances, it granted pensions, bestowed "honors" of a more prestigious position, conferred knighthoods to a minister or his children, issued titles of nobility, and appointed a minister's sons or other male relatives to government posts. While bureaucrats sought all of these rewards, knighthood and titles were particularly attractive.

The use of knighthoods to reward bureaucrats fell into two distinct periods. Prior to 1771 men entered the long-established orders of Santiago, Calatrava, Alcantara, San Juan, and very rarely, the Golden Fleece. Of the seventy-eight new men named to the Council from 1717 to 1771, twenty-four belonged to one of these orders. *Ministros de capa y espada* were especially well represented; thirteen of thirty were knights. After Charles III in 1771 established the Order of Charles III specifically to recognize and reward meritorious civil service, a larger number of men who served on the Council of the Indies became *caballeros*. Eighteen of the thirty ministers *de capa y espada* and twenty-three of the fifty-one *letrados* named after 1771 entered the new order. Moreover, one minister *de capa y espada* and nine *letrados* named to the Council before 1771 were subsequently inducted. Between 1772 and 1808, only five other ministers *de capa y espada* and two other *letrados* entered any of the older orders. Seventy-seven percent of the ministers *de capa y espada* and 49 percent of the *letrados* named after 1771 belonged to an order.

A title of nobility identified its bearer as a member of Spain's social elite. Twenty-seven ministers named from 1717 to 1808 bore titles. At least eleven titles were either inherited or received through marriage. The date of creation of two other titles, probably Italian in provenance, is unknown. Of the fourteen remaining ministers, two, Gauna y Portocarrero* and Goyeneche, received titles for their ancestors' services. Twelve men, four *ministros de capa y espada* and eight *letrados*, gained titles through their own efforts between 1719 and 1795. The Crown conferred six of the twelve from 1785 to 1795. All went to men with experience or birth in the Indies. Four of them were part of the flood of honors that Charles IV awarded following his ascension to the throne.

Service on the Council of the Indies was an honor, a responsibility, a source of income, and, with few exceptions, a secure career. Once he entered his position, a minister remained until promoted, retired, removed, or excused or until death overcame him. As in other areas, one can observe differences between the *capa y espada* ministers and the *letrados* on the Council. Since the Council of Castile lacked ministers *de capa y espada*, there was no established avenue of advancement for those on the Council of the Indies. Although commissions sometimes took them away from Madrid, as for example those received by Geraldino,* Requena, and Diego Yopulo, *capa y espada* ministers could plan on dying in their Council positions. Between 1717 and 1808, only five left their positions before death. The Crown removed Pedro Casado, excused Silva Rivera,* promoted Moñino to the governorship of the Council and then removed him five years later, and retired Machado Fiesco* and Iriarte*. Thirty-seven ministers *de capa y espada* died in office. Eighteen still held appointments in 1808.

For *letrados* on the Council the situation was quite different until 1773. Fourteen ministers named prior to that year advanced to the Council of Castile, historically the pinnacle of the *letrado* bureaucracy. In addition, three other men moved into other positions—Bazán as governor of the Council of the Exchequer and Carvajal and Gálvez into the governorship of the Council of the Indies and positions as secretaries of state. Three *letrados* retired. After Charles III declared the councils of Castile and the Indies equal, only Porlier advanced, becoming secretary of state for grace and justice before replacing Moñino as the Council's governor. Twenty-four *letrados* died at their posts and seven were retired, including an unprecedented four in 1802. Three appointees after 1773 never served and twelve *ministros togados* and two *fiscales* still held their positions in 1808.

For those ministers who secured retirement, compensation varied considerably. Areche y Sornoza,* who retired in disgrace as a result of his activities on the *visita* to Peru, received the unusually low pension of one-third salary. Cavallero y Soto,* retired in 1720, and Bernardo de Quirós,* retired in 1773, received half salary. The six men who retired after 1800 fared better. Villalengua and Valenzuela y Aguilar* each received two-thirds of their salaries. In contrast, Machado Fiesco, Iriarte y Nieves-Rabelo,* Viana,* and Cistué received full salary.

Although the Habsburg monarchs appreciated the value of appointing *letrados* with experience in the New World to the Council of the Indies, they named few such "old hands." This changed slowly in the eighteenth century. The three times the Crown expanded the number of *ministros togados*—from six to eight in 1737, to ten in 1773, and to fourteen in 1776—it named men with American experience to at least one of the new positions. Appointments with respect to this experience increased over time.

In the first period of appointments, 1717–39, only six of twenty men named *ministros togados* had lived or worked in the New World. From 1740 to the July 29, 1773, decree declaring the Council of the Indies *de término* and equal to the Council of Castile in rank, salary, and prerogatives, the number rose to eleven of twenty-one. From the 1773 decree to 1808, the number continued to climb, reaching thirty-one of thirty-nine appointments. That eleven of the last twelve and twenty-three of the last twenty-seven appointments went to persons with American experience underscores the effectiveness of the new pattern of promotion established in the 1770s.[5]

Historically the Council of the Indies had been the penultimate rung on a ladder of advancement (*ascenso*) that extended from entry positions of crown attorney or judge on a Spanish audiencia or chancellery to membership on the Council of Castile. While no individual occupied every step of the ladder, prior service in several positions was routine for men who ultimately advanced to the Council of the Indies. Tomás de Sola y Soto,* for example, began his audiencia career in 1700 with an appointment as *oidor* of the Audiencia of Galicia. He moved to the Chancellery of Valladolid as an *oidor* in 1707. Advancement to the *sala de alcaldes de casa y corte* (the criminal chamber of the Council of Castile) as a *fiscal* in 1714 was followed by an appointment as *fiscal* of the Council of War. He was named a *fiscal* of the Council of the Indies in 1718 and subsequently promoted to *ministro togado* in 1726. Forty years later, in 1766, Manuel Bernardo de Quiros also reached the Council after four previous appointments to tribunals in Spain. He began as an *oidor* in Galicia in 1740 and advanced to the same post in Valladolid in 1748. In 1753 he became regent of the Audiencia of Mallorca and then moved to the same position for the Audiencia of Zaragoza in 1760 before his promotion to the Council of the Indies. By this time, however, prior service in only two or three positions was increasingly the rule. In 1767, for example, Pedro de Avila* reached the Council after serving as *alcalde del crimen* of the Audiencia of Barcelona and then as *alcalde de casa y corte*.

The eighteen men who served on Spanish audiencias, chancellories, or councils from 1717 to 1773 and had no American experience averaged just over twenty years of previous court service, although the amount of court service varied considerably. Felipe Santos Domínguez,* appointed in 1773 after service as a *fiscal* on the Chancellery of Granada and as an *alcalde de casa y corte*, had only nine years of experience. Tomás de Sola and Manuel de Bernardo de Quiros shared the longest period of prior service with twenty-six years each. Only Antonio Jacinto de Romay lacked significant earlier government service or accomplishments. He was the only *ministro togado* on the Council from 1717 to 1808 who secured his appointment as the dowry for his wife. A professor at the undistinguished University of Santiago, Romay could claim no affiliation with a *colegio mayor* or a previous royal position. With the sale of audiencia positions rampant in the 1740s and even the sale of a post on the Chancellery of Valladolid taking place during the decade, however, the Council was fortunate that it had only one *ministro togado* named as a result of a dowry and none who had purchased an appointment. All other appointments were clearly justified by prior professional accomplishments.

Prior to the 1773 decree, ministers who had served in the colonies had a longer average length of prior service than those who had served only in Spain. Excluding the exceptional case of José de Gálvez, who was named to the Council while his *visita* was underway in New Spain, the fifteen men with American service averaged twenty-four years of prior service. In the most extreme cases, this service was for thirty-three, thirty-four, and thirty-five years respectively. In no case was it for less than fourteen years.

The modest number of men who had previously served on the House of Trade in all but one case reached the Council after fewer than twenty years of prior service. In two cases, the individuals had served only three and four years. The brevity was probably due to a belief that experience in the House of Trade was particularly useful for the Council's deliberations. In any case, both Antonio Alvarez de Abreu* and José de Valdivieso* had previous royal service, although neither had served on audiencias.

Despite the larger number of years previously served by *ministros togados* who had been in the Americas, their average age at the time of appointment was the same (fifty-six) as that of the ministers who had served only on Spanish courts. The reason for this is that peninsulars willing to go to the Indies could frequently gain an audiencia appointment at an earlier age. Men who remained resident in the *colegios mayores* at Salamanca, Alcalá, and Valladolid were often in their late thirties or even early forties before securing a post in Spain. For example, Juan Santos de San Pedro* was forty-three years old when named an oidor of the Chancellery of Valladolid and fifty-nine when he reached the Council in 1720. José Cerda y Soto,* a *colegial* of San Ildefonso at Alcalá, as had been Santos, was only twenty-seven years old when named an oidor of the Audiencia of Santo Domingo and but forty-seven years old when he reached the Council.

Of the forty-one *ministros togados* named from 1717 to 1773, twenty-one had been *colegiales* in one of the six *colegios mayores*. Only seven of these men had served in America, two with initial appointments at young ages (twenty-nine and thirty-four) to the Audiencia of Mexico, the highest-ranking tribunal in New Spain, and five with commissions to the Indies following appointments to Spanish audiencias or, in one case, the House of Trade.

The average length of service by *ministros togados* named from 1717 to 1773 was ten years, but the actual length varied considerably. Tomás de Sola and Andrés Orueta y Yrusta* died the year of their appointments. In contrast, José Cornejo y Ibarra,* named at the comparatively young age of forty-six, served for thirty years.

Prior to 1773 the Council of the Indies was part of a Spanish *ascenso*, and eight of forty-one *ministros togados* moved upward to the Council of Castile. Two of these men, Mutiloa and León y Escandón,* had previously served in the colonies, so their advancement deprived the Council of the Indies of men with first hand knowledge of America. Five of the eight men promoted, including Mutiloa, had been *colegiales mayores*.

Although the number and percentage of *ministros togados* with American experience had increased substantially from 1740 to 1773, the implementation of the decree of equality and expansion issued on July 29, 1773, and the subsequent expansion of 1776 truly transformed the Council's personnel. The apppointments after the decree of equality more than reversed the figures from the 1717–39 period and made the Council a virtual preserve of "old hands" from the New World courts.

After extensive efforts by the president and *ministros togados* of the Council of the

Indies to secure equality with the Council of Castile, Charles III acceded and henceforth *ministros togados* were no longer promoted to the Council of Castile; they ended their career on the Council of the Indies. The creation of the position of regent as the highest-ranking minister on each American audiencia in 1776, however, created an expanded *ascenso* for the New World courts that led to the Council of the Indies itself. Starting with the 1783 promotion of García León, regent of the Audiencia of Quito, almost twice as many (fifteen) regents advanced to the Council as did men of all other backgrounds combined (eight).

The regents brought a wealth of experience to the Council. Excluding the three named in 1776 who returned to Spain after relatively brief service on only one court, regents advanced to the Council had served an average of twenty-three years in America and almost uniformly in three different courts. Most of the regents, moreover, were *caballeros* of the Order of Charles III prior to their promotion to the Council. Together they formed the most illustrious group of civil servants the Council ever had.

From 1717 to 1808, the Council of the Indies had two positions of *fiscal*, one for New Spain and one for Peru, or Spanish South America. Although providing a salary equal to that of a councilor, the post of *fiscal* was considered junior, and a number of *fiscales* became *ministros togados*. As a group, however, the *fiscales* should be distinguished from the more numerous *ministros togados* on the Council.

Since the Crown charged *fiscales* on all tribunals with the defense of royal interests, it favored candidates for *fiscalías* who had demonstrated success as practicing attorneys. Some law professors became learned judges and university chairs in law were a common route to the high judiciary, but many law professors were not experienced attorneys. The *fiscales* appointed reflected the Crown's appreciation of these different backgrounds. While twenty-one *colegiales mayores* were among the forty-one *ministros togados* named from 1717 to 1773, only two of the seventeen new *fiscales* appointed during the same years were *colegiales*; both advanced as *ministros togados*.

The majority of *fiscales* on the Council had previously been *fiscales* on Spanish or American audiencias, chancelleries, or the House of Trade. From 1717 to 1808, sixteen of twenty-six fiscales had had this experience on one or more courts. Divided into the three appointment periods, the figures are four of eight for 1717 to 1739, six of nine for 1740 to 1773, and six of nine for 1773 to 1808. In contrast, only twenty of seventy-three *ministros togados* not previously counted among the *fiscales* on the Council had been *fiscales* on lower courts.

Prior to the 1773 decree of equality, a greater percentage of the Council of the Indies' *fiscales* than *ministros togados* advanced to the Council of Castile. Between 1717 and 1773 seven of the seventeen *fiscales* advanced, three as *fiscales* and four as *ministros togados*. In contrast, only eight of forty-one *ministros togados* secured the promotion, all becoming *ministros togados* on the Council of Castile.

Prior to 1773, previous experience as a *fiscal* was much more common among the Council's fiscales than experience in America. Of the seventeen *fiscales* named from 1717 to 1773, only three had been employed in New World courts. Two of them had been *fiscales*. After the 1773 decree of equality, however, all nine of the *fiscales* named had New World experience. Four had been *fiscales*, two had been regents, and two others had served as both *fiscales* and regents. The ninth man had served as an *oidor* on the audiencias of Charcas and Lima as well as on the House of Trade. With an average of twenty-two years of American experience, the *fiscales* fully met the expectations set forth in the 1770s.

For more than a century after its establishment, the Council of the Indies was the preserve of *letrados*. In 1626 this monopoly ended. Despite their numerical supremacy for most of the subsequent years, *ministros togados* henceforth would share their duties, save in judicial decisions, with *ministros de capa y espada*. From 1626 until the reorganization of 1717, fifty-four of the 186 ministers named (29 percent) were *de capa y espada*. From 1717 to 1808, a substantially higher proportion of the ministers, sixty of 139 (43 percent) were *de capa y espada*.

When Philip V reorganized the Council in 1717, he authorized two positions of *ministro de capa y espada* but in fact named three men with the proviso that the first to leave the Council would not be replaced. Subsequently, in 1760, Charles III added two more *capa y espada* seats. When he established a regular line of promotion for the chief clerks (*oficiales mayores*) of the secretariats of state in 1785, he assigned a fifth regular position. Although this was the last *número* position authorized, the number of *capa y espada* ministers burgeoned beginning in 1788 as Charles III and then Charles IV made supernumerary appointments. At the beginning of 1808, sixteen rather than five *ministros de capa y espada* held appointments to the Council, although not all were present.

The presence of two kinds of councilors had substantial implications for patronage. Unlike their *togado* peers, *ministros de capa y espada* followed no clearly understood career patterns that led to the Council. Lacking specified professional credentials, they came from a much wider range of backgrounds. For all practical purposes, the king could name any male noncleric he pleased to serve as a *ministro de capa y espada*, although persons with neither substantial individual accomplishments nor illustrious family or personal ties were effectively excluded. The consequence was that *capa y espada* ministers came from far more heterogeneous backgrounds and experiences than did *togados*. On more than one occasion, in fact, men with training in law were named *capa y espada* ministers. Nonetheless, it is possible to identify several groups of individuals that had similar backgrounds.

With respect to prior New World experience and conditions of appointment, men named *capa y espada* ministers from 1717 to 1759 resemble pre–1717 more than post–1759 and especially post–1785 appointees. From 1717 to 1759, kings Philip V, Ferdinand VI, and Charles III named twenty-eight new *ministros de capa y espada*. Given that the Council dealt with colonial affairs, the presence of ministers with personal experience was useful in its discussions. Although successive kings understood this, they named only one man born in the New World and only four others who had served there. The appointments of Francisco Fernández Molinillo,* twice an official in Mexico, and *limeño* Gabriel Munive specifically mentioned their knowledge of New World affairs. But emphasizing this background was rare, for the Crown constantly was under pressure to appoint men who had never seen the

Indies. As a result, it named the vast majority of *ministros de capa y espada* for reasons other than experience relevant to the Council's tasks.

At least seven appointments to the Council from 1717 to 1759 arose from the influence of Philip V's wife Isabel Farnese. Four men became *ministros de capa y espada* to fulfill the dowries that two of the queen's ladies-in-waiting had received from the Crown. The more spectacular case was the dowry of Isabel Piscatori, who received in 1723 a position of *ministro de capa y espada* for the man who would marry her. Pedro Casado appeared on the scene and received the appointment. Perhaps the marriage was annulled, however, for two years later Luis Yopulo was named for marrying Piscatori. His death brought forward Diego Yopulo, who received an appointment to the Council in 1735 for marrying his elder brother's widow. Nearly a decade later, in 1744, Felipe Arco married María Ana Piscatori y Baroni, probably Isabel's niece and a lady-in-waiting to Queen Isabel Farnese for fifteen years. In addition to the dowries of the Piscatori women, the appointments of Juan Pizarro y Aragón,* son of her *mayordomo mayor*, Francisco Aguirre y Salcedo,* her *mayordomo de semana*, and Juan Pérez Gamoneda,* her secretary, reveal Isabel Farnese's continued influence in high-level patronage.

Most *ministros de capa y espada* were of unquestioned nobility, and held titles and knighthoods. One was an Italian duke, nine were marquises, and one was a count. Four other ministers were sons of titled nobles. Four of the eleven titled nobles and eight other ministers were in a military (eleven) or civil (one) order.

In the absence of a clearly defined path of advancement to the Council, the services of one's father or other relatives increased in importance as a reason for appointment. Thus Mauro de Mendoza Caamaño's naming in 1735 was clearly linked to the appointment of his father, the Marqués de Villa García, as viceroy of Peru. Francisco Casado also benefited from his titled father's services as an ambassador and minister of the Council of the Indies. Gaspar Girón, too, undoubtedly was aided by his father's service as a councilor of Castile. Yet there were those whose own records formed the basis for their appointments.

Alonso Carnero* and Antonio de Ubilla,* the two *ministros de capa y espada* named by the decree of January 20, 1717, that reorganized the Council, had been appointed previously after serving as secretaries of state. Such advancements had clear seventeenth-century precedents. Later, Manuel Vadillo Estrada y Velasco,* Miguel Fernández Durán y Fernández de la Casa,* Antonio Sopeña y Mioño,* Mateo Díaz de Lavandero, and Fernando Verdes Montenegro y Castro Baamonde* were named after having served as secretaries of state. José de la Quintana, on the other hand, was named a secretary of state after several years on the Council.

Occasionally the Crown used appointment to the Council as a means to provide an ambassador with additional salary and honor or as a post following such service. The Marqués de Capecelatro,* for example, received an appointment to both the Council and the Cámara in 1729 with a specific exemption from serving while he remained ambassador to Portugal. The title of appointment stated explicitly that the appointment was to increase his income. Tomás Geraldino was named in 1739 upon returning from service as a plenipotentiary minister to England. José Torrero y Marzo,* another ambassador to Portugal, was appointed in 1746. Portocarrero, president of the Council for many years, served a number of ambassadorial positions both before and after his appointment.

Although Andrés Pez, the president named in 1717, was a naval officer with experience in the New World, a military background was rare. Rodrigo Torres y Morales* also had a naval career and Manuel de Salcedo* served in the army and as governor of Yucatán, but it was his payment of nine thousand *pesos* in 1745 that brought him his post on the Council.

Despite the occasional use of Council posts as dowries and even the sale of an appointment in 1745, after 1717 the Crown never stooped to the practices of the late seventeenth century or those of the period of the War of the Spanish Succession and appointed minors, or men of less than twenty-five years, to the Council. The last one named, Francisco Xavier de Goyeneche, served after 1717, but his appointment as a minor was never repeated. With approximate ages known for twenty-one of the twenty-eight ministers named from 1717 to 1759, the youngest, Mendoza, was twenty-seven years old when appointed. Since his title of office specified that he was not to serve until returning from Peru, however, it was clear that he would be well into his thirties before assuming his position. Only three other men were named before they attained thirty-five years of age. Another six were thirty-six to forty-five when appointed; five were aged forty-six to fifty-five; and another five were aged fifty-six to sixty-five years at the time of appointment. The oldest man named was sixty-seven years of age. Not surprisingly, his tenure was brief, only three years.

The largest group of appointees (eight) served from eleven to fifteen years. Five others served from sixteen to twenty years. Seven men served more than twenty years, although three of these held their appointments for over forty years. Just four men served less than six years and but another four held appointments from six to ten years. With twenty of the twenty-eight men serving more than a decade, it is clear that *capa y espada* ministers provided substantial stability to the Council.

The appointment of Pérez de Gamoneda by Charles III in December 1759 was the last in an era of appointments based more on favoritism or qualifications irrelevant to the affairs of the Indies than on experience in American matters. Although occasional appointments after 1759 recalled the practices of earlier times, a greater number of ministers brought knowledge and experience useful to the Council's deliberations. The appointment in 1761 of José Banfi, the chief clerk (*oficial mayor*) of the Secretariat of State for the Indies (often referred to as the Ministry of the Indies) initiated a transitional era in which the Crown advanced men who had worked with the Ministry or the Council in nonconciliar positions. Only in 1785 was the advancement of chief clerks of the several secretariats of state institutionalized, however, and the final period of *capa y espada* appointments opened.

Just seven *ministros de capa y espada* were named from 1760 to 1784. None were titled nobles, but six were members of a military order or the civil order of Charles III. Notably higher than the 18 percent of appointees named from 1717 to 1759,

43 percent (three of seven) of the ministers had substantial American experience; each had worked in New Spain, the Crown's most valuable colony at the time. Two were secretaries to viceroys and one served as secretary to the Gálvez *visita*.

The appointment in 1767 of Tomás Ortiz de Landazuri,* chief accountant for the Council of the Indies after his return from New Spain and then simultaneously with his service as councilor, inaugurated the presence of a chief accountant on the Council. His successor, Francisco Machado, the former secretary of the Gálvez *visita*, also served both posts. Pedro de Rada,* the third man with American experience, reached the Council after intervening service as chief clerk in the Ministry of the Indies.

The naming in 1774 of Fernando de Magallón y Andrés,* former secretary to the Spanish ambassador in Paris, initiated what later became an institutionalized advancement of clerks in the secretary of state's office to the Council. His successor in 1780, Bernardo de Iriarte, also came from the foreign service.

Unlike the other six appointments in the period, the naming of Francisco Moñino in 1778 probably reflected nothing more than the power wielded by his brother the Conde de Floridablanca. As such, it was reminiscent of the naked use of patronage that marked many earlier *capa y espada* appointments.

Older age at the time of appointment also distinguished men named from 1760 to 1784 from their predecessors. Although Moñino's age can only be estimated, it is probable that he was in his mid- to late thirties when appointed, making him the youngest of the seven men at the date of naming. The remaining men varied from forty-three to fifty-seven years when appointed. The older average age at appointment (forty-seven as opposed to forty-two years) was reflected in a reduction in the mean length of service from sixteen to thirteen years.

The final period of appointments for *capa y espada* ministers extended from 1785 to 1808. The opening date is important for on May 31, Charles II decreed that henceforth the chief clerks (*oficiales mayores*) of the six secretariats of state would advance along prescribed lines. One position of *ministro de capa y espada* on the Council of the Indies would be reserved for the chief clerk of the secretariat of the Indies. Ignacio de Hermosilla y Sandoval's* appointment was the immediate result. The subsequent division of the Secretariat in 1787 upon the death of Gálvez brought in its wake a second reserved position. In 1788 Manuel de Ayala y Medina,* a career bureaucrat who had become the chief clerk in the Ministry of Grace and Justice for the Indies, was named to the Council in a supernumerary capacity until a regular post became available at the same time he was named director of confiscated Jesuit properties (*temporalidades*) for the Indies. Although the official organization of the Council remained unchanged from 1785 to 1808, the number of *ministros de capa y espada* began to increase in 1788 with the appointment of Ayala as a supernumerary minister and climbed to 16 by 1808. By that year roughly two-thirds of the men with *capa y espada* appointments were, in effect, supernumeraries even if their title of appointment failed to designate them as such.

Supernumerary or not, if taken together the ministers named from 1785 to 1808 had solid professional credentials and brought to the Council experience in a number of different areas. By bringing together high-ranking officials from the Secretariats of State, War, the Navy, and Exchequer, men with experience in directing the postal service and the Almadén mercury mine, and chief accountants for the Indies, the Crown had assembled a broadly based group of specialists to complement its ministers with American experience.

At the same time, and overlapping the use of designated advancements to some extent, the appointment of men with New World experience continued. Nine of the twenty-five appointees had either served in America (six) or been born there (three). Two men, Manuel Ignacio Fernández Sarmiento y Ballón,* and Juan Ignacio de Urriza, had been intendants, Fernández in the Río de la Plata and Urriza in Cuba. Two other men, Fernando José Mangino Fernández de Lima and Vicente Hore, had been local administrators (*corregidores*), Mangino in Mexico and Hore in Peru. Francisco de Requena y Herrera* had spent many years as an engineer and administrator in present Ecuador prior to his appointment to the Council. Cenón Alonso Acosta Zorrilla y Dávila* had served as secretary to the viceroy of New Granada. Ayala, Valencia, and Tadeo Galisteo had been born in Panama, New Granada, and Guatemala respectively, although they made their careers in the Spanish bureaucracy in Madrid.

The more regularized advancements to the Council after 1785 resulted in the appointment of older men with greater experience. The mean age at the time of appointment was fifty-one years, nearly a decade older than had been the case from 1717 to 1759.

Given the bureaucratic backgrounds of the appointees, it is not surprising that their own activities rather than those of their fathers or relatives were the primary reason for their appointments. Nor did many of them (three) hold titles of nobility. The great majority (eighteen of twenty-five), however, entered a military order (three) or civil order (fifteen) before or after their appointments. Fourteen belonged to the Order of Charles III.

Taken as a group, the twenty-five *capa y espada* appointees from 1785 to 1808 suggest a conscious royal effort to bring together fairly systematically men with New World experience and a wide array of expertise gained from years of service in a number of Spanish ministries and other positions. Thus men knowledgeable in military, naval, fiscal, trade, communications, mercury production, and patronage affairs were named ministers. The degree of experience, specialization, and knowledge of New World affairs on the Council was greater in the closing decades of the Old Regime than at any prior time in its history. With American affairs divided among five secretariats of state from 1790 to 1808, the Council once again emerged as the supreme repository of expertise on the Indies.

Presiding over the Council from 1717 to 1808 was a president or governor. The difference in the two titles was primarily reflected in the amount of salary the incumbent received. A president's salary was higher than that paid to a governor. Men of both legal training and *capa y espada* backgrounds served as governor. The presidents, in contrast, were all titled nobles.

Andrés Pez, the governor named in the reorganization of 1717, had a military background and had served as general of the windward squadron (*Armada de Bar-*

lovento) as well as secretary of the navy. His successor was Baltasar Zúñiga, Marqués de Valero, a former viceroy of New Spain, who held the Council's presidency from 1724 to 1727. Following an hiatus that lasted a decade, Christóbal Gregorio Portocarrero, Conde de Montijo, was named president in 1737. A diplomat who held ambassadorial rank in England when named, Montijo continued to serve appointments abroad. Consequently, in an appointment unique in the years 1717–1808, on October 23, 1742, Philip V named José de Carvajal, a *ministro togodo* on the Council since 1738 and on the Cámara since 1740 to be interim governor when Montijo was ill or otherwise absent and unable to attend Council meetings. A full appointment as governor followed in January 1748. Upon Carvajal's death in 1754, however, the governorship ended for over twenty years. On February 20, 1763, Juan Pizarro y Aragón,* Marqués de San Juan de Piedras Albas, was named president to succeed Montijo. Pizarro, a *ministro de capa y espada* since 1728, served the presidency until his death in 1771. After the death of Carvajal and from 1771 to 1776, the Duque de Alba, grand chancellor of the Council, served as interim president by virtue of holding the grand chancellorship.

The appointment of José de Gálvez in 1776 gave the Council a permanent governor. Gálvez, a former visitor general to New Spain, *ministro togado, camarista*, and, since February 19, 1776, secretary of state for the Indies, enjoyed a concentration of authority over the Indies that was without precedent. In contrast, after Gálvez's death in 1787, Francisco Moñino held only the governorship. Moñino's appointment, moreover, can best be viewed as an effort by his brother the Conde de Floridablanca to extend his influence over the affairs of the Indies. Although Moñino had been a *capa y espada* minister since 1778, his fate was permanently linked to his brother's. Floridablanca's fall in 1792 brought Francisco Moñino's removal from the governorship within days and the subsequent appointment of Antonio de Porlier, Marqués de Bajamar. A seasoned veteran of New World audiencias and a former *fiscal* of the Council and secretary of state for grace and justice, Bajamar remained governor until after the French invasion.

From 1717 to 1808 the Council had three presidents and five governors. Four of the men had personal experience in the New World, and their tenures as presiding officers were just under half of the total period. More importantly, with the exception of Moñino, from 1776 to 1808 the governor not only had prior service as a councilor or *fiscal* but also personal experience in the colonies. The spirit of the reforms of the 1770s had extended to the very top of the Council as well as permeating the ranks of councilor and *fiscal*.

Far from being a moribund institution, the Council of the Indies in the late eighteenth century showed unmistakable signs of vitality. Charles III's decisions to elevate it to equality with the Council of Castile, to emphasize the appointment of *letrados* with experience in the New World, and to create regular lines of advancement to *capa y espada* positions transformed the Council into a repository of expertise that could be and was tapped for advice on a number of nonjudicial matters. An examination of the Council's actions and recommendations from 1717 to 1808, however, must await another historian.

The sources for this dictionary came primarily from Spanish archives. The list of ministers is based principally on titles of appointment housed in the General Archives of Simancas. Information about ministers who served on the Spanish courts prior to advancing to the Council came from documents in the section Gracia y Justicia at Simancas and Consejos in the National Historical Archives in Madrid. The latter archives also provided extensive genealogical information in the documentation required for entering a military order or the Order of Charles III. The sections Ordenes Militares and Estado house these materials. The General Archives of the Indies provided both information on ministers and their families and the documentation on the changes in the Council. Particularly helpful were the papers on the 1773 decree of equality, the 1776 expansion of the Council in size, and the abstracts of *consultas* for appointments of *letrados* to the Council. *Relaciones de méritos y servicios* on ministers were found in all of these archives. The archives of the Chancelleries of Valladolid and Granada provided otherwise often unavailable information on lawyers who reached the Council. University archives revealed ministers' place of birth and where they had studied. Notarial records in Madrid yielded the wills of a small number of ministers. Undoubtedly more material will become accessible as additional catalogs become available.

Although this work rests very heavily on archival documentation, a number of secondary works were used as well. While most provided little additional information, several deserve special mention. The most valuable genealogical work was the monumental publication by Alberto and Arturo García Carraffa, *Enciclopedia heráldica y genealógica hispano americana*. Gildas Bernard's *Le secrétariat d'état et le conseil espagnol des Indies (1700–1808)*, the only work on the Council in the eighteenth century, helped to resolve a number of questions.

In general, the information on *letrados* was more complete than on *ministros de capa y espada* and material after the middle of the eighteenth century was fuller than that for the earlier years. The relative lack of research on both Spain and the Indies in the first half of the eighteenth century persists.

This dictionary is the first attempt to bring together biographical information about the Council's ministers in the eighteenth century. As such, it provides incomplete and uneven entries that only further investigation and the release of materials still buried in the notes of countless historians can supplement. However, it is hoped that this volume will prove useful to other scholars and stimulate further biographical dictionaries of important civil, ecclesiastical, and military figures in Spain and her empire.

NOTES

1. Mark A. Burkholder and D. S. Chandler (Westport, Conn.: Greenwood Press, 1982).
2. Ernesto Schäfer, *El consejo real y supremo de las Indias*, vol. 1 (Seville: Escuela de Estudios Hispano-Americanos de Sevilla, 1935), pp. 364–65.
3. Henry Kamen, *Spain in the Later Seventeenth Century, 1665–1700*, (London: Longman Group Limited, 1980), p. 33.
4. Ibid, p. 26.
5. For a detailed examination of the 1773 decree and its consequences, see Mark A. Burkholder, "The Council of the Indies in the Late Eighteenth Century: A New Perspective," *Hispanic American Historical Review* 56 (August 1976):404–23.

ARCHIVAL ABBREVIATIONS

AGI	Archivo General de Indias, Seville
AGN	Archivo General de la Nación, Mexico
AGS	Archivo General de Simancas, Simancas
	Titles of appointment from Sección XXIII, Dirección General del Tesoro, are abbreviated by numbers indicating the inventory, *legajo*, and document, e.g. 13–9–490.
AHN	Archivo Histórico Nacional, Madrid
AHPM	Archivo Histórico de Protocolos, Madrid
AHPUV	Archivo Histórico Provincial y Universitario de Valladolid, Valladolid
ARCG	Archivo de la Real Chancillería de Granada, Granada
ARCV	Archivo de la Real Chancillería de Valladolid, Valladolid
ASC	Archivo del Colegio de Santa Cruz, Valladollid
AUAV	Archivo de la Universidad de Santo Tomás de Avila, Avila
AUS	Archivo de la Universidad de Salamanca, Salamanca
AUSE	Archivo de la Universidad de Sevilla, Seville

Biographical Dictionary of Councilors of the Indies, 1717–1808

A

Abaría y Ymaz, Esteban José de (?–March 3, 1770)

Abaría was born in the late seventeenth century in the *villa* of Villafranca, Guipúzcoa. In 1710 he began fifteen years of service for the Ministries of War and the Exchequer. Named interim principal auditor (*contador*) for the House of Trade in Cádiz on March 29, 1726, he presumably moved into a regular position upon the death or retirement of Francisco Miguelez.

Upon the recommendation of Portocarrero,* the president of the Council, Abaría was named a minister *de capa y espada* of the Council of the Indies on July 2, 1738. Simultaneously he was ordered to serve as superintendent of the accounting office (*contaduría*) of the Council. Prohibited from actually entering the Council until he had straightened out the affairs of its accounting office, Abaría completed the task in 1741 and assumed his seat. In the meantime he also served with Quintana* as a plenipotentiary following the Convention of Pardo in January 1739. Promoted to the Cámara on March 9, 1753, he was appointed on September 11, 1754 to serve as well as president of the House of Trade. On January 31, 1763 he relinquished the presidency and resumed full-time service on the Cámara.

Honored with a knighthood in the Order of Calatrava in 1733, Abaría continued to serve on the Council until his death as its senior minister (*decano*). Abaría never married. He left as his only heir his brother José, who had retired as an accountant of the Senior Accounting Office (*Contaduría Mayor de Cuentas*).

SOURCES: AGI, Indiferente 866, 885, 894, 870A, *expediente* Abaría; AGS, XXIII, 13–9–490; 2–40-(no number); *Gazeta de Madrid*, April 3, 1770; Vignau, *Calatrava*, p. 1; Bernard, "Casa," p. 279; Lanning, *Diplomatic History*, pp. 148–49.

Acedo y Ximénez, Miguel Calixto de (1730–November 8, 1814)

Acedo was born in the *lugar* of Acedo, Navarre. His parents were Diego José Acedo y Alayza, a native of Acedo, and María Teresa Ximénez Alvarez de Loyola y Echauz of the *villa* of Rincón de Soto in Castile. His father, the lord of several villages and owner of several entailed estates, held the title Conde de Echauz. Miguel's paternal grandparents were Juan Manuel de Acedo y Dicastillo and María Ana Favita Alayza y Albizú. His maternal grandparents were Joachín Ignacio Ximénez de Loyola and María Catalina Alvarez de Loyola y Echauz, both residents (*vecinos*) of Rincón de Soto. His brother José Manuel, Conde de Echauz, died leaving him a small entail in 1791. Another brother, Diego Joseph, was a military officer. His sister María Manuela married Juan Esteban de Armendariz, an army colonel who bore the title Marqués de Castelfuerte and was related to the viceroy of Peru of that title. His sister María Ana Teresa was a nun.

Acedo received his higher education at the University of Oñate, where he studied from 1749 to 1751, receiving a baccalaureate in canon law in 1751, and at the University of Salamanca, where he spent nine years and was a member of the *colegio mayor* of San Bartolomé. He left Salamanca with a licentiate in law.

Named *oidor* on the Audiencia of Santo Domingo on September 25, 1763, Acedo served there until receiving his promotion to the Audiencia of Mexico as *alcalde del crimen* on March 16, 1774. He became an *oidor* there on July 10, 1776. During his years in Mexico Acedo served as supervisor (*protector y juez conservdor*) of the Sanctuary of Guadalupe and as superintendent of its aqueduct and textile works from 1779 to late 1786 or early 1787.

During his stay in America, Acedo attempted to secure his promotion to a Spanish tribunal; in 1779 his brother Conde de Echauz wrote to Minister of the Indies José de Gálvez* on his behalf. Acedo was named *oidor* on the Audiencia of the House of Trade (*Casa de Contratación*) on March 26, 1786, and began his service there in the following year. Promoted to the Council of the Indies to replace Areche* on June 24, 1789, Acedo entered the Cámara of the Indies on September 3, 1807, and served until his death. After 1806 he suffered from ill health, including rheumatism. He spent months taking the waters at Arnedillo. He sought retirement in 1809, but was named to the Council when Ferdinand VII restored it in the summer of 1814. On September 3, 1814, he was given permission to attend the Council at his pleasure.

Acedo's wife was Javiera de Areyzaga.

SOURCES: AGI, Indiferente 869, 870A, 871, 873, 887, 888, 1980; AGS 2–47–250, 2–58–69, 13–8–346, 2–60–158, 13–9–264; AHN, Universidades 661, *expedientes* 3,4,73; AHPUV, Libro 314, 343; Roxas y Contreras, *Historia*, II, 897–99; López Sarrelangue, *Una villa mexicana*, pp. 53, 63; Howe, *Mining Guild*, p. 86.

Afán de Rivera, Pedro de (variant: Perafán de Rivera) (?–c.1727)

Afán was born in Granada, the son of Gaspar de Rivera, a knight of Santiago and alderman of the city, and Juana Gadea y Bazán. He was a student and later a professor at the University of Granada, where he received the licentiate degree.

Named an *alcalde de hijosdalgo* of the Chancellery of Valladolid in 1692, probably as a dowry for his wife, he advanced to the court's civil chamber as an oidor with an appointment of November 23, 1701. In the "new disposition" (*nueva planta*) of 1713 that reorganized the tribunals at court, Afán became an *alcalde de casa y corte* or judge for the criminal chamber of the Council of Castile. Moved to Navarre as regent of its Council in 1714, he succeeded Juan Valcárcel Dato* as the *fiscal* for Peru on the Council of the Indies with an appointment of July 11, 1721. His service on the tribunal was brief, however, for he advanced to the Council of Castile as *fiscal* on July 27, 1723. Subsequently promoted on September 24, 1726 to councilor of Castile, he remained in that position until his death.

On October 1, 1692, Afán married *madrileña* Isabel Baca de Herrera, the daughter of Cosme Baca and Manuela Hurtado de Mendoza.

SOURCES: AGS, XXIII, 13–8–579; Gracia y Justicia, 133, 136, 137, 138; AGI, Indiferente 865; AHN, Estado 6380(2); 6396(1); Consejos 13530, 13531, 13537.

Aguado Fernández de Córdoba, Antonio Francisco (c.1672–May 1741)

Aguado was born in Alcázar in the Bishopric of Toledo. He began to study civil law at the University of Salamanca in 1688 and several years later became a *colegial* in its associated *colegio mayor* of Arzobispo. A propitious marriage brought him as a dowry an appointment as *oidor* of the Audiencia of Seville in 1697. A decade later, on June 24, 1707, he was named an *oidor* of the tribunal in Valencia and simultaneously a *fiscal* of the Council of Orders. Promoted to the Council of Hacienda as a minister *togado* in 1720, he also served as intendant general of the intendancy of Soria, but the dates of his service are unclear. On February 3, 1724 he was named a minister *togado* of the Council of the Indies to replace Rodrigo de Cepeda.* Five years later, on October 30, 1729, he advanced to the Council of Castile. While on the Council he served as the protector of the University of Cervera.

A knight of the Order of Santiago, Aguado died while serving on the Council of Castile.

SOURCES: AGS, XXIII, 13–9–371; Gracia y Justicia, 137, 140; AHN, Consejo de Ordenes 5298; Estado 6380(2); Consejos 13501; AUS, Libros de Matrículas 393, 397; Ferrer Ezquerra, *Catálogo*, p. 103; Rubio y Borrás, *Historia*, I, 170–71.

Agüero Riva, José Pablo (January 20, 1713–January 12, 1782)

Agüero was born in Cádiz. Felipe Arco Riva Herrera,* his fellow councilor of the Indies, was a relative. Agüero received a bachelor's degree in canon law at the University of Osma and incorporated it into the University of Valladolid, where he was in residence from 1726 to 1741. While at Valladolid, he competed for chairs in canon law.

Agüero was named *fiscal* to the Audiencia of Santo Domingo on October 4, 1742. The English captured the ship he was taking near Cuba, however, and he did not enter his post until September 1, 1744. He then served until 1761, when he was recalled to Spain. On March 14, 1765, he emerged as *fiscal* to the audiencia of the House of Trade (*Casa de Contratación*). Despite Arco's efforts to get Agüero named to the Council of the Indies as early as 1766, Agüero remained in the House of Trade until December 5, 1773, when named to one of the two new seats on the Council. He served there for the remainder of his life.

Agüero was awarded the Order of Charles III in 1774, a means of recognizing distinguished service in the civil bureaucracy. He became a member of the influential Committee on Commerce and Money (*Junta General de Comercio y Moneda*) on March 23, 1776.

Agüero was married to Josefa Gabriela Orruño y Frias, who outlived him. The couple had no children.

SOURCES: AGI, Santo Domingo 921; Indiferente 824, 866, 870A, 894, 906, 1980; AGS, XXIII, 2–33–313; 2–49–38; 2–57–281; Arribas, *Relaciones*, p. 5; Vignau, *Carlos III*, p. 10.

Aguirre y Salcedo, Francisco Antonio (1684–November 9, 1745)

Aguirre was born in Madrid. His parents were Vicente Aguirre and María Antonia de Salcedo, a governess for the ill-fated Luis I and the first Marquesa de Montehermoso. After serving as an aide to the governor (*teniente de ayo*) of the future Charles III and *mayordomo de semana* to Queen Isabel Farnese, Aguirre was named a supernumerary minister *de capa y espada* with full salary, immediate service, and an option to the first vacant regular position according to his seniority on October 8, 1731. He served on the Council from March 27, 1732, until his death.

In 1737 Aguirre assumed the title Marqués de Montehermoso.

SOURCES: AGS, XXIII, 13–9–591; AHN, Estado 6380(1); AGI, Indiferente 866; Bernard, *Secrétariat*, p. 217; Ballesteros Robles, *Diccionario*, p. 7.

Alarcón y Vargas, Luis Ambrosio de (c. 1659–March 5, 1732)

Born in Seville, Alarcón was a member of the Colegio de Santa María de Jesús (Maese Rodrigo) and received a bachelor's degree in canon law from the University of Seville, which he attended from 1674 to 1679. In the years 1676–77 he was a student of canon law at Salamanca. He also belonged to the Colegio Mayor de San Clemente of Bologna. The Audiencia of Seville admitted him to practice law. Alarcón served as a professor at the University of Seville prior to beginning his audiencia career.

Alarcón served as *oidor* on the court of Santa Clara in Naples. He fled during the War of the Spanish Succession, losing everything to the forces of Archduke Charles. In compensation, probably in 1708 Philip V named him an *alcalde de casa y corte*, the criminal division of the Council of Castile and the judicial authority for Madrid and the court. By a decree of November 19, 1712, Alarcón was named a minister of the Council of the Indies with instructions to accompany the newly named viceroy, the Principe de Santo Buono, to Peru and to carry out certain assignments there, including two years as governor of the mercury mine at Huancavelica. Alarcón and the viceroy arrived in Lima in October 1716.

Alarcón became an *oidor* of the Audiencia of Lima by an appointment of January 10, 1720, but retained his Council appointment. He gave up his audiencia seat in

Lima in 1723 to return to Spain and assume his post there. It was some years before he actually entered the Council, however, and only on May 22, 1730, did he take his oath of office and assume the position.

Alarcón was married and had at least two daughters, Leonarda and Victoria.

SOURCES: AGI, Lima 347, 348, 596, 866, 896; AGS, XXIII, 13–8–311; 2–18–201; Gracia y Justicia 140; AHN, Estado 6380 (1); Libro de Plazas 734; AUSE, Libro 484; AUS, Libro 38; Matute, *Hijos*, II, 120.

Alesón, Juan José de (July 14, 1758–June 22, 1818)

Alesón was born in Gandía, Valencia. His parents were Juan Manuel de Alesón Romero, a native of the *villa* of Sotés, Logroño, and Inés Bueno Alapont, a native of the province of Toledo. His paternal grandparents, Diego de Alesón Marín and Catalina Romero Fernández, were from Sotés. His maternal grandfather, Sebastián Bueno de la Fuente, was a native of Santo Domingo de Silos, Burgos. His maternal grandmother, Teresa Alapont, was from Puche, Valencia. A brother, Diego, was in the Order of San Hermenegildo and in 1818 was the commander and director of pilots for the naval station at Cartagena.

Alesón began his career with an appointment as a *guardia marina* in the Royal Navy on July 14, 1776. He later claimed to have been in twenty-five naval battles prior to his retirement as a *teniente de fragata* in 1789. In 1807 he was the chief clerk (*oficial mayor*) for the secretariat of the Navy (*marina*). On March 26 of that year he was named minister *de capa y espada* of the Council of the Indies. Alesón remained on the Council until its suppression in 1812. Left without an office, he sought an appointment that would provide an equal salary to that of councilor. Retired with half salary on July 2, 1814, on August 15 he received full salary so there would be no stain on his honor.

Following his retirement from the Council, Alesón received a license to move with his family to Sotés or San Vicente in La Rioja. He owned property in both areas, although he and his wife had allegedly suffered substantial losses as a consequence of the Peninsular War.

Alesón, a *caballero* in the Order of Charles III from 1790, bore the title Barón de Casa-Davalillo. The title had been created in 1795 for his wife Andrea Davalillo Palacios y Martínez de la Piscina. She had earlier been married to Felipe García Alesón, a knight of Santiago who had been a ranking clerk (*oficial mayor segundo*) in the ministry of the Navy. At the time of his death Alesón was in Cartagena, where his brother Diego was stationed.

SOURCES: AGI, Indiferente 888, 870A, *expediente* Alesón; AHN, Estado (Carlos III), *expediente* 407, *pruebas* of Juan Josef de Alesón; García Carraffa, *Enciclopedia*, VI, 115–6; Atienza, *Nobiliario*, p. 1419.

Alonso Acosta Zorrilla y Dávila, Cenón (January 3, 1756–?)

Alonso was born in Granada, the eldest son of Salvador Antonio Alonso Zorrilla y Río and Manuela de Acosta y Dávila, both also from Granada. His paternal grandfather, Francisco Alonso y Río Tusado, was a native of Burgos who had moved to Granada and married there his second wife Francisca Josefa Zorrilla y Narváez. Alonso's maternal grandparents, Sebastián de Acosta Sánchez and his second wife, Damiana Dávila Crespo, were from Granada as well. Cenón's brother Mariano studied law and ultimately became an *alcalde de casa y corte*. His uncle Manuel Alonso y Zorrilla was a prebendary of the Cathedral of Granada.

After securing an education in Granada that, according to one contemporary, resulted in his admission to the bar, Alonso left the city in 1782 and went to Madrid. His first appointment was as a low-ranking clerk (*oficial sexto tercero*) in the Secretariat of State for the Indies. In 1786 he was sent to New Granada as the secretary to the viceroy. The following April he was present in Cartagena de Indias. After returning to Madrid in October 1790, he resumed his career behind a desk. The following year he was *oficial tercero* in the Secretariat of State for Grace and Justice, the American division. He had advanced to the position of second clerk (*oficial mayor segundo*) by the time he was named a minister *de capa y espada* on March 23, 1805. Described as a man of placid temperament when he entered the Order of Charles III in 1791, Alonso was still serving on the Council when the Spanish War of Independence began in 1808.

A *caballero* of the Order of Charles III from 1791, Alonso's career subsequent to the French invasion of 1808 is unknown. He was not listed on the Council in September 1810.

SOURCES: AGI, Indiferente 866, 887, 870A, *expediente* Alonso; AHN, Estado (Carlos III), *expediente* 531, *pruebas* of Zenón de Alonso Acosta; García Carraffa, *Enciclopedia*, VIII, 69–70.

Alvarez de Abreu, Antonio José (1683–November 28, 1756)

Alvarez was born in La Palma, Canary Islands, where his parents, natives of Seville, had established residence. Domingo Alvarez de Abreu, his father, was a military officer (*sargento mayor*). His mother was María Yáñes de Abreu. Alvarez had two brothers, Domingo and Miguel, who were clerics in the Canaries. Another brother, Santiago, was an inspector and chief accountant for the military in the Canaries. A fourth brother, Francisco, was a military officer.

Alvarez began his school in the Augustine *colegio* in La Laguna. Proceeding to the University of Salamanca, he secured a baccalaureate in canon law in 1707. Briefly enrolled at the University of Seville in 1708, he then moved to Madrid, where he took a practicum with Manuel de el Castillo. The Royal Council admitted him to practice law in 1711. He subsequently spent two years in the study of Lucas Ortiz de Aldana, an attorney in Madrid.

In 1714 Alvarez began to hold royal appointments. After service as inspector of commerce between Castile and the Indies, a post that took him to Caracas, Venezuela, he was named an *oidor* of the House of Trade on March 9, 1727. He had previously served that body as a legal adviser (*ministro asesor*). Four years later, on January 21, 1731, Alvarez was named a minister *togado* of the Council of the Indies to replace Juan José Mutiloa.* Named to the Cámara on July 22, 1733, he apparently did not assume the position until a second appointment of February 2, 1741, named him to replace Gonzalo Machado.*

Alvarez sat on committees that dealt with commercial affairs (*juntas de tabaco, comercio y moneda, minas, negocios extrangeros*) and served for a time as the superintendent of mercury production. In August, 1755, Alvarez was excused from attending Council sessions because of failing health. Nonetheless, he participated as his health permitted until November 17, 1756.

Alvarez published *Victima real legal* (Madrid, 1726; 2nd ed. 1769) defending the king's right to use freely the revenues from vacant ecclesiastical posts in America. He was rewarded with the title Marqués de la Regalía in 1739 and a pension of a thousand pesos a year for his life and that of his eldest son José Antonio. He had four other children: Félix, Jaime, Antonio, and Miguel Antonio. Jaime, a knight of Santiago, was a cavalry captain. Félix served in the diplomatic corps and ultimately in the Council of War. Alvarez married twice. His first wife was Teresa Cecilia Bertodano, a native of Castillo de Ainza, Córdoba, and the daughter of Brigadier Alberto Bertodano, a native of Tudela, Navarre, and María Juana Keneper of Luxembourg. His second wife, Rosa Yarza y Urquizu, received a pension of 6,000 *reales* a year beginning in 1757.

SOURCES: AGI, Quito 1256, *relación* of 1721; Indiferente 480, 866, 870A; AGS, Gracia y Justicia 140, 141, *relación* of 1729, XXIII, 13–9–359; AHN, Universidades 661, *expediente* 2; Consejos 12148; AUSE, Libro 484; García Carraffa, *Enciclopedia*, III, 134–5; Miralles, *Escritores*, p. 45; Bernard, *Secrétariat*, p. 217; Bernard, "Casa," p. 30; Ozanam, *La diplomacia*, p. 186 n. 1; I thank D. S. Chandler for information included in this entry.

Alvarez de Acevedo, Tomás Antonio (January 24, 1735–October 31, 1802)

Alvarez was born in the *lugar* of Lois, Asturias. Both his father, Bernardo Antonio Alvarez Acevedo, and his paternal grandfather, Rodrigo Alvarez Acevedo y Canseco, were natives of Lois as well. Alfonsa Robles y Rodríguez Lorenzana, his mother, was from the *lugar* of Otero in the Bishopric of León. His paternal grandmother was Manuela Arguelles y Pérez Estrada of the *concejo* of Piloña, Asturias, and his maternal grandparents were Juan de Robles y Ordas of Otero and Bernarda Rodríguez Lorenzana y Quiñones of Canales. Tomás had a brother named Baltazar who might have been the Baltazar Alvarez Acevedo who had a son named Tomás Antonio and who donated a million *reales de vellón* to the Crown in 1766.

Alvarez began his higher studies in 1744 and graduated with a degree of bachelor of laws from the University of Osma in 1751, incorporating it at Valladolid the same year and subsequently at Salamanca. He eventually spent nine years at the University of Salamanca where he was associated with the Colegio de San Pelayo, serving twice as its rector. Although a contestant for academic chairs at Salamanca, he never entered the professoriat.

Alvarez received an appointment as *fiscal* of the Audiencia of Charcas on December 12, 1766. While in Charcas, he was active in modernizing the curriculum of the

University of Chuquisaca. From Charcas, he steadily proceeded up the ladder of promotion. Advancement to Lima as *fiscal del crimen* was confirmed by a title of office signed on February 16, 1774, and he ascended to the civil *fiscalía* the following year. On November 14, 1776, he was named the first regent of the Audiencia of Chile, a position he assumed on December 12, 1777.

As a lieutenant of José Antonio de Areche y Sornoza* in 1778, Alvarez opened the *visita* of Chile, which lasted until 1785. As *visitador*, Alvarez oversaw bureaucratic change and expansion, but change that made the new institutions serve himself and his friends. Since the government thus remained responsive to local desires, Chile was spared the revolts that plagued Peru and New Granada. Moreover, the *visita* aided Chile in establishing financial independence from Peru. Alvarez became involved in a major fraud over an alleged mercury mine in Punitaqui. He had already left Chile for Spain, however, before its dimensions were discovered. In Chile Alvarez protected Ramón de Pedregal, the administrator of the customs and a notorious grafter, along with others, in establishing a substantial following through his uses of patronage. He established close ties with the cabildo and other members of the audiencia, ties strengthened through his *compadrazgo* with *oidores* Francisco Tadeo Díez de Medina and Joaquín Pérez de Uriondo. Although sent to Chile as a reformer, Alvarez proved a master at maintaining what Barbier has called "business as usual." When the botanist Hipólito Ruiz and his expedition reached Santiago in 1783, Alvarez entertained them. He also employed the French scientist Joseph Dombey to run tests on the alleged mercury mine in northern Chile. In 1780 he served as interim president. Following more than a decade of service, a period during which he became the leading politician in Santiago, he was named a *ministro togado* on the Council of the Indies on October 15, 1788, a position he held until his death. Traveling via Montevideo, he reached La Coruña in August 1790, and assumed his seat on November 16. On the Council he was one of the ministers charged with revising the Ordinance of Intendants. Alvarez asked for a seat on the Cámara but did not receive it.

Like many other peninsular ministers, Alvarez in 1775 married a woman of New World origins. María Josefa Salazar y Carrillo was a native of Lima, the daughter of José de Salazar Traslaviña and his second wife María Josefa Carrillo, and a relative of oidor José Clemente de Traslaviña. She was related to the Carrillo de Córdoba family. She bore at least three sons: José de Alvarez de Acevedo became an audiencia minister in America; Juan Nepomuceno attended the Seminary for Nobles in Madrid; and Tomás also attended the same Seminary. The couple had two daughters. Rufina married José María de Pando y Remírez de Laredo who was a minister to Simón Bolívar. The younger daughter, born in 1792, was named María Gregoria.

The minister's many years of service were recognized in 1785 when he was admitted to the Order of Charles III, the order established to honor illustrious civil servants.

Alvarez de Acevedo died in Madrid.

SOURCES: AGI, Charcas 196, 423; Quito 231, *títulos y grados* of 1764; Indiferente 866, 894, 870A, *expediente* Alvarez de Acevedo; AGS, XXIII, 2–50–219; 2–58–31;

2-60-286; 13-8-658; AHN, Estado (Carlos III), *expediente* 234, *pruebas* of Tomás Alvarez de Acevedo; AHPUV, Libro 201; Medina, *Diccionario*, 65; Espejo, *Nobiliario*, p. 28; Navarro García, *Intendencias*, p. 127; Barbier, *Reform*, pp. 107, 111, 114, 117, 135–39, 151, 153; Steele, *Flowers*, pp. 124–26; Lohmann, *Ministros*, pp. 4–5; Levene, *Historia*, III, 150–51; Valgoma, *La nobleza de León*, p. 17.

Amorós, Francisco (?–?)

Amorós was a clerk (*oficial*) in the Ministry of War at the beginning of 1808. On January 15 of that year he was named a minister *de capa y espada* of the Council of the Indies. In September 1808 his wife wrote Brigadier Roque Abarca, president of the Audiencia of Guadalajara, New Spain, to send via a Cádiz merchant who was the godfather of her brother Francisco Terán some of the wealth Amorós had in New Spain. Terán, an *hacendado* of San Lucar who was the intendant of the region in 1809, was accused anonymously during Spain's War of Independence of being a "blind partisan of Godoy and the French." A deputy at Bayonne when Spain's first constitution was adopted, Amorós did indeed side with the French and support José Napoleon I. Named to the Council of State by the *rey intruso*, Amorós served as *comisario regio* for the provinces of Burgos, Guipúzcoa, Alava, and Vizcaya and as president of the criminal junta of Victoria. Writing from exile in Paris, Amorós published *Representación de consejero de Estado D. . . . a Fernando VII, quejándose de la persecución que experimenta su mujer . . . de parte del capitan general de Castilla la Nueva, y defendiendo la conducta que ha tenido Amorós en las convulsiones politicas de su patria, acompañada de documentos* (Paris, 1814).

SOURCES: AGS, XXIII; 2-91-213; Gracia y Justicia 1157; AHN, Estado 29G, p. 246; Artola, *Los afrancesados*, pp. 109 n. 55, 230–31, 243–44.

Antúnez y Acevedo, Rafael de (1736–October 3, 1800)

Antúnez was born in the *villa* of Arahal, Archbishopric of Seville. His father, Manuel Antúnez y Castro, a native of Córdoba, served various appointments as a district administrator (*alcalde mayor*) before being named an *oidor* of the House of Trade in 1763. His mother was Juana Acevedo y Herrera, a native of the *villa* of Mairena, Seville.

Rafael received a baccalaureate in canon law from the University of Seville in 1764. He then followed his father in service on the House of Trade, holding the post of assistant to the tribunal's fiscal (*agente fiscal*) from June 1765 until February 2, 1771. At that date he replaced his father, receiving half salary of 15,000 *reales de vellón* until his father's death.

On July 10, 1776 Antúnez was named to replace Pedro Calderón Enríquez* as a minister *togado* on the Council of the Indies. Conferred honors of the Cámara on May 21, 1798, he was then granted a seat on that body the following August 8. Antúnez's service was interrupted for a time in 1792 and then again beginning August 21, 1794, when he started suffering from intermittent fevers accompanied on occasion by spells of vertigo. As a result of the dizziness, physicians counseled that he cease "all mental activity" until he was recovered. By the following year, however, Antúnez was sufficiently recovered that he could petition for a position of page for his younger son Antonio. He remained on the Council until his death.

Antúnez married Manuela Mosti y Arambide, a native of Cádiz, with a license granted in 1776. She was the daughter of Antonio Mosti and Faustina de Arambide, also *gaditanos*. The couple had three children. Manuel was born in Madrid in 1780, attended the Seminary for Nobles in Madrid, and served as a page. His younger son Antonio also attended the seminary. His daughter Juana married Carlos Velasco, a military officer, no later than 1800. Through his wife Antúnez was related to her cousins José Jordán y Mosti and the Condesa de Mirasol. His brother-in-law Juan Domingo Mosti was a captain of dragoons. Another brother-in-law, Ignacio Mosti y Arambide, became an *alcalde del crimen* of the Audiencia of Barcelona in 1792.

In 1794 Antúnez examined the ordinances for the new merchant guild (*consulado*) of Caracas. Three years later he published *Memorias históricas sobre la legislación, y gobierno del comercio de los españoles con sus colonias en las Indias occidentales* (Madrid, 1797). In 1799 he authored *Compendio histórico del establecimiento del Consejo de Cámara de Yndias*. From 1794 his health was deteriorating badly. Granted a license to spend six months in Andalusia in June 1800, he died before its expiration.

SOURCES: AGS, XXIII, 2–55–12, 13–8–591, 13–8–601, 13–8–592; AGI, Indiferente 866, 894, 1980, 870A, *expediente* Antúnez; 902; AHN, Universidades, 661, *expediente* 50; AUSE, Libro 598; García Carraffa, *Enciclopedia*, IX, 153.

Aparici Alvarez y Pérez, Pedro (September 25, 1738–May 25, 1817)

Aparici was born in Madrid. His father, José Inocencio Aparici, a native of Barcelona, was a treasury official who served in the general treasury of Catalonia and as an accountant for the Infante Luis. Aparici's mother was Cecilia Josefa Alvarez y Pérez, a *madrileña*. His paternal grandparents were José Aparici, a treasury official in Barcelona, and María Font, both from Caldas de Mombuy, Granollers, Catalonia. His maternal grandparents were Antonio Alvarez de Miranda, a sargeant from Santiago, Galicia, and María Juana Pérez from Pradilla de Ebro, Aragon. He had a younger brother, Luis, and a younger sister, María Antonia. His uncle Francisco Aparici was an *oidor* of the Audiencia of Barcelona.

Aparici began his bureaucratic career in 1756 as second clerk (*oficial segundo*) in the accounting section of the House of Trade in Cádiz. Seven years later he returned to Madrid as sixth clerk (*oficial sexto*) for the Secretariat of State for the Indies. Advancing through its ranks, he was the chief clerk (*oficial mayor primero*) when on January 13, 1789, he was named to the same post for the Ministry of War and the Exchequer. On June 29, 1790 he was named director of the exchequer for the Council of the Indies and given honors of minister. Four years later, on December 23, Aparici was appointed chief accountant (*contador general*) for Spain's North American colonies (America *septentrional*) and given a seat as a minister *de capa y espada* on the Council. He served until 1808 and then was named to the reestablished Council and Cámara in 1814.

Probably while serving on the staff of the House of Trade, Aparici married María de Prado y Berdeja, a native of Cádiz. She was the daughter of José García de Prado, a merchant from Lugar de Casamaría, Santander, and his wife, a Gonzalez de Berdeja from Cádiz. Their eldest son, José Manuel, was born in Madrid, entered the Order of Charles III in 1790, and married Joaquina de Cía de Velasco, a native of Zaragoza. Son José was also born in Madrid. He wed *madrileña* María del Carmen Beramendi.

In 1783 Aparici was honored with an award as a pensioned *caballero* of the Order of Charles III. Given the right to attend the Council when he chose on October 18, 1814, he died presumably still holding his appointment.

SOURCES: AGI, Indiferente 875, 888, 870A, *expediente* Aparici, *relación* of 1785; AHN, Estado (Carlos III) *expediente* 158, *pruebas* of Pedro Aparici; García Carraffa, *Enciclopedia*, IX, 185–86; Bernard, *Secrétariat*, p. 224.

Arco Riva Herrera, Felipe de (July 8, 1710, baptism–August 7, 1785)

Arco was born in the *lugar* of Villaverde in the mountains and Archdiocese of Burgos. His parents, also from the Diocese of Santander, were Agustín de Arco Agüero and Teresa María Riva Herrera. His paternal grandparents were Juan de Arco and Josepha de la Cántara, also from the Diocese of Santander. From the same region were his maternal grandparents Juan Francisco de la Riva Herrera and Antonia de la Riva Agüero. He was related to Riva Agüero.*

On July 25, 1744, Arco received an appointment without the normal tax (*media anata*) as minister *de capa y espada* of the Council of the Indies as the dowry of his wife. He entered the post five days later. Advanced to the Cámara on September 17, 1770, he served until his death.

Arco married *madrileña* María Ana Piscatori y Baroni. His wife had served for fifteen years as a lady-in-waiting for Queen Isabel Farnese. María's parents were Lucio Piscatori, Marqués de San Andrés, and Angela Baroni, both from Parma, Italy. Her maternal grandmother was Laura Baroni. María's sister married a son of Díaz de Lavandero.* Arco and his wife had a son Bartolomé who was born in Madrid and entered the Order of Santiago in 1769. Of their two daughters, Teresa died as an infant and Angela died at the age of seventeen without having married. By Catalina de la Puebla, daughter of Ambrosio de Puebla Santiago and Josefa Ruiz del Castillo, all from Heras, Santoña, Santander, Arco had a son, Felipe, a native of Gajona, who became an army captain in the Toledo regiment and, in 1773, a knight of Santiago. By María del Campo, daughter of Pedro del Campo and Isabel de la Serna Cedrón, all from the Santoña region of Santander, Arco had another son, Bernardo, a native of Villaverde de Pontones, who became a captain in the Toledo regiment and also a knight of Santiago in 1773.

In 1772 Arco became a pensioned *caballero* of the Order of Charles III.

SOURCES: AGI, Indiferente 866, 898, 870A, *expediente* Arco; AGS, XXIII, 13–8–556; AHN, Estado 6380(1); Ordenes Militares (Santiago), *expediente* 554, *pruebas* of Bartolomé de Arco Piscatori; AHPM, Protocolo 17926; García Carraffa, *Enciclopedia*, X, 255–56; Bernard, *Secrétariat*, p. 219.

Areche y Sornoza, José Antonio de (variant: Zornoza) (c.1731–October 28, 1798)

Areche was born in Balmaceda, Santander, to Marcos Areche Puente Gómez de Santiago and Angela de Fuentes Santurce y Zornoza. His brother Manuel, a knight of Santiago, was a military officer. His paternal grandparents were Miguel Areche y de la Puente and María Gómez de Santiago; his maternal grandparents were José de las Fuentes y Santurce and Angela de Zornoza y Ruiz del Arco.

Areche claimed eleven years of higher studies at the University of Alcalá in canon and civil law. His academic work began in 1746. He received the baccalaureate in 1751 and the licentiate and doctorate of canon law in 1756. He was a member of the Academy of Professors of Santa María de Regla. From 1752 he held a fellowship in the Colegio de Santa Catalina Martír de los Verdes, later serving as rector. Areche competed for the chair of canon law at Alcalá in 1759 and substituted in various others.

Charles III named Areche *oidor* of the Audiencia of Manila on July 14, 1765, a post he never served. Borrowing 5,390 pesos in Cádiz in 1767 (still unrepaid twenty years later, creditors claimed), Areche set out for Manila. While passing through Mexico, however, he was drafted by the viceroy to serve the vacant *fiscalía del crimen* of the Audiencia of Mexico despite the tribunal's objections over the legality of the appointment. Areche's work won their praise quickly, however, and a year later the ministers petitioned the king to make the appointment permanent. This took place on November 13, 1767. Areche advanced to the civil *fiscalía* on January 17, 1774, and impressed José de Gálvez* during the latter's *visita* in Mexico. While fiscal Areche supported the *acordada*, actively seeking funds to improve their quarters. He was denounced twice for possessing prohibited books, including Diderot's *Encyclopedia* and *Thoughts of Voltaire*. Noted for his harsh, acerbic view of all Mexicans, he supported the visitor general's military reforms. When Gálvez became secretary of state for the Indies in 1776, he named Areche to be visitor general of the kingdom of Peru on March 25, 1776, and simultaneously a member of the Council of the Indies. Very shortly thereafter, Areche also became a pensioned member of the Order of Charles III.

Areche carried out a stormy and controversial *visita* to Peru during the late 1770s and early 1780s, clashing with nearly all authorities there. He was to examine both the financial and judicial bureaucracies, reform corruption where he found it, investigate *repartimientos*, look into the possible implementation of the intendant system, and reform the way in which tribute was collected. Areche reached Lima on June 14, 1777. His controversies first with Viceroy Manuel de Guirior and then with Viceroy Agustín Jáuregui led to their replacement. With Jáuregui's appointment in 1780, Areche gained the duties of superintendent for financial and economic affairs. His efforts to reform the Tribunal of Accounts and the treasury system were largely unsuccessful. Jorge Escobedo Ocaña y Alarcón* reestablished the previous subtreasury system. The effort to reform municipal finances in Lima also was a failure. Areche favored the establishment of intendancies there and opposed the notorious *repartimientos*. He emphasized economy over military preparedness.

His implementation of a "military contribution" or tax on free persons of color, although allegedly voluntary, created opposition from those affected. Ordered to return to Spain in 1781, Areche was replaced by Escobedo.* He assumed his council post on September 9, 1784. On May 27, 1789, shortly after the death of José de Gálvez,* he was retired as minister with only one-third pay and ordered to vacate the court. He died in disgrace in Bilbao.

Areche became part of the craze over platinum in the late eighteenth century; he presented a three-ounce nugget from Peru to the Basque Economic Society that came to the attention of Dombey and even Buffon. Areche even collected the ossified blade of a swordfish. He apparently never married.

SOURCES: AGN (Mexico), Inquisición, vol. 1100; AGI, Quito 231; Indiferente 1519; 159 *relación* of 1757, with addendum; 894, 866, 870A, AGS, XXIII, 2–49–109; 2–51–209; 2–58–9; 13–8–143; Pérez Balsera, *Los caballeros*; Archer, *Army*, pp. 17–19; Navarro García, *Intendencias*, pp. 43–44; Sarrailh, *La España ilustrada*, p. 453; Pérez-Marchand, *Dos etapas*, pp. 102, 167, 168, 79; Calderón Quijano, *Los virreyes . . . Carlos III*, I, 251, 308; Steele, *Flowers*, p. 66n.; Campbell, *Military and Society*, pp. 91, 121; Fisher, *Government*, pp. 17–19, 21, 25, 30, 101, 104, 106, 107, 180; Vignau, *Indice . . . Carlos III*, p. 18; Fernández-Mensaque, "El tribunal," pp. 319–20; Palacio Atard, "Areche y Guirior," passim.

Avila y Soto, Pedro de (1715–January 8, 1775)

Avila was born in Villarejo, Logroño. He attended the University of Hirache, receiving a baccalaureate in canon law in 1731. Incorporating the degree at the University of Valladolid in the same year, he remained at that university for two decades. After receiving a baccalaureate in civil law in 1735, he was admitted to the *colegio mayor* of Santa Cruz in 1737. Avila substituted in different chairs at Valladolid and held the chairs of *Institutes* in 1750 and *Código* in 1751.

On August 11, 1751, Avila was named an *alcalde del crimen* of the Audiencia of Barcelona. Appointed to serve as a legal adviser (*asesor*) for the Spanish army that invaded Portugal in 1762, Avila was rewarded first with honors of *alcalde de casa y corte* on May 27, 1763, and then with a full position on March 18, 1764. On March 18, 1767 he was named to replace Gerónimo de Sola* as a minister *togado* on the Council of the Indies. His service was brief, however, for he was promoted to the Council of Castile as a minister *togado* on July 28, 1768, and assumed this new post on October 26.

Avila was named a *caballero* of the Order of Charles III with pension in 1772.

SOURCES: AGI, Indiferente 894, 869, *expediente* Goyeneche; AGS, Gracia y Justicia 152, 158; XXIII, 13–8–544; *Gazeta de Madrid*, March 24, 1767, January 24, 1775; ASC, Libro 22, p. 174b; Alcocer, *Universidad de Valladolid*, V, 33; González García, *Datos*, I, 156.

Ayala y Medina, Manuel José de (March 26, 1728–March 8, 1805)

Ayala was born in Panama City. He was the youngest son of Tomás Francisco de Ayala and his second wife Juana de Medina Calderón, a native of Panama. His father, a native of the *villa* of Fuenmayor in La Rioja, Spain, had gone to Panama

City as a young man. There he served as treasurer of the royal exchequer. He enjoyed considerable success and by the early 1730s was able to loan more than three thousand *pesos fuertes* to newly arrived *oidor* Jacobo Sánchez Samaniego and to put up him and the cousin who traveled with him in one of his properties. His own house was described as "one of the richest and most opulent" in the city. Manuel José de Ayala's paternal grandparents, both from Fuenmayor, were Miguel de Ayala and Francisca Torrealva Salazar. His maternal grandparents, both from Panama, were Luis de Medina, a military captain, and Ysabel María Calderón y Hurtado. He had two half sisters, María Ambrosia and María Marcelina Ayala y Tobar, two brothers, Feliz José, who served as a treasury official in Portobelo, and Antonio, an attorney who was with him in Madrid in 1768. He also had three sisters. Eugenia and Angela entered religious houses; Isabel married José Vitor de la Guardia. His uncle, Manuel Ayala, was a knight of Calatrava and an accountant for the treasury in Lima, Peru.

Ayala received his early education at the seminary in Panama City. Moving to Spain in 1757, he quickly established contact with merchants in Cádiz. Settling in Madrid, he worked in the Ministry of the Indies. Julián de Arriaga, the secretary of state for the Indies, named Ayala in 1760 to found the archives for the secretariats of the Council of the Indies. Ultimately he became a chief clerk (*oficial primero*) in the Ministry of Grace and Justice. Named the director of confiscated Jesuit properties (*temporalidades*) in the Indies in 1788, he was simultaneously named a supernumerary minister *de capa y espada* of the Council of the Indies. Two years later, on February 8, 1790, he was granted a regular seat on the Council to replace Manuel Ignacio Fernández.*

In Madrid, Ayala had a number of close friends who also had ties to the Indies. Among them were Sánchez Samaniego, who died on the Council of Castile; Pedro León y Escandón*; the former visitor of the mines of Potosí, Ventura de Santelices;* and Juan José de Rovina, an accountant for the Tribunal of Accounts in Lima.

Ayala devoted a tremendous amount of time compiling a collection of royal *cédulas*, orders, regulations, decrees, *consultas*, and opinions related to the Indies. The collection was particularly valuable for he had gathered back together a number of documents that the secretariats of state had lost in the palace fire of 1734. In addition, Ayala provided more than 5,000 notes to the 6,400 laws in the *Recopilación*. The final collection was some 450 volumes. Although not all evaluators, notably Marcos Jimeno* and Francisco Echavarri,* approved his efforts, there was recognition that the effort was of some utility. Tangibly, Ayala received a pension of 1,000 *pesos fuertes* as a reward. He believed, however, that he deserved more and in 1797 claimed to have spent 23,000 pesos of his own money on the expenses of the collection.

Ayala married Ana María Fariña, a native of the *villa* of Neda, Galicia, and the widow of Francisco Lastarria, Chief of a squadron in the Royal Navy, with a license issued in 1775. The couple had no children. In 1785 Ayala became a *caballero* of the Order of Charles III with pension.

SOURCES: AGS, XXIII, 13–8–341; AGI, Indiferente 869A, 894; AHN, Estado (Carlos III), *expediente* 210, *pruebas* of Manuel José de Ayala; Estado 4817, *expediente* 18; Hacienda 505, No. 455; AHPM, Protocolo 22424; *Diccionario de historia de España*, I, 425.

B

Banfi y Parrilla, José (December 22, 1704–August 20, 1776)

An eldest son, Banfi was born in Trujillo, Cáceres, Extremadura. His father, Juan Bautista Banfi, a native of Madrid and lawyer, was serving as a provincial administrator (*alcalde mayor*) in Trujillo at the time of José's birth. His mother, Josefa Parrilla y Montoya, was a native of the *villa* of Escalona, Toledo. Banfi's paternal grandparents were Julio Banfi, a military officer who had been born in Melegnano, Milan, and María Teresa Torijano of Alcalá de Henares. His maternal grandparents were Francisco Parrilla of Castillo del Garcimuñón, Extremadura, and María Teresa de Rozas y Villalobos of Escalona. Banfi had a sister named María Teresa.

Banfi, who never went to the Indies, began his career in the Secretariat of the Ministry of the Indies on February 25, 1732, upon the proposal of José Patiño, the secretary of state for the Indies, navy, and exchequer. A decade later, at the behest of José del Campillo, the secretary of state for the Indies, navy, war, and the exchequer, he became a chief clerk (*oficial mayor*) in the secretariat. He was responsible for the issuance of decrees. On June 29, 1761 he was given honors of minister *de capa y espada* of the Council of the Indies and a supernumerary appointment to that body. On November 13, 1765, he entered a regular position vacated by the death of Fernández Molinillo.* Although blind by 1775, he remained on the Council until his death following a long and painful illness.

Banfi, a knight of Calatrava from 1752, was married to *madrileña* Manuela Montato, the daughter of Marcos Montato. The couple had at least two children, María Catalina, who married Francisco Xavier del Moral, and Nicolás José, born in Trujillo, a page for the king, and, in 1752, a knight of Calatrava.

SOURCES: AGS, XXIII, 13–8–167; Indiferente 870B, *expediente* Banfi; AHN, Ordenes Militares (Calatrava), *expediente* 222, *pruebas* of José Banfi y Parrilla; *expediente* 112, Manuel Ignacio Fernández Sarmiento; AHPM, Protocolo 19133; *Gazeta de Madrid*, September 3, 1776; García Carraffa, *Enciclopedia*, XIII, 134.

Bazán y Melo, Joachín Antonio (c. 1682–February 16, 1754)

Bazán was born in either Seville or Jerez de los Caballeros, Extremadura, the son of a Portuguese *caballero* and a woman from Extremadura. His paternal grandfather was Juan Carlos de Bazán, Marqués de San Gil, *comendador* of the Order of Alcántara, councilor of Castile, and ambassador to Savoy. His uncle García Fernando Bazán also served as a councilor of Castile.

Bazán went to Italy with his grandfather and attended a seminary in Rome. In 1697 he matriculated in the faculty of canon law at the University of Salamanca. Subsequently, in 1704, he received a baccalaureate in canon law from the University of Seville. He entered its *colegio* of Maese Rodrigo.

The first appointment Bazán received was in 1706 as a judge (*juez*) of the Corte de la Vicaria in Naples. Two years later, the year he returned to Spain, he was named an *oidor* of the Chancellery of Valladolid. Promotion to Seville as regent of the Audiencia followed in 1733. Named ambassador to the United Provinces of the Netherlands, he was appointed to the Council of the Indies as a minister *togado* on December 10, 1734 to replace Diego de Rojas y Ortega.* He reached the Hague on January 28, 1735, and remained an ambassador until September 11, 1746. In an unusual action, however, following a *consulta* by the Council on September 16, 1737, Philip V declared Bazán's Council post to be *de capa y espada*. An appointment as governor of the Council of the Exchequer followed on September 1, 1746.

Bazán, who married Juana Josepha Ortega Riaño y la Cerda, held the family title of Marqués de San Gil. The couple apparently had no children.

SOURCES: AGS, XXIII, 13–8–440; Gracia y Justicia, 139, 140, 141, 142; Secretaría y Superintendencia de Hacienda 1, 4; AHN, Estado 4814, 6380(1); Ordenes Militares (Alcántara), *expediente* 167, *pruebas* of Juan Carlos Bazán; AUSE, Libro 596; AUS, Libro 401; AGI, Indiferente 824, 894.

Bernardo de Quirós, Manuel (1699–March 10, 1784)

Bernardo de Quirós, a second son, was born in the *lugar* of Villa, *concejo* of Langreo, Asturias. His parents were Martín Bernardo de Quirós Estrada and Isabel Valdés Navia Osorio. His paternal grandparents were Martín Bernardo de Quirós y la Madrid and María de Junco Estrada. His maternal grandparents were Andrés de Valdés, señor of the House of Valdés in the *concejo* of Llarena and Antonia Navia Osorio.

Bernardo de Quirós spent five years at the University of Oviedo and then about two decades at the University of Salamanca. He was in the minor *colegio* of San Pelayo before entering the *colegio mayor* of Oviedo.

On January 25, 1740, Bernardo de Quirós was named a judge (*alcalde mayor*) of the Audiencia of Galicia. Advanced to Valladolid as an *oidor* of its chancellery on February 21, 1748, he subsequently spent about two years as *corregidor* of Guipúzcoa.

Promoted to the Audiencia of Mallorca as regent on November 19, 1753, he then moved to the same post of the Audiencia of Zaragoza on January 30, 1760. On June 22, 1766, Bernardo de Quirós was named a minister *togado* of the Council of the Indies to replace Juan Vázquez de Agüero.* He entered the post the following August 29. His health failing within several years, Bernardo de Quirós was in Oviedo in late 1772 soliciting retirement. His request was granted on May 15, 1773 and he was given half pay as a pension. He died in Oviedo, apparently a bachelor.

SOURCES: AGS, XXIII, 13–8–400; Gracia y Justicia 153; AGI, Indiferente 894, 1519, 871, *expediente* Bernardo de Quirós; 872, *expediente* Santos; AHN, Consejos 13532, 13495, 18735, 17954; Alvarez de la Rivera, *Biblioteca*, II, 157.

Borrull y Ramón, José (1685–November 29, 1750)

Borrull was born in Valencia to Pedro José Borrull y de Arbizu, a councilor of Castile, and Bernarda Ramón. His paternal grandparents were Sebastián Borrull, a notary (*notario*) and Teófila de Arbizu. José's eldest brother was Juan, an attorney and legal adviser (*asesor*) for the *diputación* of Valencia. Other brothers were Vicente, an audiencia minister in Spain, and Francisco Xavier, Bishop of Tortosa.

Borrull received his university education at Salamanca where he was a *manteista*, or student unaffiliated with a *colegio mayor*. Vice-rector of the University in 1706–1707, he secured a doctorate and for approximately a decade was the first professor of civil law. In addition, Borrull held a benefice in the parish of Jávea in Valencia.

Borrull began his audiencia career with an appointment as criminal *fiscal* of the Chancellery of Granada on July 17, 1724. The following year, on August 22, he advanced to the civil *fiscalía*. Promoted to *oidor* of the same court on November 29, 1728, his service in the magistracy was highly regarded. Named to replace Martínez Carvajal* as *fiscal* for New Spain on the Council of the Indies on February 27, 1738, he entered the post on March 26. Although conferred honors of Councilor of Castile in October, 1748, Borrull remained on the Council of the Indies until his death.

Borrull was a friend of the celebrated Valencia intellectual Gregorio Mayans and served as his protector.

SOURCES: AGS, XXIII, 13–8–213; Gracia y Justicia 135; AUS, *Libros* 411, 427; AGI, Indiferente 865, 885; AHN, Consejos 13519; Molas, *Magistrados*, p. 114.

C

Calderón Enríquez, Pedro (variant: Calderón de la Barca Enríquez) (February 17, 1704, baptism–May 1, 1781)

Calderón was born in the *lugar* of Terán, Valle de Cabuérniga, Diocese of Burgos, into a noble family. His parents were Sebastián Calderón Enríquez and Margarita de Ceballos, of Terán and the *villa* of Cabezón de la Sal, Santander. His paternal grandparents were Nicolas Calderón and María de los Ríos of Terán and the *lugar* of Valle. His maternal grandparents were Pedro de Ceballos Cos of Cabezón de la Sal and Francisca Cossio Barreda of the *villa* of Sotillana. One of five children, Pedro had two older brothers. Juan Antonio received the post of secretary to the king in 1748. By 1731 Manuel was in Peru.

Calderón boasted fourteen years of higher studies. After a fellowship in the College of San Gregorio in Valladolid, he proceeded to the University of Valladolid, where he received the baccalaureate in canon law in 1724 and in civil law in 1725. He performed his practicum with Pedro Manuel Esteban Montero, professor of *Institutes* at Valladolid, from 1726 to 1732. Calderón substituted in academic chairs at Valladolid and competed for professorships. The Chancellery of Valladolid accepted him as an *abogado* in January, 1732, and the Royal Council did so later in the year.

Calderón received his first audiencia appointment as supernumerary *oidor* of the Audiencia of Manila on September 8, 1736, taking possession on August 17, 1738. In the late 1730s Calderón moved against the Jesuits on charges of collecting rent from natives upon land for which the Jesuits did not have title. The charge was proved and the Crown upheld him. In 1745 Calderón was sent to deal with a Tagalog revolt over land usurpation by large estates. His mixture of force and leniency was successful and his support of the natives in securing protection from the encroachment by mostly Church estates won royal approval. While in Manila he served as *consultor* for the Inquisition in 1746. He pushed hard for the occupation and settlement of Upper California and was a strong supporter of the Philippines Company. During a dispute in 1759 over which ecclesiastical authority should become interim governor, Calderón was briefly excommunicated.

Having set out for Spain with a royal license, Calderón was captured by the British on the way. Notified in 1766 of his selection on June 29, 1764, as *oidor* of the Chancellery of Valladolid, Calderón never served there; his long experience in the Orient and during the English invasion won him a post on the Council of the Indies to replace León y Escandón* on August 23, 1766. He served in that post from October 13, 1766, until he was retired with full salary on April 23, 1776, as a result of an unsuccessful cataract operation. Calderón has been described as one of the new breed of officials critical of many features of the old regime and open to the new ideas of the century.

Calderón married María Teresa Fernández Toribio, daughter of Francisco de Fernández Toribio, an oidor of the Audiencia of Manila, and a native of the audiencia district of Manila. Their son José became an army officer in Manila and a knight of Santiago in 1773. Their daughter was named María Josefa. A third child, Manuel, served as an *alcalde* for the noble estate in Terán. In 1739 Calderón published *Discurso iurídico, en que se defiende la Real iurisdicción*. Although named a knight of Calatrava in 1742, it was not until 1751 that his genealogical materials were approved and he entered the order. He died in his home *lugar* of Terán.

SOURCES: AGI, Panama 124, *títulos* of 1733; Filipinas, 273; Indiferente 1519, 866, 894, 870B; AGN (Mexico), Inquisición, vol. 898; AGS, XXIII, 2–30–372; 2–31–394; 13–8–546; 13–8–535; Gracia y Justicia 158; AHN, Ordenes Militares, (Santiago), *expediente* 265, *pruebas* of José Calderón Enríquez; (Calatrava), *expediente* 398, Pedro Calderón y Ceballos; Cushner, *Landed Estates*, pp. 59–64; Pardo de Tavera, *Biblioteca*, p. 77; Schurz, *Manila Galleon*, pp. 53, 244, 410; Arribas, *Relaciones*, pp. 38–39; Medina, *Imprenta en Manila*, p. 131; *Gazeta de Madrid*, June 8, 1781; Blair and Robertson, *Islands*, XLIX, 178–79; Cunningham, *Audiencia*, pp. 419–20.

Capecelatro, Marqués de (var. Capezalatro) (?–?)

Capecelatro served on the Council of Italy prior to his appointment in 1716 as the Spanish ambassador to Portugal. In order to increase Capecelatro's income so he could continue in Portugal, on May 4, 1729, Philip V gave him an appointment as minister *de capa y espada* of both the Council and Cámara of the Indies with an exemption from service while he remained an ambassador. Replaced as ambassador on May 24, 1737, on September 16 of that year he was allowed to attend the Council at his pleasure as a result of the miserable state of his health.

SOURCES: AGS, XXIII, 13–8–448; Gracia y Justicia 166; Secretaría y Superintendencia de Hacienda 2; AGI, Indiferente 824, 865, 885; *Catálogo . . . Pellicer*, III, 16.

Carnero, Alonso (?–April 28, 1721)

Carnero served as a secretary of state with an appointment of 1694. His father Antonio Carnero had held the same position. Replaced the following year, he was named to the Council and Cámara of the Indies on July 6, 1695. He survived the various perturbations of the Council during and immediately after the War of the Spanish Succession and was reappointed as a minister *de capa y espada* when the Council was reorganized on January 20, 1717. He served until his death.

SOURCES: AHN, *Libro de Plazas* 731; Bernard, *Secrétariat*, p. 213; Escudero, *Los secretarios*, III, 655, 723.

Caro de Briones, Teodomiro (1715–June 15, 1774)

Caro was born in Carmona, Andalusia. He had at least four siblings.

Caro received his early education at the University of Granada as a student in the Colegio de San Miguel. After receiving a baccalaureate in canon law, he proceeded to the University of Salamanca, incorporating his degree in 1745. A *colegial* in Cuenca, he served as the *colegio mayor*'s rector. He also taught in the chair of *Decretales Menores*.

Caro was named an *alcalde del crimen* of the Audiencia of Valencia on April 10, 1755. Advanced to the tribunal's civil chamber as an *oidor* on February 1, 1763, he subsequently was named regent of the Audiencia of Asturias on March 28, 1770. On May 16, 1773, he was named to replace Manuel Pablo de Salcedo* as a minister *togado* of the Council of the Indies. He entered the post on July 17, 1773.

Named a *caballero* of the Order of Charles III with pension in 1773 while still the regent in Asturias, Caro died in his position as councilor. His wife María Luisa Lozella was probably the daughter of Francisco Lozella, an audiencia minister in Spain who ultimately reached the Council of Castile. The couple had a son named Juan.

SOURCES: AGS, XXIII, 2–57–61; Gracia y Justicia, 154, 161; Dirección General del Tesoro, Inventario 39, legajo 13; AGI, Indiferente 894; AHN, Consejos 13379 (2), *relación* of 1753; 18214, 18215, 13489; Vignau, *Carlos III*, p. 36; Molas, *Magistrados*, p. 100.

Carvajal y Lancaster, José de (March 16, 1698–April 8, 1754)

Carvajal was born in Cáceres, Extremadura, to Bernardino Carvajal y Vivero, the Duque de Linares and second Conde de la Quinta de la Enjarada, and Isabel de Lancaster y Noroña. Paternal grandparents were Juan de Carvajal y Sande Perrero, first Conde de la Quinta de la Enjarada and María de Viveroy Motezuma. Maternal grandparents were Agustín de Lancaster y Sande, Duque de Abrantes, and Juana Noroña Castro y Silva. His brother Nicolás, a gentleman of the royal chamber and military officer, through his wife became the Marqués de Sarria. His sister María received a substantial pension following Carvajal's death.

Carvajal began his studies at the University of Alcalá in 1711, received a baccalaureate in canon law from the University of Salamanca in 1717, and entered its *colegio mayor* of San Bartolomé in the same year. While at Salamanca awaiting a suitable position, he secured a licentiate. Named *alcalde de hijosdalgo* of the Chancellery of Valladolid on November 29, 1728, Carvajal took the highly unusual step of refusing the appointment on the grounds that it was inappropriate for a person of his background. The king accepted the argument, and on August 8, 1729,

Carvajal was named to the higher position of *oidor* on the Chancellery. When the Council of the Indies was expanded in 1738, he was named on February 27 to one of the two new places. Given a supernumerary position on the Cámara on April 29, 1740, he accompanied Portocarrero* as "second ambassador" to the Diet in Frankfurt, which elected Charles VII Holy Roman Emperor. After a falling out with Portocarrero, however, Carvajal returned to Madrid in 1742. He served as the Council's interim governor from October 23, 1742, until Portocarrero's return to Madrid in 1744 and as governor with an appointment of January 27, 1748. Named secretary of state and *decano* of the Council of State on December 4, 1746, during the early years of Ferdinand VI's reign he was a leading proponent of reducing Spain's ties with France and adhering to an independent foreign policy that would reduce tension with England. He labored tirelessly to make Spain a great power again. Among his other positions, Carvajal served from 1746 as president of the General Committee of Commerce, Money, Foreign Affairs, and Mines (*Junta General de Comercio, Moneda, Dependencias de Extrangeros, y Minas*) and beginning in 1747 as the superintendent general of the postal service.

A gentleman of the royal chamber, Carvajal was a knight of the Golden Fleece. He never married and left as heirs a brother, a niece, and a nephew, the Duque de Abrantes.

SOURCES: AGS, 13–8–205, 13–8–214, 2–40–233; Gracia y Justicia 137, 140, 145, 147, *titulos* of 1724; AHN, Consejos 13432; AGI, Indiferente 894, 885, 870B, *expediente* Carvajal; Agúndez, *Juristas*, p. 51; *Catálogo . . . Pellicer*, IV, 141; Escudero, *Los secretarios*, III, 726; Ozanam, *La diplomacia*, passim.

Casado, Pedro (?–?)

Casado was the son of Isidro Casado y Acevedo, Marqués de Monteleón, an outstanding diplomat who, among other positions, served as ambassador to Genoa and from 1711 to 1717 held an appointment as a minister *de capa y espada* on the Council of the Indies. Isidro was an influential adviser of Philip V. Pedro's brother was Francisco Casado.* His paternal grandfather was Pedro Casado, a senator of state in Milan.

On April 27, 1723, Pedro Casado was given an appointment as minister *de capa y espada* as a dowry for Isabel Piscatori, a lady-in-waiting for Queen Isabel Farnese and the daughter of Laura Piscatori, a native of Piacenza who was the queen's extremely influential former wet nurse and for many years her first lady of the bed chamber. Casado assumed his position but, having ceased to attend on December 18, 1725, was formally removed from his post on October 30, 1729. Luis Yopulo* was given a postion as a dowry for Isabel Piscatori in 1725.

SOURCES: AGS, XXIII, 13–8–576; AGI, Indiferente 844; Baudrillart, *Philippe V*, II, 238; III, 5; García Carraffa, *Enciclopedia*, LXXII, 229; Coxe, *Memorias*, II, 231, 304–5; Bernard, *Secrétariat*, p. 216.

Casado y Velasco, Francisco (Variant: José Francisco) (?–July 23, 1744)

Casado was the son of Isidro Casado y Acevedo, Marqués de Monteleón, who was retired in 1717 as a supernumerary minister *de capa y espada* of the Council of the Indies. Pedro Casado* was his brother.

Casado was granted a *futura* with salary and honors of minister of the Council of the Indies on October 31, 1726, as a reward for the services of his father. He was not to assume his place until a vacancy appeared on the Council. He died following an illness of two and half years, leaving his widow, Francisca Antonia de Ulloa, in debt.

SOURCES: AGS, XXIII, 13–9–597; AGI, Indiferente 866, 892.

Castaño, José Agustín (1726–March 12, 1807)

Castaño was born in the *villa* of Hellín in the Diocese of Cartagena. His parents, also from Hellín, were Salvador Castaño and Francisca Altes de Moya.

Castaño was a student in the Colegio de San Fulgencio in Murcia and received a baccalaureate in canon law from the University of Orihuela. From 1750 to 1757, he took a practicum in law in the office of José de Gálvez.* The Royal Council received him as an attorney in 1758 and he, in turn, trained other attorneys.

At the suggestion of his powerful *paisano* José Moniño, *fiscal* of the Council of Castile and later Conde de Floridablanca and a secretary of state, Castaño was named an official (*agente fiscal*) of that council in 1768. He served until 1782 when he was named governor and superintendent subdelegate of the mercury mines at Almadén. An appointment as *oidor* of the House of Trade followed on November 16, 1785. When that body was abolished on August 4, 1790, Castaño was given a supernumerary position as minister *togado* on the Council of the Indies. As a result of the successive moves to Almadén, Cádiz, and Madrid, Castaño was in debt in 1791 and unable to provide a dowry for his daughter. His plea was successful and in April, 1791, his salary was increased to the normal 55,000 *reales de vellón* although no regular position had become available on the Council.

Castaño married Josefa Ruiz de Funes, the daughter of Francisco Ruiz de Funes of Murcia and Antonia Torrecilla of the *Villa* of Autón de Santillana in Granada. Their son Pascual, born on March 24, 1770, was named an *oidor* of the Audiencia of Manila on September 16, 1797. Their son Aquilino, born in Madrid in 1769, was educated at the University of Granada and admitted to practice law by the Royal Council in 1790. Both he and his brother José became presbyters. The couple also had a daughter. After his wife's death, in the mid–1770s Castaño married Clara Sánchez Doncel, a native of the *villa* of San Torcaz.

Castaño was suffering from ill health from at least 1793 when he went to Trillo to take the waters. He died fourteen years later in Madrid.

SOURCES: AGS, XXIII, 13–8–83; AGI, Indiferente 885, 866, 894, 870B, *expediente* Castaño; 872, *expediente* Santos Domínguez; AHN, Consejos 12126, *expediente* 60; 12152, *expediente* 102; 12149, *expediente* 2; Burkholder and Chandler, *Biographical Dictionary*, p. 78.

Castillo y Negrete, Manuel del (c. 1750–?)

Castillo was born in the *villa* of Peñalver, Toledo. His parents were Manuel Castillo y Negrete and María Fernández Ropero. He attended the University of Sigüenza, gaining the bachelor's degree in canon law in 1767. In 1768 he joined the Academy of Canon and Civil Law of Madrid, teaching civil and canon law there and becoming vice-president. He became a *colegial* in Santa Catalina Martír in 1767 and transferred his bachelor's degree to the University of Alcalá in 1771, receiving the licentiate in canon law there. Castillo substituted in various academic chairs at Alcalá and competed there for others. He practiced law in Alcalá and Madrid from 1768 to 1776. Castillo entered a competition for a canonry at the Cathedral of Sigüenza and also at the *colegial iglesia* of the Royal Palace of San Ildefonso. In 1775 he was designated inspector general to the Bishopric of Sigüenza. The Royal Council admitted him as an *abogado* in 1777.

The king named Castillo a supernumerary *oidor* to the Audiencia of Manila on October 9, 1777; Castillo entered the post on July 29, 1778. He served as interim *fiscal* in 1781 and 1784–86. In the latter year he became the general legal adviser (*asesor general*) of the government. In Manila he was an opponent of the economic changes introduced by *oidor*/intendant Ciriaco González Carvajal. Castillo was ordered to the Audiencia of Guadalajara as *oidor* on June 7, 1787, but remained in the islands on orders of the governor as legal adviser of the superintendency of the treasury, writing new instructions and ordinances for all the provincial governing entities before proceeding to Guadalajara. The king ordered Castillo to Santa Fe as *oidor* on September 10, 1795, for marrying a native of the audiencia district of Guadalajara without permission. The move never occurred, however, for Viceroy Marqués de Branciforte detained him in Mexico City to deal with a backlog of criminal cases on the audiencia, and on May 16, 1797, the king regularized the appointment. Castillo served until elevated to the post of regent of the Audiencia of Guatemala on May 4, 1803. In 1804 he was one of several ministers there who expressed public thanks for the arrival of the first smallpox vaccine. Two years later Castillo returned to Mexico as regent of that audiencia with an appointment dated October 30, 1805, taking possession on July 7, 1806. On June 22 of the following year Castillo was promoted to replace Hernández de Alva* as *fiscal* for New Spain of the Council of the Indies, but as late as September 1809 he was still present in Xalapa, New Spain, waiting for a ship. He finally reached Spain and on March 22, 1810, assumed the position of *fiscal* for the recently and temporarily combined councils of Castile and the Indies. The Regency named him a *ministro togado* of the Council on October 27, 1810.

Castillo married Felipa María Soto Posada of Guadalajara de Indias in the early 1790s. Her father was Francisco Basilio Canal Soto Posada, *alguacil mayor* of the audiencia and a cousin of Ramón de Posada y Soto.* When Castillo made his testament on June 6, 1812, probably just before his death, his wife was deceased and he had seven minor children: Manuel, Luis, Joaquín, José, Francisco Xavier, María Guadalupe, and María de los Angeles. Luis, born in Mexico around 1799, was a provincial administrator in Spain during the 1830s.

Castillo wrote *Remedio político y civil para corregir los defectos de una República . . .* (Sampaloc, Philippines, 1779) and *Ordenanzas o instrucciones que se proponen para el régimen y gobierno del Hospicio general para los pobres Mendigos, Mugeres de Mala vida.* He also wrote *Discurso político y ordenanzas para fundar Hospicio en Manila* while serving there. For this effort he was incorporated in the Royal Academy of History in 1780. In 1792 he published *Manifiesto sobre la distribución que hizó de sus rentas decimales el Iltmo. Señor D. fr. Antonio Alcalde, Obispo de Guadalajara.*

SOURCES: AGI, Chile 172, *consulta* of March 3, 1777; 258; Charcas 423; Guadalajara 245; Mexico 1641, 1642, *relación* of 1791; AHN, Consejos, 13370–114, *relación* of son, 1831; Indiferente 865, 887, 869B; AGS, XXIII, 2–61–141; 2–71–143; 2–79–214; 2–81–82; 2–87–84; 2–89–152; 13–9–256; 2–92–306; AHPM, Protocolo 23639; Catalina García, *Biblioteca*, p. 64; Lanning, *Enlightenment*, p. 256; Navarro García, *Intendencias*, pp. 49–50; Lafuente Ferrari, *Iturrigaray*, pp. 117, 126; Pardo de Tavera, *Biblioteca Filipina*, p. 92; Medina, *Biblioteca*, V, 105, 312–13; Beristain, *Biblioteca*, 2nd ed., I, 273; Medina, *Imprenta en Manila*, 201.

Castro, Jacinto Miguel de (1707–March 13, 1773)

Castro was born in the *villa* of San Pedro de Latarce, Bishopric of Zamora. He received a baccalaureate in civil law from the University of Burgo del Osma and subsequently studied at the University of Valladolid. He took his practicum with Juan Martín Rico beginning in February 1730. Following Rico's death in July 1732, Castro concluded his training with Patiño.* The Chancellery of Valladolid admitted him to practice law in February 1735. He competed for chairs at the university on at least two occasions and offered clerking opportunities for men aspiring to become lawyers.

On March 16, 1752, Castro was named criminal *fiscal* of the Audiencia of Valencia. After a routine move into the civil *fiscalía*, he was named an *oidor* of the court on February 21, 1761. Promoted to regent of the Audiencia of Mallorca on March 16, 1765, he advanced to the Council of the Indies on September 27, 1770, as a minister *togado* to replace José de Rojas y Contreras.* Castro's service was brief. He entered his new post on February 6, 1771, and advanced to the Council of Castile as a minister *togado* on July 20, 1772. He died in that position.

Castro was married. His son Jacinto Xavier held several appointments as *alcalde mayor* and *corregidor* in Spain before being named to the Audiencia of Barcelona in 1777. He died as an *oidor* of the Audiencia of Valencia in 1793.

SOURCES: AGS, XXIII, 13–8–153; Gracia y Justicia, 158; AHN, Consejos 12116, 18213, 18221, 18735; AGI, Indiferente 866, 894; ARCV, Secretaría del Acuerdo, *caja* 16; *Gazeta de Madrid*, March 23, 1773; Alcocer, *Universidad de Valladolid*, III, 77; V, xlv.

Cavallero y Soto, Juan (1681–1741)

Cavallero was born in Medina de Rioseco, Bishopric of Palencia. He received a baccalaureate in canon law from the University of Alcalá in 1700 and incorporated it at Valladolid in 1705.

In 1706 Cavallero was named an *alcalde de la quadra* in Seville, a position he assumed in May. He was subsequently named *alcalde del crimen* of the Audiencia of Valencia but apparently never assumed the position, for he was still on the court in Seville when named *fiscal* of the Council of the Indies March 5, 1717, to replace Martín de Mirabal.* Cavallero began to serve four days later, but remained little over three years. On July 11, 1720, he was retired with half salary for poor health and, shortly afterward, given honors of minister *togado* of the Council.

Cavallero was married to a woman from Seville.

SOURCES: AGS, XXIII, 13–8–254, 13–8–247; Gracia y Justicia 135; AHN, Consejos 13501; AGI, Indiferente 865, 885, 1519; AHPUV, Libro 200.

Cavallero y Tineo, Bernardo (1701–July 1, 1774)

Described by a contemporary as "well born," Cavallero attended the University of Oviedo and competed for chairs there. Admitted to practice law by the Royal Council, he ran an open study at court from 1728. He made contacts in Madrid and on November 27, 1748, was named *fiscal* for the Audiencia of Galicia. Promoted to the Audiencia of Mallorca as regent, probably in 1761, he was advanced to the Council of the Indies on February 14, 1765. There he replaced Luis Francisco Mosquera y Pimentel* as fiscal for New Spain. His tenure was extraordinarily brief on the Council of the Indies, for in August 1766 he was named a minister *togado* of the Council of Castile. He served there until his death. Cavallero apparently never married.

SOURCES: AGS, 13–9–425; Gracia y Justicia 150; AGI, Indiferente 894, 870A, *expediente* Marqués de Aranda; *Gazeta de Madrid*, July 12, 1774; Canella Secades, *Universidad de Oviedo*, p. 451.

Cepeda y Estrada de Jerez, Rodrigo de (September 19, 1663–February 13, 1730)

Cepeda was born in the *villa* of Talavera de la Reyna, Toledo, to Rodrigo de Cepeda y Tofiño, a knight of Santiago, and Catalina de Estrada Gil Gibaja, both natives of the same district. His paternal grandparents were Rodrigo de Cepeda, also from the Talavera district, and Petronila Tofiño of the *villa* of Torrejón de Velasco, near Madrid. His maternal grandparents, both from Talavera, were Juan de Estrada de Jerez and Catalina González Gil de Gibaja.

Cepeda spent the years from 1683 to 1700 at the University of Salamanca. A *colegial* of Arzobispo from 1693 to 1700, he also held the chair of *Código*. Named *fiscal* of the Chancellery of Valladolid, probably in 1700, he became an *oidor* on that court on January 14, 1705. Subsequently he was named regent of the Audiencia of Valencia and intendant of the province of Cuenca. He may have briefly served in the Council of Orders. On February 8, 1718, Cepeda was named a minister *togado* of the Council of the Indies and granted honors of the Council of Castile. On October 25, 1723, he was promoted to the Royal Council, where he served until his death.

Cepeda married Rosa María Garma de la Puente, a *madrileña*. Their son Bernardo, born in Valencia, became a knight of Santiago in 1717. Cepeda, himself a knight of Santiago from 1707, was recognized as an author. While on the Council of Castile he served for several years as protector of the University of Cervera.

SOURCES: AGS, XXIII, 13–8–607, 13–8–606; AHN, Consejos 13531, Estado 6380(2); Ordenes Militares (Santiago), *expediente* 1875, *pruebas* of Rodrigo de Cepeda Estrada; Rezabal, *Biblioteca*, p. 452; Vignau, *Santiago*, p. 78; García Carraffa, *Enciclopedia*, XXVI, 43.

Cerda y Soto, José Antonio de la (August 13, 1727–February 21, 1797)

Cerda was born in the *villa* of Tendilla, the second son of Manuel de la Cerda y Soto, a native of the *villa* of Fuente el Viejo, and María Baquero Remírez de Arellano of the *villa* of Gascueña in the Diocese of Cuenca. The couple married in Tendilla in 1709. Cerda's paternal grandparents were Francisco de la Cerda, a militia captain, and native of Tendilla, and María Remírez de Arellana of Fuente el Viejo. His maternal grandparents were Juan Baquero Remírez de Arellano of Fuente el Viejo and María García Baquero of Gascueña. José's only and older brother Manuel Francisco died in 1766. His uncle Phelipe de la Cerda had been a *colegial* in the *colegio mayor* of Arzobispo at the University of Salamanca, turned down an appointment as a *fiscal* of the Audiencia of Quito, and accepted a position on the cathedral chapter of Ciudad Rodrigo. A number of more distant relatives had held prominent civil and ecclesiastical positions.

Cerda began his higher studies in 1738. In 1743 he received the bachelor's degree in canon law, and in 1749 he obtained the licentiate and doctorate in that faculty from the University of Alcalá. In 1744 he assumed a fellowship in the *colegio mayor* of San Ildefonso. During his years at Alcalá, Cerda competed for and substituted in various academic chairs.

On December 29, 1754, Cerda was named *oidor* of the Audiencia of Santo Domingo. He took the *residencia* of the former governor in 1758–60 and served as interim captain general in 1760. Cerda requested an appointment to the Audiencia of Aragon in 1765; in 1766 he received a license to return to Spain, and following his arrival in March 1767 the Cámara of Castile was ordered to consider him for appointments. On December 9, 1767, he was named *alcalde del crimen* of the Audiencia of Aragon. Two years later, on December 17, he was named *oidor* of the Chancellery of Granada. On October 10, 1774, Cerda was appointed a *ministro togado* of the Council of the Indies. *Preeminencias* followed on April 27, 1794. Cerda served on the influential Committee of Commerce and Money from 1774, and was the senior member by 1794. Although not required to attend the Council since 1794, he continued to serve by commission the post of legal adviser and general superintendent of the mercury monopoly until his death in Madrid.

Cerda married María Teresa Sebes de Caseba, possibly while still in America. After her death and with a license issued in 1774, he married Melchora Martínez de Bustos y Martínez, whose brother Patricio was a minister of the Council of Hacienda. Cerda's only child, Manuel, studied at Alcalá and received a baccalaureate in canon law. Cerda became a *caballero* with pension of the Order of Charles III in 1786.

SOURCES: AGI, Charcas 195, *relación* of 1753; Indiferente 865, 869, 870B, 886, 892, 894, 902; AGS, Gracia y Justicia 159, 160; XXIII, 2–40–157; 2–58–290; 13–8–78; AHN, Consejos 13521, 17957; Estado (Carlos III), *expediente* 238, *pruebas* of José

Antonio de la Cerda. AHPM, Protocolo 19734; *Gazeta de Madrid*, March 14, 1797; Mejía Ricart, *Historia*, VI, 388.

Cerdán y Pontero, Ambrosio (variant: Cerdán Simón Pontero) (February 7, 1752, baptism–1803)

Born in Barcelona, Cerdán was the son of an *oidor* and grandson of a councilor of Castile. His father, Dionisio Cerdán de Landa, a native of Cuenca and knight of Alcántara, was serving on the Audiencia of Barcelona at the time he died. His maternal grandfather, Andrés Simón Pontero, a native of Chillarón del Rey in the Bishopric of Cuenca, served in a series of Spanish courts before reaching the pinnacle of the Council of Castile; he married Teresa Torroba of Soria. Cerdán's paternal grandparents were Francisco Javier Cerdán de Landa, an alderman (*regidor perpetuo*) and native of the city of Cuenca, and Juana María Cerdán de Landa, also of Cuenca. After his father's death, Cerdán's mother, María Carlos Simón Pontero, a native of Teruel, Aragon, married Juan Moreno Beltrán, a bureaucrat who ended his career on the Council of Orders. Cerdán's full sister María Teresa, who died in Madrid in 1781, had married José Merchante y Contreras, an audiencia minister in the Indies. Cerdán also had three half brothers (Cayetano, Fernando, and Mauriano) and a half sister (María Teresa) who entered a religious house in Granada. Carlos Simón Pontero, a minister of the Council of Orders, was Cerdán's uncle.

Cerdán began his higher studies in 1763. At the University of Siguenza he received the bachelor's degree in canon law in 1768. He enrolled in the first year of civil law at the University of Valladolid in 1768, then transferred the degree in canon law to the University of Alcalá in 1770. Cerdán claimed a licentiate, perhaps by virtue of being an attorney, belonged to the Academy of Civil and Canonical Law of the Royal Court, the Royal Academy of San José at Alcalá, the Royal Academy of Public Law of Madrid, and was a professor in the Academy of Canons, Liturgy and Ecclesiastical History of San Isidro at court.

Allowed to practice law by the Royal Council in 1772, Cerdán received his first audiencia appointment on August 25, 1776, with the expansion of the court in Chile. As its first *fiscal del crimen*, he took possession on April 3, 1777. Cerdán was important in reopening a former Jesuit college for Indian nobles and establishing the Caroline Academy, an academy for practical jurisprudence. He wrote regulations for both. A bachelor upon his arrival in Santiago, Cerdán soon prepared to marry locally born Josefa Encalada, daughter of the Marqués de Villapalma. The Crown granted his request for a license but transferred him to Lima as an *alcalde del crimen* on March 6, 1779. Cerdán arrived in Lima with Viceroy Agustín de Jáuregui on January 2, 1780. Promotion as an *oidor* followed on December 4, 1784. Two years later he wrote a set of regulations for Lima's theater (*coliseo de comedias*). An unsolicited advancement to Guatemala as regent followed on November 29, 1794. When Cerdán arrived in Guatemala in 1796 his ship was placed in quarantine because a number of persons aboard, including three of his five daughters, had recently had smallpox. In 1800 his uncle Carlos Simón Pontero, then on the Council of Orders, unsuccessfully sought Cerdán's appointment as a minister *togado* on the Council of the Indies. Although subsequently named to replace Cistué as *fiscal* for Peru of the Council of the Indies on March 5, 1803, Cerdán never served, for he died en route in Vera Cruz of yellow fever.

Cerdán's marriage to Josefa Encalada in 1779 linked him to a growing familial web of audiencia marriages. Other daughters of Manuel Calvo de Encalada, Marqués de Villapalma, and Margarita Recabarren y Pardo de Figueroa married Lorenzo Blanco Cicerón, Fernando Márquez de la Plata y Orozco and José Lucas de Gorvea y Vadillo.* Josefa was also a cousin of Gaspar Antonio Remírez de Laredo. Cerdán and his wife had five children. Their son Dionisio and another son were in the first class admitted to the ill-fated College for American Nobles that was to have opened in Granada. The English seized their ship, however, and they arrived in Spain without any belongings.

Cerdán was thoroughly imbued with the ideas of the Enlightenment as it filtered through Spain. He opposed traditional formal and professionally oriented universities, and as protector of the Convictory of San Carlos in Lima, approved the revised plan of studies prepared by Toribio Rodríguez de Mendoza and Fray Diego Cisneros. An active participant in Lima's Economic Society, he wrote for its paper, the *Mercurio peruano*, under the name "Nercadio" and became president of the society following José Xavier de Baquíjano's departure for Spain. In Guatemala, however, he was hostile to *oidor* Jacobo de Villaurrutia and the *Gazeta de Guatemala*, probably from personal antagonism and jealousy rather than principle, and was considered to be part of the conservative group. Cerdán published *Oratio de juris publici, et hispaniarum legum studio* (Madrid, 1773) and *Tratado sobre las aguas que fertilizan los valles de Lima* (Lima, 1793), which was reprinted several times. He was a *caballero* of Charles III from 1794.

As a result of the Crown's catastrophic financial condition, the requests of his children that their official pension be increased were denied in 1807.

SOURCES: AHN, Estado (Carlos III), *expediente* 165, *pruebas* of Ambrosio Cerdán de Landa y Pontero; AGI, Guadalajara 242; Guatemala 525; Santa Fe 547; Charcas 501, *relación* of 1773; Indiferente 871, 872 *expediente* Saavedra; Ultramar 861; AGS, XXIII, 2–60–195; 2–63–20; 2–68–227; 2–78–173; 13–9–40; AHPUV, Libro 80; Espejo, *Nobiliario*, p. 255; Medina, *Diccionario*, p. 999; AHN, Consejos 20344; Cooper, *Disease*, p. 95; Lanning, *Enlightenment*, pp. 84, 89, 90, 333; Luque Alcaide, *Sociedad económica*, pp. 36, 51, 125–26; Lohmann Villena, *Ministros*, pp. 33–34; Vargas Ugarte, *Historia*, V, pp. 45–46; Góngora, *Studies*, p. 190; Vargas Ugarte, *Impresos*, X, 295; Lohmann Villena, "Las relaciones," pp. 323–24n.5

Cistué y Coll, José de (December 27, 1725–January 1, 1808)

Cistué was born in the *villa* of Estadilla, Aragon, to Francisco Antonio Atilano de Cistué y Ejea, *Señor* of Estadilla and a native of the town, and Rosa Coll y Chia of Calasanz. His paternal grandparents were José Cistué y Puyuelo of Estadilla and Antonia de Ejea y Ejea of Fonz. His maternal grandparents were Nicolás Coll y Viverón of Calafanz and Geronima Chia y Balafanz of Capella. His older brother

Pedro, the first Barón de la Menglana, was also an attorney and served as his *apoderado*. From his brother José Cistué inherited the title of second Barón de la Menglana. His only sister, María Antonia, married Antonio Mozarbe.

Cistué claimed twenty years of higher studies in 1755—three in philosophy at the University of Zaragoza and the other seventeen in law at the University of Huesca. At Huesca he spent fourteen years as a *colegial* in the *mayor* of San Vicente Martír, where he was rector. He received baccalaureates in civil and canon law from Huesca, and eventually doctorates. Cistue served the chair of *Decretos* in 1746, the second chair of canon law in 1749, and from 1752 to 1754 the chair of *Institutes* at Huesca. He also served a term as vice-rector of the university. The Bishop of Lérida named him his *vicario general* and *provisor*.

In 1754 Cistué received one first place and one second place vote on a *consulta* for *oidor* in Santo Domingo; in 1756 he received a third-place vote for *oidor* in Guatemala, and on March 4, 1758, he was selected to be *fiscal* in the Audiencia of Quito. While there he became godfather to the Marqués de Selva Alegre, who was a leader in the 1809 conspiracy and revolt in Quito. The Crown moved Cistué to Guatemala as *oidor* in 1772 because of his unpopularity with the plebeians of Quito after introducing new revenue measures (popular with the Crown, although they touched off the uprising of 1765). Although he briefly supported public opposition to the taxes, he soon thought better of it and fled to Latacunga for safety. On February 7, 1773, the king named him instead to the *fiscalía* of Guatemala, a position he served until promoted to *alcalde del crimen* in Mexico on June 21, 1775. As *fiscal* in 1775, Cistué rendered a sound plan for constructing the new Guatemala City in the wake of the devastating earthquake of 1773. He described buildings that would be as earthquake-proof as possible yet attractive and functional. Unfortunately his plan was not followed closely by the builders. Named *fiscal* for Peruvian affairs on the Council of the Indies to replace Piña* on October 28, 1777, Cistué assumed his position on June 15, 1778. On October 26, 1787, he was given a vote in the Cámara of the Council of the Indies when his activities as *fiscal* allowed him to participate. He served on the influential General Committee of Commerce, Money and Mines. Cistué retired with full salary on September 25, 1802, with "broken health."

Cistué received a license in 1782 to marry María Josefa Martínez de Jiménez Pérez y Manrique de Lara, lady-in-waiting to the future Queen María Luísa. They had at least three children: Luis María, who was admitted to the Order of Charles III in 1802, fought against the French at Zaragoza, later became *oidor* of the Audiencia of Valencia, and ultimately was a field marshal under Isabel II; José María, who also fought at Zaragoza and later married the sister of the Marqués de Campo Sagrado; and Francisco.

In 1782 Cistué was admitted to the Order of Charles III, with pension. He died in Zaragoza.

SOURCES: AGI, Quito 124, *relación* of 1755; Indiferente 870A, *relación* of 1773, 870B, 902, 865, 886, 1519; Guatemala 515, *relación* of 1753; 425; AGS, XXIII, 2–43–79; 2–57–12; 2–59–70; 2–60–159; 13–8–142; 13–8–80; 13–9–221; AHN,

Estado (Carlos III), *expediente* 130, *pruebas* of José de Cistué; Pérez Valenzuela, *Nueva Guatemala*, pp. 104–5; Carrera Andrade, *El camino*, p. 300; Zúñiga, *Montúfar*, p. 114; *Gazeta de Madrid*, March 11, 1808, p. 254, February 16, 1790; García Carraffa, *Enciclopedia*, XXVI, 207–8.

Contreras y Zúñiga, Pedro Domingo de (Variant: Contreras y Guillamas) (c. 1675–?)

Contreras was born in Segovia. His uncle Francisco Contreras was president of the Council of Castile, and his uncle Antonio Contreras served on the Cámara of Castile. His brother Manuel was an army officer.

Contreras was associated with the universities of Alcalá, Salamanca, where he enrolled as a second-year student in canon law in 1692–93, and Avila, from which he received a baccalaureate and licentiate in canon law in December 1696. At Salamanca he was a *colegial* in Arzobispo for over twenty years and taught in different chairs of civil law.

In 1716 Contreras left Salamanca to assume an appointment of June 17 as *fiscal* of the Audiencia of Seville. Advanced to *oidor* of the court on January 22, 1720, he subsequently rose to the Council of Hacienda in 1729. On November 22, 1731, Contreras was named visitor general of New Spain. He remained there only briefly, however, for he was back in Madrid in October 1734, assuming a post of minister *togado* on the Council of the Indies to which he had been named on September 22. Replacing Gonzalo Machado* on the Council, he served until December 31, 1751.

SOURCES: AGS, XXIII, 13–8–564; Gracia y Justicia 133, 140, 143; AHN, Consejos 13501; AGI, Indiferente 164, 137, 869, 870B, *expediente* Contreras; AUS, Libros 397, 405; AUAV, Registro de Grados 1696; Ferrer Ezquerra, *Catálogo*, p. 105; Larios, *Nobiliario*, V, 76.

Cornejo y Ibarra, José (March 20, 1688–December 12, 1764)

Cornejo was born in Seville and one of six children still living in 1717. His father was Alonso López Cornejo, a native of San Lucar la Mayor in the Archdiocese of Seville who owned property including some vineyards outside of the city of Seville. His mother, Andrea de Ybarra y Góngora was from Seville. His paternal grandparents were Antonio Cornejo and Ana Sebastiana María Soldán, a *vecina* of Seville. His maternal grandparents were Blas Ybarra, a native of Seville, and Beatriz de Góngora.

Cornejo studied canon law and received a baccalaureate in the faculty from the University of Seville on October 23, 1707. He ultimately secured a doctorate in canon law. Beginning in 1708, he began to compete for chairs at the University of Seville. The only contestant for the one of *Decretales Mayores* in 1711, he was duly named to fill it. The following year, however, he was in Madrid and the chair was declared vacant. His father later related that he had spent 1500 *ducados de vellón* on his son's degrees and travel to Madrid.

Cornejo began his government service in 1712. After working as an interim *agente fiscal* for the Peruvian desk, on February 3, 1716, he was named the regular *agente fiscal* for the New Spain desk. Cornejo was subsequently named superintendent of mines at Almadén. For his services he was given honors of minister of the House of Trade on February 22, 1728, and a regular post of oidor there on January 23, 1731, but with orders to remain temporarily in Almadén.

On July 29, 1734, Cornejo was named a minister *togado* to replace Andrés Orueta.* Taking possession of the post on August 3, 1734, Cornejo advanced to the Cámara on March 9, 1753. Not long before his death, on January 12, 1764, he received the right to attend the Council at his pleasure.

As a minister *togado*, Cornejo analyzed reports on the Huancavelica mercury mine in Peru. From his recommendations for reform and direct control of the mine by the Council of the Indies came Gerónimo Sola's* appointment as superintendent general of the mines.

In Toledo in 1725 Cornejo married Teresa Leocadia Castaño, daughter of Andrés Castaño y Vargas and Juana Francisca de Estrada, all natives of the city. The couple had at least three sons. José Antonio Cornejo y Castaño, born in Almadén, became a knight of Santiago in 1736. Manuel, born in Madrid, entered the same order simultaneously. A third son, Andrés Bruno, also a knight of Santiago, served on the Chancellery of Valladolid for many years after having been a *colegial* in the *colegio mayor* of San Ildefonso at the University of Alcalá de Henares. He married María Josepha de Jaureguizondo.

SOURCES: AGS, XXIII, 13–8–256, 13–8–223, 13–8–256; Gracia y Justicia 914; AGI, Indiferente 1628, 870B, *expedientes* Contreras and Cornejo; AHN, Ordenes Militares (Santiago), *expediente* 2131, *pruebas* of Andrés Bruno Cornejo Castaño; AUSE, Libros 596, 930; *Gazeta de Madrid*, January 1, 1765; García Carraffa, *Enciclopedia*, XXVII, 172; Bernard, "Casa," p. 30; Whitaker, *Huancavelica Mercury Mine*, pp. 23–24.

Cortines, Francisco Ignacio (August 11, 1745–March 14, 1806)

Cortines was born in Seville. His father, also a *sevillano*, was the treasurer for Seville's city income (*tesorero de propios y arbitrios*). His mother was *sevillana* María Antonio de Andrade y Herrera. His paternal grandfather, Fernando González de Cortines, was from the *lugar* of Zizera, in the mountains of Santander, Archbishopric of Burgos. His paternal grandmother was *sevillana* María Sipriana Crespo de Cortines. His maternal grandparents were Francisco de Andrade, a native of Seville who had been a chief notary for the navy (*escribano mayor de la real marina*) and Juana de Herrera y Peralta, a native of the *villa* of Umbrete, close to Seville. His siblings, all younger, were Ramón, Nicolas Antonio, Manuel, and María de la Paz.

At the University of Seville Cortines studied three years of philosophy and four of theology in addition to canon law, in which he received the baccalaureate, the licentiate and the doctorate in 1762. In 1763 he received bachelor's degrees in philosophy and theology. He also presided over an Academy of Canon Law for two years and was an honorary member of the Academy of Bellas Letras in Seville. While in Seville he served as regent in the chair of *Código* and the second chair (*vísperas*) of canon law. He became an attorney before the Audiencia of Seville, the Royal Council in 1771, and a member of the Colegio de Corte in 1772. He attended the study of the Conde de Floridablanca from 1769 to 1772 for his practicum and assisted the *agente fiscal* of the Council of Castile.

In 1774 Cortines was named *fiscal* of the royal irrigation works of Xarama y Colmenar, and five years later, on November 10, he was appointed lieutenant governor and legal adviser and judge for military affairs (*teniente de gobernador* and *auditor de guerra*) of the province of Venezuela, a post he assumed on July 16, 1780. On October 17, 1786, Cortines won the second place of *oidor* of the new Audiencia of Caracas; he assumed his seat on April 12, 1787. From his days as a lieutenant governor, Cortines had trouble with the Caracas city council, and the *caraqueños* viewed with pleasure his promotion on July 28, 1801, as regent of the Audiencia of Quito. He never served that appointment, however. Promoted to the Council of the Indies to replace Valenzuela* on March 20, 1806, he died in Venezuela before the title of appointment was even issued.

In 1779 Cortines joined the Economic Society of Madrid. He had earlier authored a *Discurso político sobre el establecimiento de los hospicios en España* (Madrid, 1768). In 1797 he entered the Order of Charles III.

His wife was Josefa Espinosa y Cortines, who was in Madrid in late 1802 and at the time of his death, possibly living there permanently. Her brother Manuel Sixto Espinosa, the accountant for seized Jesuit properties in the Indies in 1795, later served on the Council of Hacienda.

SOURCES: AGI, Indiferente 870B, 872, 1627, 871, 869, *relación* of 1794; Charcas 510, *relación* of 1775; Chile, 173; Santa Fe 548; Ultramar 862; AGS, XXIII, 2–63–151; 2–70–225; 2–85–104; 13–9–105; Secretaría y Superintendencia de Hacienda 396; AHN, Estado (Carlos III), *expediente* 1011, *pruebas* of Francisco Ignacio de Cortines; Matute, *Hijos*, I, 263; García Chuecos, *Estudios*, II, 12, I, 7–9.

D

Díaz de Lavandero y Martín, Mateo Pablo de (May 5, 1681–April 18, 1746)

Díaz was born in Pelahustán, Diocese of Toledo, to Miguel Díaz de Don Pablo and María Martín de Córdova. His father was from Las Navas del Marqués, Avila; his mother from Pelahustán. Díaz's paternal grandparents were Juan Díaz de Lavandero and Ana de Don Pablo y Gómez. His maternal grandparents, both natives of Pelahustán, were Juan Martín y Martínez and Ana de Córdoba. Díaz had three siblings: María, Ana, and Miguel.

Díaz began his government services in 1715. He had attained high positions, including that of director general of the tobacco monopoly, by at least the 1730s. He became the superintendent general of the Royal Exchequer, treasurer general, and, on November 7, 1736, replaced José Patiño as the secretary of state for the Ministry of the Indies and the Navy. On March 14, 1739, he was named a minister *de capa y espada* and given a seat on the Cámara of the Indies.

Díaz married *sevillana* Manuela Petronila Ortusaustegui y Fernández Hidalgo in 1709. The couple had three sons, Miguel, who married María Teresa de Piscatori y Baroni, niece of Teresa Piscatori, Duquesa de San Blas and sister of Arco's* wife, and succeeded his father as Marqués de Torrenueva; Raymundo, who died as a boy; and Antonio. In addition they had nine daughters, one, Teresa Petronila, who married Francisco Antonio Piscatori Mentegasi, Marqués de San Andrés.

Díaz was granted the title Marqués de Torrenueva in 1732 and made a knight of Santiago in 1734.

SOURCES: AGS, XXIII, 13–8–434, 13–9–435; AHN, Ordenes Militares (Santiago), *expediente* 2458, *pruebas* of Mateo Pablo Díaz de Lavandero; AGI, Indiferente 894,

866; Alvarez y Baena, *Hijos de Madrid*, II, 260–61; García Carraffa, *Enciclopedia*, XXIX, 85–88; Escudero, *Los secretarios*, III, 738.

Díaz Freyle, Manuel (November 1711–December 26, 1777)

Díaz was born in the *lugar* of Chinchón, Toledo, the son of Manuel Díaz and María Freyle, also from Chinchón. His paternal grandparents were Gabriel Díaz and Clara Sesena; his maternal grandparents were Francisco Freyle and Luisa Rodríguez. He had at least two brothers, Juan Ventura and Antonio Nicolás.

Díaz began his higher studies at the University of Alcalá in 1727, receiving the baccalaureate and licentiate degrees in canon law in 1732 and 1737. He took the doctorate in 1737 also. He became a *colegial* at San Felipe y Santiago of Alcalá in 1734, serving as rector in 1746. Díaz was a candidate for and a substitute in various academic chairs at Alcalá.

On December 26, 1752, Ferdinand VI named Díaz *oidor* of the Audiencia of Guatemala, a post he assumed on August 17, 1754, and held until 1766. Díaz served at times as interim *fiscal* and from 1758 also as legal adviser for military affairs (*auditor de guerra*) for the captaincy general of Guatemala. He received a license dated August 24, 1765, allowing him to go to Spain to recover his health and to seek a position there. Informed in Spain, on May 3, 1767, that the king had selected him to be an *oidor* in the Chancellery of Granada, he took possession of the post on July 6 of that year. The king named Díaz on March 16, 1774, to replace Mosquera y Pimentel* on the Council of the Indies. He served in that position from March 24 until his death.

Díaz's first wife died on the way to Guatemala, and in 1762 he unsuccessfully sought a license to remarry. He persevered, however, and with a license granted in 1767 married Josefa Olarte of Málaga, daughter of José Olarte, administrator of the tobacco monopoly for the province of Madrid. After his death she declared herself poor as a result of the trip back from America twelve years earlier.

SOURCES: AGI, Indiferente 569, 894, 901B, 1507, *relación* of 1767; Guatemala 525; AGS, XXIII, 2–39–176; 2–58–68; Dirección General del Tesoro, Inventario 39, Legajo 12; AHN, Hacienda 504, *expediente* 267; *Gazeta de Madrid*, December 26, 1752; January 13, 1778.

E

Echavarri y Ugarte Elcorobarrutia, Francisco Antonio de (1701–April 16, 1774)

Echavarri was born in Vitoria, Alava. His parents were Pedro González de Echavarri and Corona Ignacia Ugarte y Aguirre. He attended the University of Valladolid, attained the bachelor's degree in law in 1725, and then transferred to the University of Alcalá, where he eventually obtained the licentiate in law. He entered the *colegio mayor* of San Ildefonso in 1733, with a supernumerary fellowship, and competed for various chairs at Alcalá.

On March 6, 1735, the king named Echavarri *oidor* in Mexico, a position he held from 1736 until he retired. His recommendation of employing pardons to end the Yaqui Rebellion in 1740 was followed. Echavarri thought the lamentable condition of the Indian villages (*reducciones*) and perhaps the treatment missionairies gave the Indians were responsible for the problem. In 1742 he became superintending judge (*juez superintendente*) of the aqueduct works at the Shrine of Guadalupe. An extreme devotee of the Virgin, Echavarri refused any extra pay for the commission and spent his own funds for construction projects. His service was brief, however, for he had to depart for Spain on a royal commission. In 1749 Echavarri received an option on the first vacancy in the Chancelleries of Granada and Valladolid but apparently chose not to exercise it. Five years later, back in Mexico, he was supervising judge (*juez privativo conservador*) of the estate and marquisate del Valle, a lucrative commission. From February to April 1760, having been senior judge since 1743, he served as interim captain general following the death of Viceroy Marqués de las Amarillas. Echavarri began soliciting retirement as early as 1761; he went to Spain seeking to restore his health in 1766 and in 1768 even had an audience with the king. Retirement with half pay for reasons of health was officially granted on October

19, 1769, along with honors of the Council of the Indies. Echavarri's health improved after leaving Mexico, however, and on April 4, 1770, he was appointed to the Council of the Indies as minister *togado*, a position he served from June 1, 1770, until his death.

Although refused a license to marry a native of the audiencia district of Mexico in 1739, Echavarri later did so in Oaxaca. Barbara Rita de Tamayo became his wife, but estrangement followed and the couple lived apart after 1751. Later she accused him of nonsupport. Echavarri attained the *hábito* of the Order of Santiago in 1753, from a nomination of 1735, and in 1771 asked for but did not receive a Navarrese title of nobility. Regarded by Viceroy Conde de Revillagigedo I as indiscreet and ambitious, Echavarri owned property in Mexico City and two country houses in the suburban areas of San Angel and San Agustín de las Cuevas (now Tlalpan). He apparently died without children for he founded an entailed estate for his nephew Luis de Echavarri.

SOURCES: AGI, Indiferente 869, 894; Mexico 384, 385, 452, *títulos* of 1734, 1697; AGS, XXIII; 2–30–65; 2–53–181; 2–53–178; 13–9–563; Alanis Boyso, *Elecciones*, p. 36; Martínez Cosío, *Caballeros*, p. 86; López Sarrelangue, *Una villa mexicana*, pp. 84, 87, 150, 217; Calderón Quijano, *Los virreyes . . . Carlos III*, I, 7, pp. 503–4; Arrangoiz, *México*, p. 242; *Gazeta de México*, No. 92 (July 1735), p. 736; Vignau and Uhagón, *Indice*, p. 148; *Gazeta de Madrid*, April 19, 1774; Konetzke, *Documentos*, III, tomo 1, 224–5; Hamnett, "Mexican Bureaucracy," p. 14; Navarro García, "La sublevación Yaqui," pp. 511–12.

Escarano, Francisco Antonio (December 14, 1730, baptism–September 17, 1794)

Escarano was born in Zamora. His father, Antonio Genaro Escarano, was a native of the city of Naples who served in the Spanish army and then in the militia of Lugo. His mother, Josefa Torres Tribiño, was from Alexandria de la Palla, Milan. His paternal grandparents, both from the city of Naples, were Thomas Escarano and Cam ila Caxavita. His maternal grandparents were José Mathias Torres Tribiño, a native of the *villa* of Moya, New Castile, and an infantry captain, and Mariana Teresa de Chaves, from Alexandria de la Palla, Milan. His brother Manuel, born in Lugo in 1735, was an accountant (*contador principal*) for the royal lead monopoly.

Early in his career, Escarano was a lieutenant in an infantry regiment and stationed at the Spanish embassy in Paris in 1766. Subsequently, he was a clerk (*oficial*) for the Secretariat of State serving as secretary of the Spanish embassy in London. Present there in 1769, he was honored with a knighthood in the order of Santiago that year. Later returning to Spain, Escarano became the director general of the postal service (*correos y caminos*). He was named a supernumerary minister *de capa y espada* of the Council of the Indies on March 19, 1794. He served, if at all, very briefly for he died in Bilbao within months of his appointment.

Escarano married María de la Concepción Zuaznavar y Azcuea, a lady-in-waiting to the future Queen María Luisa. He died leaving several young children.

SOURCES: AGS, XXIII, 13–9–515; AHN, Estado (Carlos III), *expediente* 1516, *pruebas* of Josef Escarano; Ordenes Militares (Santiago), *expediente* 2710, *pruebas* of Francisco

Antonio Escarano y de Torres; Estado 3427, *expediente* 22; Hacienda 506, *expediente* 1; AGI, Indiferente General 869, *expediente* Escarano.

Escobedo Ocaña y Alarcón, Jorge (April 4, 1743, baptism–May 11, 1805)

Escobedo was born in Jaén. His father, a native of Martos, Extremadura, was Jorge María Escobedo y Serrano, Conde de Cazalla, a militia brigadier and perpetual alderman (*regidor perpetuo*) of Madrid. His mother, from Pozuelo, was María Antonia Alarcón y Ocãna, Señora de Pozuela. The paternal grandparents were Diego Ignacio Escobedo Osorio, Conde de Cazalla del Río, a native of Zafra, and Elvira Serrano Mecía, Ponce de León from Jaén. His maternal grandparents were Antonio Ocaña y Alarcón, a native of Havana, Cuba, and María de Montalvo of Puerto de Santa María, Spain.

Escobedo received his early education in Granada, where after eight years of study he obtained a bachelor of canon law degree from the university in 1762. He studied two years with Licenciado Ramón Moreno of Granada, gaining practical experience. Incorporating the degree in the University of Salamanca in 1762, in the same year he entered its *colegio mayor* of Cuenca with a fellowship. He remained at Salamanca, served as rector of Cuenca, earned the bachelor of law degree, and competed for chairs, as he had done at Granada, until receiving his first audiencia appointment.

On April 25, 1776, Escobedo was named an *oidor* of the Audiencia of Charcas. Although he received appointments to Lima as an *alcalde del crimen* on November 30, 1778, and *oidor* on January 29, 1780, he devoted his time to assisting the *visita* of that kingdom headed by José Antonio de Areche,* assuming the appointment as *oidor* on January 18, 1781. As subdelegate for the *visita*, he reformed and reorganized the Potosí mint, which resulted in great savings. On September 13, 1781, Escobedo was himself named visitor general and given honors of the Council of the Indies on July 3, 1783, and membership in the Order of Charles III in 1784. He led the *visita* to its conclusion starting in June 1782. From 1782 to 1784 he reorganized the provincial treasuries to pave the way for the intendant system, while voluntarily accepting only half salary during the war years of the early 1780s. He strongly favored the intendant system and thought its implementation was the *visita*'s greatest accomplishment. He himself served as intendant of Lima and helped to name the other initial intendants. Unlike Areche, he enjoyed good relations with the viceroy for some time. Deterioration occurred after 1785 over both Lima's municipal affairs and mining jurisdiction and the creation of a mining tribunal. In 1787, when he was ordered to Spain, the post of superintendent of treasury affairs was reassumed by the viceroy.

Under Escobedo's supervision, tribute revenue in Peru increased and detailed knowledge of the provinces was enlarged. He also sought to revive Lima's city council. While in Peru he supported the botanical expedition of Ruiz and Pavón, sent plants to Spain, and even took two folio volumes of the expedition's records to Spain with him on his return. Advanced to the Council of the Indies on April 27, 1785, and returning to Spain in July 1788, Escobedo entered his post on

November 4. He reached the Cámara on December 22, 1792, a position he held until his death. In 1803 he was instrumental in pushing for reform of the intendancy system and in recognizing the shortfall between the promise and actuality of the system. He was one of the committee that drafted the New Ordinance of 1803 for the intendant system.

Married before leaving Spain to Gertrudis Velasco, daughter of Captain Juan Alonso de Velasco y Castillo, permanent councilman of Gibraltar and María Lorenza de Arcos y Aranda, Escobedo had one son, Jorge, who was born in Madrid, and two daughters, María Josefa de los Dolores and Francisca Xaviera. Jorge died in 1788, shortly after his father reached Spain. His brother-in-law Juan Gutiérrez Gayón sought to benefit from Escobedo's prominence in securing an appointment as administrator of customs in Chile.

Escobedo held the family title at the time of his death, presumably inherited from his elder brother Manuel Joaquín. He left his widow and two daughters as heirs.

SOURCES: AGI, Charcas 510, *relación* of 1775; Ultramar 867, *relación* of 1802; Guatemala 409; Chile 258; Contratación, 5522, No. 47; Indiferente 894, 885, 886, 869 (*expediente* Ecobedo); Ultramar 867; AGS, XXIII, 2–60–93; 2–62–224; 2–64–2; 13–8–104; 13–8–86; 13–8–52; 2–86-no number; AHN, Estado (Carlos III), *espediente* 179, *pruebas* of Jorge de Escobedo y Alarcón; AHPM, Protocolo 20224; Brading, *Miners*, pp. 88, 89, 91; Barbier, *Reform*, p. 186; Steele, *Flowers*, pp. 115, 136, 140, 160n; Lohmann Villena, *Ministros*, pp. 41–42; Fisher, *Government*, passim.

Ezpeleta y Amatriain, José de (1694–November 29, 1757)

Born in Pamplona, Ezpeleta was the third son of Miguel de Ezpeleta y Rada, a Navarrese noble, and his wife Antonia de Amatriain. His paternal grandparents were Ignacio de Ezpeleta y Arizcun and Juana de Rada y Elío. His sister Inés married Andrés de Baquedano. His brother Fermín was a canon in Pamplona. Agustín, José's oldest brother, followed a military career and held the family properties and titles (*señoríos*).

Ezpeleta was a student at the University of Alcalá, receiving a baccalaureate in canon law in 1715 and a licentiate in 1719. He belonged to its *colegio mayor* of San Ildefonso. While at Alcalá he competed for chairs in canon law.

On October 16, 1727, Ezpeleta was named an *alcalde del crimen* of the Chancellery of Valladolid. Advanced to the civil chamber as an *oidor* on September 13, 1734, he was subsequently promoted to *alcalde de casa y corte* on September 12, 1744. On March 22, 1752, he was named a minister *togado* of the Council of the Indies, a post he held from the following day until his death.

SOURCES: AGS, XXIII, 13–8–192; Gracia y Justicia 139; AHN, Universidades 46(1), *expediente* 86; Libro 1147, p. 160; Consejos 13532, 13643; AGI, Indiferente 866, 894.

F

Fernández de Córdoba, Francisco (?–?)

Fernández was born in Almogía, Málaga. His parents were José Fernández de Córdoba of Almogia and Dorotea Zayas y Ramos of Iznate, Málaga. His sister María Josefa married Antonio Mora y Peysal who served as intendant of Oaxaca, Mexico, from 1787 to 1808 and was a *caballero* of the Order of Charles III. Fernández's aunt Ana Zayas y Ramos married Matías de Gálvez, brother of José,* and Viceroy of New Spain. His sister Ana married Ramón de Posada.*

Fernández began his career as a clerk (*oficial sexto*) in the Ministry of the Indies in 1776. After several years of service, he was named secretary of the cámara of the viceroy of New Spain, a post he assumed on January 30, 1784. Three years later, on February 14, 1787, he was appointed superintendent of the mint in Mexico City. On February 4, 1799, Charles IV designated him a minister *de capa y espada* of the Council of the Indies. By the time of the French invasion of Spain in 1808, however, Fernández had not yet assumed his new position. Nonetheless, honors of the Cámara followed on May 26, 1810. On January 9, 1817, his appointment to the Council was reconfirmed and he was told to return to Spain to serve for his knowledge of New Spain would be valuable. He died, however, without entering the position.

Fernández married María Guadalupe de Moncada y Berrio, the first Marquesa de San Román and the daughter of Brigadier General Pedro de Moncada y Branciforte, Marqués de Moncada, and Mariana de Berrio y de la Campa y Cos, Marquesa de Jaral del Berrio. María Guadalupe was a native of Puebla and served as a lady-in-waiting to Queen María Luisa. The couple had three children, all of whom married cousins. Joaquín married Dolores Moncada Sesma. Manuel married Mariana Moncada

Sesma. Guadalupe married Juan Isidro Moncada. Fernández was a pensioned *caballero* of Charles III from 1786.

SOURCES: AGS, XXIII, 2–98–1; AGI, Mexico 1906; *Gazeta de Madrid*, February 19, 1799; García Carraffa, *Enciclopedia*, LX, p. 232; Vignau, *Indice*, p. 62; Ladd, *Mexican Nobility*, 213; Magdaleno, *Catálogo XX*, pp. 79–81, 177; Hamnett, *Politics*, p. 158.

Fernández Durán y Fernández de la Casa, Miguel (April 17, 1681–October 11, 1721)

Fernández was born in the *lugar* of Braojos in the Archdiocese of Toledo. His parents were Miguel Fernández Durán of Peñuezar and Magdalena Fernández de la Casa of the *villa* of Buitrago, Braojos. His paternal grandparents, Juan Fernández Durán and María González, and maternal grandparents, Pedro Fernández de la Casa and Magdalena Hernández, were also from the same region.

Fernández was a knight of Calatrava from 1706 who held the title Marqués de Tolosa from its creation in 1719. In 1708 he held the right to a future appointment as secretary of the Council of Orders. After service as secretary of state for the navy, war, and the Indies through three reorganizations of administration from 1714 to January 8, 1721, he was appointed a minister *de capa y espada* of the Council of the Indies on the latter date. He died within the year.

Fernández was married first to María de Vega. After her death, in December, 1719, he married Isabel María de Tejada, the widow of Juan Prieto de Aedo, a knight of Santiago and the chief accountant (*contador mayor*) for the military orders. She was the daughter of Antonio López de Tejada, Marqués de Gallegos and a knight of Santiago, and María Francisca de la Veldad. Miguel, the only son of Fernández's second marriage, succeeded him as Marqués de Tolosa, became *mayordomo de semana* in 1748, and entered the Order of Calatrava in 1749.

SOURCES: AGS, XXIII, 13–8–46; Gracia y Justicia 922; AHN, Ordenes Militares (Calatrava), *expediente* 915, *pruebas* of Miguel Fernández Durán; Atienza, *Nobiliario*, p. 1665; Vignau, *Calatrava*, p. 55; Escudero, *Los secretarios*, II, *cuadro sinóptico*; III, 732, 961.

Fernández Molinillo, Francisco (March 14, 1688–May 14, 1765)

Fernández, a second son, was born in the *villa* of Brunete, in the Archbishopric of Toledo. His parents, also natives of Brunete, were Gabriel Fernández Molinillo y Cardeña, who held a variety of honorific positions in Brunete, and María García del Moral. Also from Brunete were his paternal grandparents Marcos Fernández Molinillo and Ana Cardeña. His maternal grandparents were Juan García del Moral of the *villa* of Colmenar Viejo, Toledo, and María de la Torre of Brunete. His brother Gabriel served as a cavalry captain and superintendent of the mint in Mexico and was a knight of Santiago. His sister Micaela married her relative Diego Fernández Molinillo y Tello de Meneses. He had two other brothers named Alfonso and Ysidro.

Fernández began his government service during the War of the Spanish Succession. He worked for some time in the Ministry of the Indies before going to New Spain, where in 1727 he was secretary to Viceroy Marqués de Casa Fuerte. Returning to Spain, he was subsequently named secretary to the commandant general of Mallorca. Appointed secretary to the viceroy of New Spain Conde de Fuenclara on April 23, 1742, simultaneously he was named a supernumerary minister *de capa y espada* of the Council of the Indies, with service to begin upon his return from Mexico. The appointment emphasized his knowledge of American affairs. Given a regular (*número*) seat on the Council on August 26, 1747, he was advanced to the Cámara on March 9, 1753. A knight of Santiago from 1728, Fernández served until his death. Apparently he never married, for he left nephew Francisco Dionisio Fernández Molinillo as his sole heir.

SOURCES: AGS, 13–9–580, 13–9–578; AHN, Estado 6380(1); Ordenes Militares (Santiago), *expediente* 2987, *pruebas* of Francisco Fernández Molinillo; AGI, Indiferente 869, 885; AHPM, Protocolo 17560; *Gazeta de Madrid*, May 21, 1765; García Carraffa, *Enciclopedia*, XXXIV, 81–82; Lohmann Villena, *Americanos*, II, 50; Arnold, "Bureaucracy and Bureaucrats," p. 15.

Fernández Sarmiento y Ballón, Manuel Ignacio (December 14, 1738, baptism–January 4, 1790)

Fernández was born in La Coruña, Galicia. His father, Manuel Fernández Sarmiento de la Cruz, was from the *lugar* de Silva-Redonda, seven leagues from La Coruña. Having gone to Mexico City with his uncle Diego Antonio de la Cruz y Figueroa at the age of six, as a result of being orphaned, Manuel retained commercial interests in Mexico for the remainder of his life. Upon the death of his second wife, María Isabel Ballón y López, he returned to Mexico, where his uncle had remained, but died on the voyage back to Spain. Manuel Ignacio's paternal grandparents were Alberto Fernández and Dominga Gertrudis de la Cruz. His maternal grandparents, also from Galicia, were Juan Ballón and Ynés López Mariño. Fernández had a half sister, Magdalena Fernández y Vázquez, who received a dowry of 4,000 *ducados* when she married Antonio López, and two full sisters, María Ignacia who married Juan Núñez Baamonde y Espantosa, and María Antonia.

After the death of his father, in 1753 Fernández went to El Ferrol and became a clerk (*oficial*) in the accounting department (*contaduría*) of the naval station there. For fourteen years he served the Ministry of Marine in El Ferrol, Cádiz, and Cartagena. Advanced to the position of *comisario real* of the army, he served for nine years in Valencia, Alicante, Cádiz and Orán. His activities included participating in preparations for the Algerian campaign in 1775. He accompanied the Pedro de Cevallos expedition to the Río de la Plata in 1776 as intendant general of the army. Soon, on March 21, 1778, he was named superintendent general of finances for the viceroyalty. Charged with increasing government revenue and encouraging production, Fernández successfully implemented a policy of economic protection that resulted in a rapid growth of prosperity. His energetic activities led to jealousy on the part of Viceroy Cevallos. An opponent of the general visitation by José Antonio de Areche* being extended to the Río de la Plata, Fernández was reprimanded for his conduct. Fernández, who had proved himself a strong-willed administrator, was advanced to the Council of the Indies as a minister *de capa y espada* on September 1, 1785. Previously rewarded with membership in the Order of Charles III in 1781, he served in his new position from September 7, 1785, until his death. He died without having married.

SOURCES: AGS, XXIII, 13–8–357; AHN, Estado (Carlos III), *expediente* 112, *pruebas* of Manuel Ignacio Fernández Sarmiento; AGI, Indiferente 894; *Gazeta de Madrid*, March 16, 1790; Vignau, *Carlos III*, p. 64; Lynch, *Spanish Colonial Administration*, pp. 43, 56, 122–23.

Fondevila y Guerra, Francisco Xavier (Variant: Xavier) (March 6, 1730, baptism–January 5, 1801)

Fondevila, one of three children, was born in the city of Santander; he usually used just Xavier as his first name. His parents were Gerónimo Fondevila y Condor of Ager, Lérida, and María Rosa Guerra de la Vega of Santander. His paternal grandparents, both from Ager, were Jaime Fondevila y Hortiello and Jerónima Magdalena Condor y Folch. His maternal grandparents were Fernando Guerra and María Gómez of the city of Santander. His brother Gerónimo became a merchant in Cádiz. His brother Joaquín was an *asistente* in Pamplona, New Granada, in 1774.

Fondevila began his career in the mid–1740s. He spent thirteen years in the army and artillery corps and twenty-four years in the War Ministry, rising to the post of chief clerk (*oficial mayor*). On April 22, 1793, he was named a supernumerary minister *de capa y espada* of the Council of the Indies. Upon the death of Gabriel de Munive y Tello,* he advanced to a regular (*número*) seat. He held his office until his death.

Fondevila married Manuela Causada y Bernal. She predeceased him by at least a decade. The couple had three daughters. The eldest, María, married Francisco de Bustamante y Guerra, a *caballero* of Charles III and member of the Cádiz merchant guild. Manuela married Luis Antonio Flores, a knight of Calatrava and naval captain. The third daughter, Ana, was single in 1801.

SOURCES: AGS, XXIII, 13–8–696; AGI, Indiferente 869, *expediente* Gamiz; AHN, Estado (Carlos III), *expediente* 544, *pruebas* of Francisco Xavier Fondevila; *Gazeta de Madrid*, April 14, 1801; García Carraffa, *Enciclopedia*, XXXV, 180.

G

Galisteo y Manrique, Tadeo José de (October 27, 1758–October 3, 1810)

Galisteo, the younger of two children, was born in Guatemala City. His father, Manuel Severino de Galisteo y Gigorro, was a native of Villarejo de Salvanés in the Archbishopric of Toledo. Having emigrated to Guatemala after receiving basic schooling, he held a variety of posts in the area, including that of factor for the royal tobacco monopoly in Costa Rica. His mother, Josefa Manrique, was a native of Guatemala. His paternal grandparents were Francisco de Galisteo y Pérez of the *villa* of Fuentidueña de Tajo and Ysabel Gigorro y Díaz of the *villa* of Valdelaguna. His maternal grandparents were Alexo Martín Manrique, a merchant in Guatemala who had been born in the *lugar* of Magán in Toledo and Ana Gutiérrez of Guatemala. His brother Domingo was a cleric in Apestepeque, Guatemala.

Galisteo went to Spain as the page of the bishop of Tortosa, Pedro Cortés y Larraz. After service as secretary to the chief general of the army of Rosellon for about six months, Galisteo began his career in the Secretariat of State in its "ninth and last" position. He advanced steadily, however, and in 1798 was in the fourth-ranked clerk position (*oficial quarto primero*). By 1801 he was its deputy chief clerk (*oficial mayor segundo*). On November 28, 1801, he was named a minister *de capa y espada* to replace Bernardo de Iriarte.* He served on the Council until his death.

Galisteo, a pensioned *caballero* of the Order of Charles III since 1801, married María de la Paz Enderiz in 1799. Her parents were Manuel Antonio de Enderiz, a *comisario ordenador de marina*, and María Josepha López y Angulo.

SOURCES: AGS, XXIII, 13–9–290; AGI, Indiferente 872, *expediente* Requena, 892; AHN, Hacienda 512, *expediente* 2428; Estado 3421, *expediente* 2; Estado (Carlos III), *expediente* 1147, *pruebas* of Tadeo Galisteo y Manrique; Vignau, *Carlos III*, p. 68.

Gálvez y Gallardo, José de (January 7, 1720, baptism–June 17, 1787)

Gálvez was born in the *villa* of Macharaviaya, Málaga, the second son of Antonio Gálvez y Carvajal and Ana Gallardo y Jurado both from the town. His paternal grandparents were Francisco de Gálvez of Macharaviaya and Elena de Carvajal of the *villa* of Benaque. His maternal grandparents were Matías Gallardo and Catalina de Cabrera y Jurado, both of Macharaviaya. As a consequence of his own success, Gálvez was able to promote his three brothers. Matías, the eldest, was named viceroy of New Spain. Miguel reached the Council of War. Antonio became the commandant general for the customs house in Cádiz and a field marshal. Matías's son Bernardo was the governor of Louisiana, celebrated for his victories against the British in the Seven Years' War.

Gálvez left his mountainous village to study first in the Royal Seminary of San Sebastián in Málaga and then law at the University of Salamanca. After receiving a baccalaureate in civil law in 1739 from Salamanca, he went to Madrid and attended from 1741 to 1744 the study of attorney Manuel Ignacio de la Serna. After the Royal Council admitted him as an attorney in 1743, Gálvez established a private practice in Madrid. By 1756 he was recognized as a representative for French, Dutch, Swedish, and Hanseatic interests, some religious houses, and some grandees. About 1761 he became the *fiscal* for the *aposento*. Allegedly aided by French support, Gálvez began a rapid ascent in 1764 with an appointment on November 25 as *alcalde de casa y corte*. Almost immediately, on February 20, 1765, he was named visitor general for New Spain. His visitation there from 1765 to 1771 was a major effort to improve government, administration, and royal finances, and to expand Spanish authority into California. Given honors of the Council of the Indies with his appointment as visitor, he was granted honors of the Cámara and given an appointment to the Council on December 28, 1767. Following his return to Spain, Gálvez was ordered to assume his place on the Council to replace Jacinto Miguel de Castro* and to enter the Cámara on July 7, 1772. Two years later he was named to a position on the General Committee for Commerce, Money, and Mines. By a decree of February 19, 1776, Charles III named Gálvez secretary of state for the Indies to replace the deceased Julián de Arriaga. On March 31, 1776, Charles further named him to fill simultaneously the post of governor of the Council of the Indies in the absence of the Duque de Alba. Gálvez continued as governor following the Duque's death on November 15, 1776. For the remaining years of his life, Gálvez wielded immense power over Indies affairs, instituting general visitations for South America, establishing the intendant system in most of the empire, extending "free trade within the empire," and continuing a policy of favoring peninsulars at the expense of Americans for high positions in the New World.

Gálvez married María Magdalena Grimaldo and then, in 1750, a French woman, Lucia Romet y Pichelin. Romet, too, had died before Gálvez began the *visita* in Mexico. His third wife, whom he married in 1775, was María de la Concepción Valenzuela y Fuentes, daughter of Antonio de Valenzuela, Conde de la Puebla de los Valles, and Beatriz de Fuentes. The couple had one child, María Josefa.

Gálvez was honored richly for his royal service. In 1772 he was given the Large

Cross of Charles III with pension. Two years later he was granted a pension of 2,000 pesos a year. On April 23, 1780, he was named to the Council of State. Finally, in 1785, he received the title Marqués de Sonora.

SOURCES: AGS, XXIII, 2–58–325, 13–8–150, 2–60–59, 2–49–40; Gracia y Justicia 158; AGI, Indiferente 865, 894, 892, 869, *expediente* Gálvez, Santa Fe 285, *relación* of brother Miguel of 1755; AHN, Estado (Carlos III), *expediente* 60, *pruebas* of Miguel de Gálvez; AHPM, Protocolo 18469; *Gazeta de Madrid*, October 28, 1777, July 3, 1787; Vignau, *Carlos III*, p. 68; García Carraffa, *Enciclopedia*, XXXVI, 200–201; Valgoma, *Mecenas*, I, 243; Aiton, "Spanish Colonial Reorganization"; Priestley, *Gálvez*, passim.

Gamiz y Espinosa, Antonio de (?–February 7, 1833)

Gamiz was born in Madrid, probably in the early 1760s. His parents were Fernando Gamiz Mesía y Portugal, a native of Jaén, and Ana de Espinosa of Granada. He had at least three sisters. María was still single in 1833. Manuela married Miguel de Sierra y Cienfuegos. Gertrudis married Hermenegildo Rodríguez de Rivera, an *oidor* of the Chancellery of Valladolid.

Gamiz followed a naval career. Beginning as a *guardia marina* in 1779, he rose to the rank of lieutenant (*teniente de fragata*). Named archivist for the Ministry of the Navy, by 1801 he was the chief clerk (*oficial mayor primero*) of the ministry and held the rank of ship's captain. On January 15 of that year he was named a minister *de capa y espada* to assume the seat reserved for chief clerks and left vacant by Xavier de Fondevila.* He remained in Madrid during the initial French occupation, serving on the Council until José Napoleon I abolished it. When the French withdrew, he was elected a substitute deputy (*suplente*) to the Cortes. He fled Madrid when the French withdrew, but was robbed and mistreated on the road to Andalusia. He explained later that he had remained in Madrid and worked for the French because he had no other source of income to support his aged mother, siblings, and nephews. His explanation was accepted and in 1814 Ferdinand VII named him to the restored Council. In 1816 he became a brigadier general of the Royal Armada. Although plagued with ailments, including the loss of sight in one eye in 1818, he held his seat on the Council until his death.

Gamiz never married.

SOURCES: AGS, XXIII, 13–9–1; AGI, Indiferente 825, 866, 869, *expediente* Gamiz; AHN, Estado 175; Hacienda 510, *expediente* 2033.

García León y Pizarro, José (October 11, 1730–March 30, 1798)

García was born in Motril, Granada, the son of José García de León of Arévalo, Avila, and Francisca Pizarro y Rivera of Motril. His father was an infantry colonel and served as governor of Mazalquivir. His paternal grandparents were Lázaro García Madrigal of Arévalo and Juana de León of Coca. His maternal grandparents were Alonso Pizarro Padilla of Truxillo and Ysabel de Rivera y Santa Marina of Motril. García's brother Ramón served several governorships in the New World, and was governor and captain general of Charcas by an appointment of 1796.

García completed his advanced studies at the University of Granada and graduated with a doctorate. While at the university he taught in the faculties of civil and canon law. He was a member of the Royal Madrid Academy of Spanish Law. After his practicum in Granada, the Royal Council admitted him to practice law in 1751.

García followed the *carrera de varas* (career in municipal and provincial administration), serving as *alcalde mayor* in Alhama (1760), Ubeda (1763), and Jerez de la Frontera (1767) and then as *corregidor* of Baena (1771). Named *fiscal* of the Audiencia of Seville on August 20, 1775, he was quickly tapped to inaugurate the new position of regent and president of the Audiencia of Quito on November 18, 1776. Serving in Quito from 1778 to 1784, he proved himself an effective tax collector as he implemented financial reforms. With his brother Ramón, the governor of Guayaquil, García and his family dominated the presidency politically. Despotically, he used his office for personal gain and self-aggrandizement. Seeing military reform as a needed complement to fiscal reform, he introduced a "disciplined militia" that was, in fact, ill disciplined and served García rather than the Crown by aiding him to gain control of potential laborers. Overall he proved effective in playing upon the aristocracy's fears of a social rebellion to gain support for financial reforms and incorporating them into the defense system of the presidency. He tried unsuccessfully to become captain general as well as president and regent of Quito. González Suárez considered him one of the most effective presidents of the colonial period. As for many other regents, the position served as a stepping stone to the Council of the Indies, and García was advanced with an appointment as a *ministro togado* on March 14, 1783 to replace Villarrasa.* He returned to Spain via Havana and La Coruña, assuming his post on August 14, 1786. Later he joined the Cámara of the Indies with an appointment of November 18, 1791, serving until his death.

García married María Frias y Pizarro of Ronda before going to Quito. Their son José, a *caballero* of Charles III, was a celebrated official in 1812–13 and was called to the *Junta Central* by the Conde de Floridablanca. Daughter Josefa María married Juan José de Villalengua.* A third daughter was named María de los Dolores. In 1782 García received the Cross of the Order of Charles III. His wife outlived him.

SOURCES: AGI, Indiferente 866, 885, 894, 869; AGS, XXIII, 2–60–291; 13–8–103; 13–8–60; Gazeta de Madrid, No. 28, April 6, 1798; AGS, Gracia y Justicia 157, 161; AHN, Consejos 13502; Estado (Carlos III), *expediente* 137, *pruebas* of José García de León y Pizarro; Medina, *Imprenta en Quito*, p. 44; Magdaleno, *Catálogo XX*, p. 620; Flores y Caamaño, *Don José Mejía Lequerica*, p. xlviii; Kuethe, *Military Reform*, pp. 90, 118–25; 182; González Suárez, *Historia*, V, 309; Zúñiga, *Montúfar*, p. 319.

Gauna y Portocarrero, Juan de (Variant: Gaona) (February 13, 1696–January 4, 1760)

Gauna was born in the *villa* of Almagro. His parents were Juan de Gauna Abad, a native of Almagro and a *familiar* of the Inquisition of Toledo, and Aldonza Portocarrero of the *villa* of Cabra. His paternal grandparents were Ignacio de Gauna and Francisca Abad, both of Almagro. His paternal grandparents were Vicente

Portocarrero, who was born in Valencia when his father was captain of the viceregal guard and considered Cabra his true home, and María Manuela de Aranda of Cabra.

At the age of three, Gauna was made a knight of Calatrava as a reward for the services of his grandfather Vicente Portocarrero. Shortly afterward, in 1705, he received the title Conde de Valdeparaíso.

Gauna engaged in service at court. A hereditary alderman of Almagro, by 1740 he was also the first equerry (*primer caballerizo*) to the princess. On October 4, 1740, he was named a supernumerary minister *de capa y espada* of the Council of the Indies with the right to advance into a regular position according to seniority but without salary. On October 24, 1741, he entered a regular position. Subsequently, on July 22, 1754, he was named secretary of state for the exchequer and superintendent general of revenues (*rentas*), allegedly for his part in the disgrace of the Marqués de la Ensenada. Later appointed ambassador to Poland by Charles III in the new king's first change of a minister, Gauna died before assuming the post. He retained his Council position until death, although from January 1, 1744, he enjoyed the privilege of attending at his pleasure. He was also the first equerry and *mayordomo* to Ferdinand VI's wife Queen María Barbara of Portugal.

Gauna was married, but his wife predeceased him. He left as co-heirs his sons Elías Gauna, the Marqués de Añavete, and Juan Francisco Gauna. His niece Isabel Portocarrero y Alfaro married Francisco Xavier de Torres, a *colegial* of San Bartolomé who became an *oidor* of the Cámara de Comptos of the Council of Navarre.

SOURCES: AGS, XXIII, 13–9–442; Gracia y Justicia 194; AHN, Ordenes Militares (Calatrava), *expediente* 1038, *pruebas* of Juan de Gauna y Portocarrero; AGI, Indiferente 892, 894; Bernard, *Secrétariat*, p. 218; Vignau, *Calatrava*, p. 63; Coxe, *Memoirs*, III, 177–78, 237.

Geraldino, Tomás (var. Jeraldino; Thomas FitzGerald) (1681–June 14, 1755)

Geraldino was from Jerez de la Frontera, a member of a far-flung extended family that also had branches in England, Ireland, and France. He began his career in royal service with an appointment as Spain's representative on the board of directors of England's South Sea Company. Following the departure of Portocarrero,* in 1737 he began to serve as minister plenipotentiary in London. He was recalled in disgrace on the eve of the War of Jenkins' Ear (1739–48), leaving England on September 19, 1739. He held an appointment in the accounting office (*contaduría mayor*) in Madrid when named a minister *de capa y espada* of the Council of the Indies on December 22, 1739. He entered the position the following day. He died in Jerez de la Frontera where he was serving on a committee charged with overseeing a canal project designed to bring fresh water to the city.

Geraldino married Michaela Barreda, who predeceased him. The couple had three children: Teresa, Francisco, and Miguel José.

SOURCES: AGS, XXIII, 13–8–671; Secretaría y Superintendencia de Hacienda 2; AGI, Indiferente 892, 894, 897; AHN, Estado 2689, 4814; *Gazeta de Madrid*, July

8, 1755; Nelson "Contraband Trade," pp. 56, 58; Lanning, *Diplomatic History*, passim; Price, *France and the Chesapeake*, I, 559–61.

Girón Venegas de Córdoba, Gaspar Cayetano (Variant: Jirón) (c. 1657–December 15, 1727)

Girón was born in Madrid. His father, Juan Girón de Zúñiga, also from Madrid, was a *letrado* who culminated his career on the Council of Castile and enjoyed an *encomienda* of the Order of Santiago. His mother was Catalina Venegas de Córdoba of Luque. When she married in 1637, she brought as a dowry the position of *aposentador mayor* of the Tribunal of the Royal Junta of Aposento. Girón's paternal grandfather was Egas Venegas y Girón, a native of Granada, knight of Santiago, minister of the Council of Orders, and husband of *sevillana* Ana de Zúñiga. His maternal grandparents were Salvador Egas Venegas de Córdoba, a native of Luque, knight of Santiago, and Conde de Luque, and María Manrique de Aguayo.

As a youth of six or seven, Girón entered the Order of Santiago, receiving the *encomienda* of Pozorrubia that his father had held. In 1665 he received the position of *aposentador mayor*, but until 1682 it was filled for him by other persons for he had not reached the age of majority. He retained the post, however, until his death. Girón also served as a page for the Queen Mariana of Austria. In 1724 he held the post of *mayordomo* of the king and was a gentleman of the royal chamber. On March 16 of that year Luis I named him a supernumerary minister *de capa y espada* of the Council of the Indies, a post he held from the following day until his death.

Girón married twice. His first wife was María Teresa de Zárate, a daughter of Iñigo López de Zárate. His second wife was María Josefa Manso de Zúñiga, the daughter of Francisco José Manso, Conde de Erbias, and María Magdalena de Zúñiga Tenorio, Señora de las Cuevas y Montalvo. He had no children to succeed him from either marriage.

SOURCES: AGS, XXIII, 13–9–626; AHN, Estado 2672; 6400 (2); Ordenes Militares (Santiago), *expediente* 3419, *pruebas* of Gaspar Cayetano Girón Venegas de Córdoba; AGI, Indiferente 844, 866; Alvarez y Baena, *Hijos de Madrid*, II, 312–13; Ballesteros Robles, *Diccionario*, pp. 254, 665; Bernard, *Secrétariat*, p. 216.

Gómez de Grijalva, Francisco (?–January 21, 1809)

Gómez de Grijalva attended the universities of Valladolid and Alcalá de Henares. He began his government service in 1778 with an appointment of February 27 as sixth clerk (*oficial sexto*) of the Ministry of the Indies. Six months later, on August 22, he was promoted to fifth clerk. Advancement to fourth clerk came on August 7, 1782. Shortly afterward, however, on October 28, he was named chief accountant for the House of Trade. When that body was abolished in 1790, he advanced to the Council of the Indies as a supernumerary minister *de capa y espada*.

Married to a woman whose last name was Cárdenas, Gómez had a daughter named Angela. On August 21, 1807, a license was granted permitting her to marry José Félix de Campoblanco, a recently appointed *oidor* of the Audiencia of Charcas. Gómez bore the title Marqués del Surco, a title created in 1716 for Fernando Suárez de Figueroa.

SOURCES: AGS, XXIII, 13–8–342; AGI, Indiferente 870B, 885, 887, 869A, 1980; Magdaleno, *Catálogo XX*, pp. 80–81; Bernard, "Casa," p. 280; Atienza, *Nobiliario*, p. 1659.

Gómez Jara y Diosdado, García (November 7, 1762, baptism–?)

Gómez was born in Fuente del Maestre in the province of Badajoz. His parents were Francisco María Gómez Jara y Baena of Mérida and Isabel Diosdado of Fuente del Maestre. His paternal grandparents were García Gómez Jara y Pérez, a native of the *villa* of Valverde de Mérida and an attorney of the Royal Council, and Leonor Baena Guerrero of Fuente del Maestre. His maternal grandparents were Francisco Diosdado Cavallero and Leonor González Periana. His brother Francisco José was a cantor in Cartagena and a senior minister (*auditor decano*) on the Rota, an ecclesiastical tribunal.

Gómez enjoyed the favor of Manuel Godoy as a result of his father's services as administrator of the royal favorite's pastures. He was the deputy chief clerk (*oficial mayor segundo*) in the Ministry of State when named a minister *togado* of the Council of the Indies on December 10, 1800. He replaced Rafael de Antúnez.* In Lisbon serving as secretary to the Spanish ambassador to Portugal when appointed, it is unknown when Gómez entered his post. He was present when the French invasion occurred in 1808.

Gómez became a knight of Santiago in 1797.

SOURCES: AGS, XXIII, 13–9–611; AGI, Indiferente 866, 870, 886, 871, *expediente* Mangino; AHN, Ordenes Militares (Santiago), *expediente* 3459, *pruebas* of García Gómez Jara; *Gazeta de Madrid*, October 4, 1808; García Carraffa, *Enciclopedia*, XXXIX, 272; Cadenas, *Caballeros*, p. 165; Antón Olmet, *El cuerpo diplomático*, I, 318.

González Bustillo y Villaseñor, Juan Manuel (1725–March 31, 1797)

González was born in Salamanca, to José González Barrientos and Josefa Bustillo Villaseñor. He had at least one sister, María Antonia. He was a *deudo* of Simón de Baños of the Council of Castile.

González received the bachelor's degree in laws from the University of Salamanca in 1745, having begun his studies there in 1738. He claimed seventeen years of higher studies by 1754 and was a candidate for vacant academic chairs at Salamanca. A member of the Academy of Nuestra Señora de los Angeles there and also the Academy of San Millán, González was admitted to practice law by the Royal Council in 1751.

The king selected González to be *oidor* in the Audiencia of Guatemala on August 14, 1756. He arrived one year later on August 13. From 1771 to 1773 he served as interim president and captain general of Guatemala prior to the arrival of Martín de Mayorga. Following the 1773 earthquake, he published in 1774 several influential reports on its effects, including *Razón particular de los templos, casas de comunidades, y edificios, públicos y por mayor del número de vecinos de la capital de Guatemala: y del* *deplorable estado a que se hallan reducidos por los terremotos . . . del año próximo pasado de setenta y tres* (Guatemala, 1774). He advocated relocating the capital, and this position carried over the opposition of the largely clerical party. González received advancement to Mexico as *alcalde del crimen* on March 16, 1774, primarily due to his services during the earthquake emergency. He assumed the post on June 8, 1775, but by that time the decree had been issued advancing him to the post of *fiscal* of the audiencia of the Casa de Contratación. Elevated to the Council of the Indies on May 3, 1778 to replace Díaz Freyle* as *ministro togado*, González entered his post on June 6. He was considered a strong regalist among its members. González had health problems from 1786 but held his position until death.

González never married. He left as his universal heir his sister María Antonia, the wife of José Fuentes Mangas, an *alcalde mayor* in Spain. González was the uncle of José, María Eugenia, and María Vicente Fuentes González. José received an appointment as *oidor* of the Audiencia of Cuzco while his uncle was on the Council.

SOURCES: AGI, Charcas 195, *títulos* of 1754; Indiferente 869, 894, 866, 1980, 873; AGS, XXIII, 2–42–92; 2–58–67; 2–60–49; 13–8–135; Gracia y Justicia 819; Farriss, *Crown and Clergy*, p. 105n.; Calderón Quijano, *Los virreyes . . . Carlos III*, II, 28; Markman, *Colonial Central America*, pp. 27–8; Meyer, *Historical Dictionary of Nicaragua*, p. 64; Pérez Valenzuela, *Nueva Guatemala*, pp. 19ff; Zilbermann Morales and Luján Múñoz, "Santiago de Guatemala," p. 561.

González de Mena y Villegas, Pedro (1722–November 18, 1773)

González was born in Burgos and attended the University of Santiago, where he received a baccalaureate in civil law in 1743. Incorporating the degree in the University of Valladolid, he received a baccalaureate in canon law there in 1747. While in Valladolid he competed for chairs at the university and took his practicum with Manuel Patiño.* The Chancellery of Valladolid admitted him to practice law in 1748.

In 1753 González became an attorney (*abogado fiscal*) for both the Inquisition in Valladolid and the tobacco monopoly there. On March 17, 1764, he was named a judge of the Audiencia of Asturias. Three years later, on June 16, 1767, he was selected to replace Manuel Patiño as *fiscal* for Peru on the Council of the Indies. Advanced to the post of *fiscal* on the Council of Castile on May 10, 1772, to replace José de Moñino, he served until his death.

González was married and had at least three children.

SOURCES: AGS, 13–8–542; Gracia y Justicia 158; Hacienda 249, *títulos* of 1764; AHN, Estado 6380(2); AGI, Indiferente 865, 894, 869, *expediente* González Mena; *Gazeta de Madrid*, January 4, 1774.

Gorvea y Vadillo, José Lucas de (variant: Gorbea, Badillo) (October 18, 1746–October 18, 1809)

Gorvea was born in Orduña, Vizcaya, to Pedro de Gorbea of the *lugar* of Retes and Agueda Gertrudis de Vadillo of Orduña. His paternal grandparents were Pedro Simón de Gorbea, of the *lugar* of Erbi in the same region of Ayala, Calahorra, and

Francisca de Echaurren of Retes. His maternal grandparents were Francisco Vadillo of the *lugar* of Villaño in the jurisdiction of Orduña and Lucía de Madaria of Orduña. His brother Manuel was prior of the Lima merchant guild, 1819–20.

Gorvea studied first at the University of Valladolid beginning in 1759 and then, from 1765 to 1771, was at the University of Toledo, from which he received a bachelor's degree in civil law in 1767. In the early 1770s Toledo conferred upon him the licentiate and doctorate of civil law as well. He joined the Royal Academy of Civil and Canon Law of San Juan Nepomuceno and remained for four years. While at the University of Toledo, Gorvea served as regent of the chair of *Institutes* in 1769 and 1770. In 1772 he was admitted as an *abogado* by the Royal Council and the next year to the Colegio de Corte. He belonged to the Royal Academy of Practical Jurisprudence at court.

On April 21, 1777, Gorvea was named an *oidor* of the Audiencia of Chile, a position he occupied in April 1778. He received a permit to marry in 1782 but was told that the woman must not be a local. Nonetheless, Gorvea married a *chilena* in 1785. Advanced to Lima as *fiscal del crimen* as a consequence, he moved into the civil *fiscalía* in 1785. He convened a group of Basques in Lima in 1794 for the purpose of sending relief to Vizcaya as a result of the French invasion. In 1801 he was an executor for Viceroy Marqués de Osorno. Refusing a proffered appointment as regent of the Audiencia of Manila in 1802, he was named to the same post for the court in Buenos Aires on May 13, 1803, before being promoted to the Council of the Indies to replace Cerdán* as fiscal for Peruvian affairs on March 15, 1804. Unkind sources in Buenos Aires a few years later claimed the promotion came because Gorvea's brother was an associate of Manuel Godoy, the powerful royal favorite. Given Gorvea's position and years of service, the promotion was not unusual, however. Delayed in Buenos Aires for three years as a result of successive British invasions and local disturbances, Gorvea was commissioned along with other notables by the city government to locate Viceroy Marqués de Sobremonte and urge upon him Santiago Liniers as his deputy, a job that Gorvea apparently performed and that Argentine historians have regarded as the first step toward independence. In February 1807 Gorvea played a role in the deposition of Sobremonte by proposing that the viceroy be declared ill and unfit to govern. This view was supported by Martín de Alzaga and other local leaders and was adopted by authorities in Buenos Aires. Gorvea reached Spain after a trip that took him to England in early January, 1808 to serve his post. He entered the position on February 10 but died soon afterward in Madrid.

A bachelor upon his arrival in Chile, Gorvea married into the Calvo de Encalada family. By his wife María Teresa Calvo de Encalada, he had at least one son, Manuel, who later also had a career serving in the judicial bureaucracy. Through marriage he was united to four other audiencia ministers in America: Ambrosio Cerdán,* Lorenzo Blanco Cicerón, Fernando Márquez de la Plata* and Gaspar Antonio Remírez de Laredo.

In 1796 Gorvea was admitted to the Order of Charles III.

SOURCES: AGI, Chile 173; Indiferente 869, *expediente* Gorbea, 871, 865, 887, Lima 877; Santa Fe 547; Charcas 501, *relación* of 1773; 510, *relacion* of 1774; AHN, Consejos

13372, *relación* of son; Estado (Carlos III), *expediente* 983, *pruebas* of José Lucas de Gorbea y Vadillo; AGS, XXIII, 2–61–47; 2–68–226; 2–87–95; 13–9–217; Lohmann Villena, *Ministros*, pp. 51–2; Udaondo, *Diccionario*, p. 415; Gandia, *Orígenes*, pp. 51–2, 60; Vargas Ugarte, *Impresos*, X, 305; López, *Historia de la republica*, p. 20.

Goyeneche y Balanza, Francisco Xavier de (December 16, 1690–March 4, 1748)

Goyeneche, a second son, was born in Madrid. His father was Juan de Goyeneche y Gastón, a native of Arizcun, Navarre, treasurer for the queen, and a much lauded industrialist in early-eighteenth-century Spain. His mother was María Francisca de Balanza of Madrid. His paternal grandparents were Martín de Balanza of Aoiz and María de Ambrona of Cigudosa, Soria. His younger brother Francisco Miguel served as treasurer to the queen, was a knight of Santiago, and became the first Conde de Saceda.

As a youth Goyeneche traveled extensively. His father sent him with a tutor to France and Italy where Goyeneche acquired a reasonable mastery of French and Italian. He translated from French into Spanish *Comercio de Holanda, ó el gran tesoro historial y político del floreciente comercio que los Holandeses tiene en todos los estados y señorío del mundo* (Madrid 1717, reprinted 1746).

Goyeneche was named a minister *de capa y espdada* of the Council on November 11, 1707, long before he was twenty-five years of age and thus eligible to vote. He attended the sessions until 1715 but was suspended just before he reached his majority. A decree of January 20, 1707, ordered that he remain retired but be allowed to retain the honors of his post and half salary. On February 16, 1722, however, he was restored to his position. On March 11, 1744, he advanced to the Cámara, where he served until his death.

Goyeneche was a knight of Santiago from 1701 and held the title Marqués de Belzunce from 1731. He apparently never married for his brother Francisco Miguel was his heir.

SOURCES: AGS, XXIII, 13–9–600; AGI, Indiferente 865, 885, 869, 873, 894; AHN, Estado 6380 (1); *Gazeta de Madrid*, March 12, 1748; Alvarez y Baena, *Hijos de Madrid*, II, 245–46; Valgoma, *Mecenas*, I, 284; Figueroa, *Estudio*, V, 833; García Carraffa, *Enciclopedia*, XLI, 26; Callahan, "Don Juan de Goyeneche."

Gutiérrez de Piñeres, Juan Francisco (August 25, 1732–October 7, 1802)

Gutiérrez was born in the *lugar* of Lebeña, León, to Francisco Gutiérrez de Piñeres of Lebeña and Lucía Pariente of the *lugar* of Arguevanes. His paternal grandparents, both from Lebeña, were Juan Gutiérrez de Piñeres and María López. His maternal grandparents, both from Arguevanes, were Tomás Pariente and María Vélez de las Cuevas. His older brother Antonio, born in 1724, was the father of Fernando Antonio Gutiérrez de Piñeres, a *fiscal* on the Audiencia of Manila.

Gutiérrez studied philosophy in the College of Santo Tomás in Seville for three years. Turning to the study of law, he attended academies in Seville and in 1758 was accepted by the Audiencia of Seville as an attorney. After joining the College of Lawyers of Seville in 1759, he was recognized by the Royal Council in 1762. For several years he taught law in his own academy in Seville.

In 1763 Gutiérrez was named to the first of a series of local positions, that of *alcalde mayor* of public weights and measures of Seville. The following year he became a criminal judge for the city. In 1768 he was named chief deputy municipal administrator (*alcalde mayor primer teniente de asistente*) of Seville, a post that placed him directly under Pablo de Olavide. In 1772 he was named administrator and judge (*alcalde mayor*) of Cádiz and two years later advanced to the Chancellery of Valladolid as Juez Mayor de Vizcaya, a judge named to the Chancellery to hear cases involving Vizcayans. Named an *oidor* of the Audiencia of the House of Trade on June 29, 1776, within months, on December 18, he was appointed inspector general (*visitador general*) for New Granada and the first regent of its Audiencia of Santa Fe. In 1777 he added the office of intendant of the royal armies. Gutiérrez reached Santa Fe in January 1778 with authority to reform the royal treasury. Immediately, he was at odds with Viceroy Manuel Antonio Flórez. By not pushing the formation of a militia he gained the support of the local aristocracy. Gutiérrez energetically implemented royal efforts to centralize and rationalize administration. He sought to enforce existing tax and monopoly laws and to eliminate wasteful government expenditures and fraud. On the need to increase revenues he was unwilling to compromise or slow down his pace. Early on he purged Santa Fe's fiscal offices of their entrenched creoles and implemented a broad policy of Europeanizing the high bureaucracy. Authorized in 1779 to increase the sales tax and the prices on tobacco and *aguardiente*, Gutiérrez placed enforcement primarily in the hands of peninsulares. His actions met with widespread antipathy, and a popular rebellion, the Comunero Revolt, began largely as a result of his administration. To the rebels Gutiérrez, not the king or viceroy, was the enemy. In the face of the rebellion, Gutiérrez fled Bogotá on May 12, 1781. Although he had effectively been the viceroy since August 1779, his power ended with his flight. He returned to the city on February 13, 1782, and remained in office until December 7, 1783. With an appointment of February 10, 1783, he advanced to the Council of the Indies to replace Villarrassa* as a *ministro togado*. Entering his post on June 18, 1784, he held it until he died in Madrid.

Gutiérrez married María Manuela Vélez de las Cuevas, a native of the *villa* of Saldaña, Palencia, who as late as 1809 was living in Toledo. Her parents were Domingo Vicente Vélez de las Cuevas and Teresa de Quijano. The couple had no children. Gutiérrez was admitted to the Order of Charles III in 1782.

SOURCES: AGI, Indiferente 869, *relación* of 1781, 870A, 894, 1980, 866, 886; AGS, Gracia y Justicia 153, 161; XXIII, 2–60–146; 2–60–316; 24–187–304; AHN, Estado (Carlos III), *expediente* 1357, *pruebas* of Fernando Gutiérrez de Piñeres; Kuethe, *Military Reform*, pp. 74, 77, 80, 82–3, 85; Phelan, *People*, passim; Restrepo, *Mandatarios*, pp. 509–14; *Gazeta de Madrid*, December 3, 1802, p. 1215.

H

Hermosilla y Sandoval, Ignacio Agustín de (c. 1718–November 29, 1794)

Hermosilla was born in the city of Llerena. His parents were Rodrigo de Hermosilla and María Teresa de Sandoval. He had a sister named Tomasa.

Hermosilla studied jurisprudence in Spain and for four years in Rome. He spent some time in the Ministry of Grace and Justice for Castile before working in the Ministry of the Indies. The first clerk (*oficial mayor primero*) in 1785, he was named on September 1 of that year a minister *de capa y espada* to replace Felipe de Arco.* He served until his death.

Hermosilla was a member of the Royal Academy of History and the Academy of Fine Arts (*Bellas Artes*). In 1772 he was made a *caballero* of the Order of Charles III with pension.

Married to Andrea de Mena y Salazar, Hermosilla had no children. He left his wife and niece, Manuela de Hermosilla y Sandoval, as his co-heirs.

SOURCES: AGS, XXIII, 24–187–178; AGI, Indiferente 866, 894, 869, *expediente* Hermosilla; Vignau, *Carlos III*, p. 85; Bernard, *Secrétariat*, p. 223.

Hernández de Alva Alonso, Lorenzo Serapío (November 21, 1740–May 20, 1806)

Hernández, the eldest of three sons, was born in the Villa de Arévalo, Avila, the son of Pedro Hernández de Alva y Piral and Ana Alonso, both of Arévalo and married in 1740. His paternal grandparents were Pedro Hernández de Alva y Montero and Gregoria Piral, both of Arévalo, and married in 1714; his maternal grandparents were Manuel Alonso of the *lugar* of Celecinos de los Barrios, Bishopric of León, and Manuela Carpizo of Arévalo. Lorenzo was a brother to Juan Hernández de Alva

Alonso, an audiencia minister in America. He had a second brother, Valentín, whose son Lorenzo was dean of the Cathedral of Toledo and member of the Order of Charles III, in 1830.

Hernández studied philosophy three years in the Convent of Saint Francis of Arévalo and entered the University of Valladolid to study canon law in 1759. He graduated with a baccalaureate in the faculty. A member of the *gimnasio* for legal study, he did practica with Antonio Leca y Huerta of Valladolid from 1760 to 1763, with the future councilor of Castile Santiago Ignacio Espinosa in Valladolid from 1760 to 1762, and with Joachin Anton Ximénez in Madrid from September 1762 to April 1766. The Royal Council admitted Hernández as an *abogado* in 1766 and he then joined the Colegio de Corte.

The following year Hernández served as attorney for the poor in Madrid. He became attorney to the Duque de Alba in 1769 and in 1770 to the Conde de Huescar, son of the Conde de Oropesa. He served in a similar capacity to the Duque de Medina Sidonia, the Marqués de Castelmoncayo, and the Duque de Werbic. In 1770 he became attorney of the estate of Veragua y Liria and in 1773 to the Marqués de Villena. The bishop and chapter of the Cathedral of Jaén named him attorney in 1774. The Crown made Hernández *fiscal de lo civil* of the Audiencia of Santo Domingo on August 30, 1777, and promoted him to *fiscal del crimen* of the Audiencia of Mexico on March 20, 1780. On November 10, 1784, he advanced to the civil *fiscalía* there, taking possession on March 3 of the following year. For unspecified reasons, royal favorite Manuel Godoy considered his opinions suspicious during the French subversion scare in Mexico in 1794–95 and informed Viceroy Marqués de Branciforte of his concern. The impact on Hernández's career, however, was negligible, and on January 22, 1795 he was advanced to the post of *fiscal de hacienda* in Mexico. Promoted to the Council of the Indies as *fiscal* for New Spain to replace Posada* on September 12, 1802, he served from September 5, 1803 until his death in Madrid within days after suffering a stroke that left his right side paralyzed.

Hernández married Rita Sánchez Jiménez Carvajal of Yepes, Toledo, in Madrid in 1769. Her parents were Tomás Sánchez Jiménez and Jacinta Carvajal. Their son Juan Manuel served on the Audiencia of Guadalajara in New Spain; another son, Lorenzo, later served as intendant of Puerto Príncipe; a daughter María Guadalupe married Juan Gabriel Jabat y Aztal, captain in the navy, minister to the Ottoman Porte, Order of Charles III, and commissioner of the Junta of Seville to Mexico in 1808; and daughter María Josefa received a permit to marry Pablo Martín de Jáuregui of Spain in 1794; a son named Pedro Regado predeceased his father. After Hernández's death, his widow was permitted in 1807 to draw her pension from Mexico while living in Spain.

SOURCES: AGI, México 1137; Indiferente 894, 865, 886, 887, 1323, 869, *relación* of 1802; Ultramar 861; AGN (México), Historia, vol. 120–18, *relación* of 1795; AGS, XXIII, 2–61–109; 2–64–25; 2–68–205; 2–79–5; AHN, Estado (Carlos III), *expediente* 2112, *pruebas* of Lorenzo Hernández de Alba; Consejos 12137, 12126; AHPUV, Libro 77; Lafuente Ferrari, *Iturrigaray*, pp. 190, 317; Calderón Quijano, *Virreyes de Carlos IV*, I, 394–95.

Herrera y Rivero, Vicente de (November 10, 1733–February 27, 1794)

Herrera was born in the *lugar* of Miengo. His parents were Fernando Manuel de Herrera y del Corro, a native of Miengo, and Ana Tomasa Rivero y Gómez de la Madrid of Llanes. His paternal grandparents were Captain Fernando José Herrera y Campuzano of Miengo and Josefa del Corro y Rivero of San Vicente de la Barquera. His maternal grandparents, both from Llanes, were Juan Francisco Rivero y Cienfuegos and Antonia Francisca Gómez de la Madrid. Fernando, his oldest brother, inherited the family *mayorazgo*. Antonio, another brother, was a *colegial* in the *colegio mayor* of San Bartolomé at the University of Salamanca and became a canon of the Cathedral of Zamora. Ana Xaviera, a sister, married José Velarde. Another sister, Barbara Ignacia, was unmarried in 1767.

Herrera was a member of the *colegio mayor* of San Bartolomé, receiving a licentiate from the University of Salamanca. He became *fiscal* of the Audiencia of Santo Domingo on June 18, 1764, and served there until promoted to *alcalde del crimen* in Mexico on March 18, 1770. Three years later he advanced to the civil *sala* as of May 6 and on November 1, 1776, was promoted to be the new regent of the Audiencia of Guatemala. He reluctantly left Mexico City on November 14, 1777, and assumed the post in January 1778. While an *oidor* he was denounced for possessing prohibited books. He served as protector and judge for the Shrine of Guadalupe from 1774 until he left. On November 11, 1782, Herrera returned to the Audiencia of Mexico as regent by an appointment of January 24 and served there until promoted to the Council of the Indies to replace Lanz de Casafonda* on March 30, 1786. He held the post from September 28, 1787, until his death in Madrid.

As regent Herrera helped to divide Mexico City into districts for better administration in 1782–83. From November 1784 to June 1785 he led the audiencia as captain general in his capacity as regent, a service for which he was paid 6,000 pesos. Herrera was opposed to extending legal jurisdiction to other agencies and thus diminishing the importance of the audiencias and removing large groups from ordinary justice. He also opposed the rule of military men in civil government. Although he opposed its separate legal jurisdiction and the consequent weakening of the audiencia, Herrera strongly supported strengthening the mining guild as the only way to prop up the industry. Such views did not adversely affect his career. After reaching the Council of the Indies in the early 1790s, he wrote an influential *informe* that supported the mining guild. He was considered to be very able and responsible in his actions.

Over her protests Herrera married María Dolores Romero de Terreros, a native of Mexico, while serving there. She was a younger sister of the second Conde de Regla, the third Marquesa de San Francisco, and a prize heiress. He had received a license for the marriage in 1783. The couple had no children. Herrera had a nephew named José Rivero, born in 1758, who asked permission to go to Mexico with his uncle in 1773. Herrera's cousin, Felipe Rivero, was on the Council of Castile. Herrera became a member of the Order of Charles III in 1781 and took the titles of Marqués de Herrera and Vizconde de Santo Domingo in 1790. By 1793 he had donated 3,000 pesos to the war effort.

SOURCES: AGI, México 1859; Guatemala 525; Indiferente 866, 872, 869, 906, 1814; AGS, XXIII, 2–48–174; 2–54–43; 2–57–56; 2–60–271; 2–66–5; 24–187–46; AHN, Estado (Carlos III), *expediente* 102, *pruebas* of Vicente de Herrera y Rivero; Ladd, *Nobility*, pp. 177, 199; López Sarrelangue, *Una villa mexicana*, p. 63; Pérez-Marchand, *Dos etapas*, pp. 101, 168; Calderón Quijano, *Los Virreyes . . . Carlos III*, II, 304–6; Howe, *Mining Guild*, pp. 201–4; Arrangoiz, *México*, p. 249; Tutino, "Creole Mexico," pp. 81–82; *Gazeta de México*, II, No. 30 (March 13, 1787), p. 316; *Diario curioso*, November 14, 1777, and August 7, 1785 (courtesy of Linda Arnold).

Hore Dávila, Vicente (November 5, 1752–?)

Hore was born in Calzada de Calatrava, La Mancha. His parents were Vicente Hore, a native of Alicante, Valencia, who held the rank of *sargento mayor* in the infantry and served as a local magistrate (*alcalde ordinario*) in Calzada de Calatrava, and his third wife Ana Teresa Dávila Carrillo, a native of Daymiel, La Mancha. His paternal grandparents were Jacinto Hore of Alicante and Juana Cabrera of Murcia. His maternal grandparents were Sancho Dávila Carrillo of Daymiel and Mariana Calvillo of Torralva. Hore's father had been married first to María Ana Gónzalez of Palermo. From this marriage were seven children: María Manuela, Ramón, María Amoma, Juan Joseph, Francisco Xavier, and María Luisa. By his father's second wife, María Manuela Hore, Vicente Hore y Dávila had a half sister María Juana. In addition, he had seven full siblings: Sancho, María Teresa, María Ana, María Francisca, Rafael, María Gracia, and Serafín. His cousin Ramón Hore y Valiente was a knight of Calatrava who had served as governor of Acapulco in New Spain.

Hore studied philosophy and jurisprudence at the University of Granada, taking a degree in canon law but not pursuing his studies to become a lawyer. On April 16, 1771, he entered the navy as a *guardia marina*. Promoted to a post as clerk (*oficial*) on June 22, 1774, he participated in the Algerian campaign of 1775. The following year he went to Lampa, Peru, to serve as a substitute *corregidor* for his father-in-law the Marqués de San Antonio de Saldaña. He reached Peru with his wife and children only to find that the viceroy had already filled the position. Consequently it was not until late 1780 that Hore assumed possession. The timing was unfortunate for him. During the Túpac Amaru revolt, rebels sacked the merchandise Hore was going to distribute to Indians and burned his house. He claimed later to have lost capital of 40,000 pesos. Returning to Lampa in September 1782, he found his post eliminated fourteen months later when the intendant system was established in Peru.

Hore apparently continued his military career after the disastrous experience as *corregidor*. Although named secretary to Viceroy Francisco Gil de Taboada in Peru about 1794, he never served. By 1795 he was a colonel in the infantry. On June 26 of that year he was given a supernumerary position as minister *de capa y espada* on the Council of the Indies, but without salary. His zeal in serving on the Council, however, was such that on March 28, 1797 he was awarded the standard annual salary of 55,000 *reales de vellón*.

In 1806, when admitted to the Order of Calatrava, Hore was in Seville serving as *asistente* on commission since November 28, 1805. He continued as *asistente* and intendant of Andalusia until removed by the Junta Central on October 21, 1808. While the Junta had decreed on October 14, 1808, that Hore should go to Calzada de Calatrava, believing his life to be in danger, it modified its order upon receiving evidence that the people of Seville were very pleased with their intendant. Ordering Hore to Córdoba, which he had requested, the Junta left him with full salary as councilor of the Indies.

Hore married twice. His second mother-in-law, the Condesa de Casa Real, possessed wealth in Potosí. On May 13, 1807, Hore received honors of councilor of state.

SOURCES: AGS, XXIII, 13–8–678, 13–8–679; AGI, Indiferente 886, 866, 869, *expediente* Hore; AHN, Ordenes Militares (Calatrava), *expediente* 47 *moderno*, *pruebas* of Vicente Hore y Dávila; Estado 53A, 878, *expediente* 55; Vignau, *Calatrava*, pp. 74–75.

Huerta y Cigala, Jacobo Andrés de (February 2, 1712–March 13, 1790)

Huerta was born in Las Palmas, Canary Islands. He was the son of Cayetano de Huerta, secretary of the Tribunal de la Santa Cruzada and accountant of Church accounts, and Luisa Bernarda Cigala, both of the Canary Islands. His maternal grandparents were Captain Julián García Macías de la Cruz and Ana María Cigala Iglesias de Aguilar. Huerta, the third son, had four brothers. Andrés became a canon in the Canaries; Pedro went to the Indies; José became an infantry captain; and Agustín was a priest. His sister Antonia married her cousin Colonel Cristobál Adrián de Graf Sarmiento, the *justicia mayor* of Neyba, New Granada.

Huerta studied in the School of the Augustinians in the Canaries for three years and won a fellowship at the Colegio de San Miguel de Granada from 1731 to 1735. He received the baccalaureate in canon law from the University of Granada and, in 1737, the licentiate and doctorate in that faculty. He was a member of the College of Santa Catalina Martír of Granada and substituted in various chairs at the university. The Royal Council approved him to practice law in 1738.

Huerta began to be considered for audiencia positions in America in 1739 and obtained an appointment as *oidor* on the Audiencia of Guatemala on March 7, 1742. He assumed the post in April 1744. When that audiencia was purged of its deadwood in 1745, Huerta was the only minister then serving who was allowed to remain. He served there until about 1756, when after prolonged petitioning by his brother Andrés he was allowed to return to Spain with assurance of an appointment. After fifteen months in Spain, in April 1760 he was named an *oidor* of the Audiencia of Barcelona. He advanced to the first of three new positions of *ministro togado* of the Council of the Indies on May 4, 1776, serving there until his death.

Huerta married *canariana* Isabel María de Ceballos y Ceballos, the daughter of Diego de Ceballos Carvajal, permanent city councilman (*regidor perpetuo*) of Puerto de Santa María, commander of militia, and Isabel Ana de Ceballos y Fernández de

Castro. Their only child, Joaquín de Huerta Ceballos, succeeded to the family *mayorazgo* and was given a pension of 500 ducats a year by Charles III.

Huerta possessed a *mayorazgo* in the Canary Islands. Considered for membership in a military order in 1751, he was supposed to have received one but whether he did is not clear.

SOURCES: AGI, Indiferente 866, 807B, 892, 894, 1628; 154, *relación* of 1753; Guatemala 525; AGS, Gracia y Justicia 155, 157; XXIII, 2–33–285; 13–8–144; AHN, Consejos 18515; García Carraffa, *Enciclopedia*, XLIV, 127–28.

I

Ibáñez de Mendoza y Córdoba, Mateo (October 4, 1661, baptism–May 7, 1738)

Ibáñez, a second son, was born in Madrid. His parents were *madrileños* Gaspar Ibáñez de Mendoza, Marqués de Agropoli and, by marriage, the Marqués de Mondejar, and María Gregoria Mendoza y Aragón, the ninth Marquesa de Mondejar, grandees of Spain. Gaspar was a celebrated author. Mateo's paternal grandparents were Mateo Ibáñez de Segovia, a native of Segovia and knight of Calatrava, and Alvira de Peralta of Madrid. His maternal grandparents were Núño Córdoba Bocanegra y de la Cueva, a native of Texcoco, New Spain, knight of Alcántara, and Marqués de Agropoli, and María de Mendoza of Madrid. Ibáñez had three brothers. José inherited his father's titles. Núño held *togado* positions and reached the Council of Orders. Vicente served in the navy.

Ibáñez studied at the Universities of Alcalá, where he was accorded the unique distinction of being matriculated as *señor*, and Salamanca. He received a baccalaureate in canon law from Salamanca in 1676, entered the *colegio mayor* of San Ildefonso at Alcalá in 1681, and received a licentiate from that university in 1683. While at Alcalá he competed for and substituted in academic chairs.

On October 16, 1690, Ibáñez was named an *oidor* of the Chancellery of Granada. He subsequently advanced to the Council of Orders with an appointment as *fiscal* on May 22, 1698. Named a supernumerary minister *togado* of the Council of the Indies on February 16, 1700, he served until Philip V exiled him in 1706. On December 23, 1726, he was reappointed to replace Tomás de Sola.* A decade later, on August 6, 1736, he advanced to a seat on the Cámara. He served until his death.

SOURCES: AGS, XXII, 13–8–488; Gracia y Justicia 966; AHN, Estado 6380 (1); Ordenes (Calatrava), *expediente* 1264, *pruebas* of Mateo Ibáñez de Mendoza; Consejos 13518;

Libro de Plazas 732; Universidades, Libro 456F, 1233F, 1146F; AGI, Indiferente 865; Roxas y Contreras, *Historia*, II, 183, 187; Alvarez y Baena, *Hijos de Madrid*, II, 304–12; Ballesteros Robles, *Diccionario*, p. 314; Bernard, *Secrétariat*, p. 216.

Iriarte y Nieves-Rabelo, Bernardo de (February 18, 1735–July 11, 1814)

Iriarte was born in Puerto de la Cruz, Canary Islands. His parents were Bernardo de Iriarte y de Cisneros, a native of Orotava, Canary Islands, and a lieutenant in the provincial militia, and Barbara Nieves-Rabelo y Hernández de Oropesa from the same town. His paternal grandparents were Juan de Iriarte y Echevarría, a noble from Oñate, and Teresa de Cisneros y Excañuela from Orotava. His maternal grandparents were Domingo Lorenzo de la Nieves-Rabelo and Catalina Josefa Pérez Motáñez, both from the Canaries. Bernardo had five younger siblings. Brother Domingo became a career diplomat. Tomás, a famous fabulist, served as chief archivist for the Council of War. José became intendant general for the Canaries. Juan Tomás entered the Dominican order. Carolina married infantry captain Francisco del Castillo de Santelices.

Iriarte began his career in 1756 when he went to Parma as a secretary for the Spanish embassy there. In 1758 he returned to Spain as eighth clerk (*oficial octavo*) in the Ministry of State. As part of his career in that ministry, he later served in Vienna and London, where he was secretary to the Spanish ambassador. The senior chief clerk (*oficial mayor decano*) of the Ministry of State in 1780, he was named on May 14 of that year to replace Fernando de Magallón* as minister *de capa y espada* on the Council of the Indies. Advanced to the Cámara on May 19, 1793, to replace Gabriel de Munive,* he secured the right to attend at his pleasure on December 31, 1797. Among his activities, Iriarte was vice-president of the Philippines Company. On April 8, 1802, he was retired with full pay. On August 29, 1803, he was informed that he could live anywhere in Spain except Madrid. He selected Valencia.

Iriarte married Antonia Sáenz de Tejada, probably in 1797. After his death in Bordeaux, she died in Bremen. Iriarte, a pensioned *caballero* of the Order of Charles III from 1772, reportedly had an excellent private collection of paintings.

SOURCES: AGS, XXIII, 13–9–404, 13–9–421; AGI, Indiferente 892, 869, *expediente* Iriarte; AHN, Hacienda 511, *expediente* 2232; *Enciclopedia Universal Ilustrado*, XXVIII, 1937; García Carraffa, *Enciclopedia*, LVI, 9–10; Vignau, *Carlos III*, p. 90.

Isla, Luis Fernando de (Variant: Luis Fernández de Ysla) (1676–August 15, 1755)

Isla was born in Urueña, Bishopric of Palencia. After receiving a baccalaureate in civil law from the University of Valladolid in 1695, he was admitted to the *colegio mayor* of Oviedo at the University of Salamanca, served as a professor of Institutes there, and, in 1704, was rector of his *colegio*.

After twice substituting as a judge for Basque affairs (*juez mayor de Vizcaya*) on the Chancellery of Valladolid, Isla purchased an appointment as a supernumerary *oidor* of that court on September 3, 1710. For some time, however, he served as *corregidor* of Vizcaya, concluding this post in 1722. Named *alcalde de casa y corte* on September 1, 1727, Isla advanced to the Council of the Indies to replace Mateo Ibáñez de Mendoza* as a minister *togado* with an appointment of August 28, 1738. He assumed the position on September 1. A final advancement came on September 27, 1741, when he was named a minister *togado* of the Council of Castile, a post he held until his death.

Among other responsibilities, Isla served as legal adviser (*asesor*) for the Council of War and as superintendent general of the *presidiarios*.

SOURCES: AGS, Gracia y Justicia 138, 139, 142, 146, 147; AHN, Consejos 13531, 13532, 13643, Estado 6380(2); AGI, Indiferente 897; AUS, Libro 409; AHPUV, Libro 199; *Gazeta de Madrid*, August 16, 1755.

J

Jacot Ortiz Rojano Ruiz de la Escalera, Melchor (1732–1807)

Jacot was born in Málaga to José Jacot y Ruiz de la Escalera of Málaga and María Ortiz Rojano from Baena, Córdoba. Both his father and paternal grandfather were regidors in perpetuity in Málaga, and in due course Melchor too held the office. His paternal grandparents were Melchor Jacot Varenne and Leonor Ruiz de la Escalera, both from Málaga; his maternal grandparents were Antonio Ortiz Rojano of Baena, a knight of Calatrava, and Josefa de Miranda y Trillo of Madrid. His paternal great grandfather came from Antwerp. Jacot had three brothers: José, the eldest son; Francisco, a *caballero* of Charles III; and Juan.

In 1752 Jacot won a fellowship to the Colegio de San Bartolome y Santiago el Mayor in Granada, an award he held three years. He competed for chairs at the University of Granada and was elected the substitute professor of *Código*. After he had spent four years in the office of Antonio López del Rincón, who would later become an audiencia minister in Spain, and another four years in the office of José Fernández de la Fuente, the Chancellery of Granada admitted him to practice law in 1756, and the following year he was incorporated to practice before the Royal Council.

In 1758 Jacot began to serve *alcaldías* of Spain. In 1766 he received honors of *alcalde de la quadra* of the Audiencia of Seville. His first audiencia appointment was as an *alcalde del crimen* of the Chancellery of Valladolid in 1769. Five years later he advanced to *oidor* of the court and on November 14, 1776, was named the first regent of the Audiencia of Lima, a post he assumed on June 12, 1777. He was also assigned to take the *residencia* of departing Viceroy Manuel de Amat. In Lima, Jacot immediately found himself at odds with Visitor General José Antonio de Areche* and leading ministers of the Audiencia of Lima as well as Viceroy Manuel de Guirior.

Reportedly, he left a *relación* for his successor dated November 20, 1787. On May 19, 1788, Jacot was admitted to the Order of Charles III. That same year he joined what would soon be a parade of regents advanced to the Council of the Indies, to the dismay of a number of Lima's residents. Named by a decree of February 12, 1787, he assumed the post on June 2, 1788. He received the title Conde de Pozos Dulces in 1790. On July 9, 1800, he entered the Cámara of the Indies, having received honors of the prestigious body the previous year. He served until his death.

Jacot was first married to Francisca Paula Cascajedo. They had a daughter named María del Carmen born in Madrid in 1761. In 1788 Jacot sought a license to remarry. The following year he wed Maria Luisa López de Maturana, a native of Huaura, who eventually died in Madrid in 1832. Her parents were Gregorio López de Maturana and María Irene Eguilaz. The marriage joined Jacot to "the most important and noble families of Lima." Luisa's uncle Julián de Maturana was a knight of San Juan and the treasurer of the Cathedral of Lima. Other uncles were José and Pedro Tagle, audiencia ministers in Lima. Jacot's brother Francisco entered the Order of Charles III in 1788 and served as permanent city councilman of Malaga.

SOURCES: AGI, Indiferente 865, 866, 886, 1507, *relación* of 1757; 869 *expediente* Jacot; 870A *expediente* Antúnez; 871 *expediente* Pozos Dulces, *relación* of 1791; AHN, Estado (Carlos III), *expediente* 283, *pruebas* of Melchor Jacot Ortiz Rojano; Consejos 13532; 13533; AGS, Gracia y Justicia 150, 156, 161; ACRG, *cabina* 321, *legajo* 4291, *pieza* 2; Lohmann Villena, *Ministros*, pp. 57–58; Lohmann Villena, "Las relaciones," p. 337; Matilla Tascón, *Rentas vitalicias*, pp. 57–58.

Jimeno Rodríguez, Marcos (var. Ximeno) (June 19, 1702, baptism–August 28, 1781)

Jimeno was born in the *villa* of Rueda, Valladollid, and was probably the fourth of eight children. His parents were Marcos Jimeno y Ramos and Francisca Rodríguez Benito, both from Rueda. His paternal grandfather, Bernabé Jimeno Moro, was from Villaverde de Medina. His paternal grandmother, María Ramos Perez, and his maternal grandparents, Pedro Rodríguez Campo and María Benito Blanco, were from Rueda. His siblings were Bernabé, Cristóbal, Valerio, Isabel, Teresa, Francisca, and Catalina.

Jimeno received a baccalaureate in canon law from the University of Valladolid and a baccalaureate, licentiate, and doctorate in civil law from the University of Salamanca. At Salamanca he spent twenty-seven years in the *colegio mayor* of Oviedo and held a succession of academic chairs, culminating with the distinguished first chair of civil law.

On April 26, 1749, Jimeno was named a criminal *fiscal* of the Chancellery of Granada. Routinely advancing briefly into the civil *fiscalía* in early 1752, he was named an *oidor* on the court on July 25, 1752. Promoted to Valencia as regent on February 19, 1757, he moved to Madrid with an appointment of February 20, 1764, as minister *togado* of the Council of the Indies to replace the long-deceased Antonio Romay.* Advanced to the Cámara on March 18, 1767 to replace Gerónimo de Sola,* he was given the right to attend at his pleasure on November 30, 1778.

Jimeno became a pensioned *caballero* of the order of Charles III in 1777. His nephew Juan Bonilla Ximeno served as an *oidor* on the Audiencia of Manila. Jimeno died a bachelor in Madrid. He left a library worth 5,000–6,000 *reales de vellón* and some entailed land in Rueda.

SOURCES: AGS, XXIII, 13–8–406, 13–9–481; Gracia y Justicia 158; AHN, Consejos 13520, 18213, *títulos* of 1742; Estado (Carlos III), *expediente*, 45, *pruebas* of Marco Ximeno y Rodríguez; AGI, Indiferente 824, 894, 1630, 869, *expediente* Jimeno; AHPM, Protocolo 19893; *Gazeta de Madrid*, September 18, 1781; Vignau, *Carlos III*, p. 93; García Carraffa, *Enciclopedia*, XLVII, 137.

L

Lanz de Casafonda, Manuel Miguel (December 24, 1721–November 27, 1785)

Lanz was born in Peñaranda de Bracamonte, Bishopric of Salamanca. His parents were Manuel José Lanz de Casafonda, a native of Sangüesa, Navarre, who practiced medicine in Peñaranda, and Thomasa María de Ozcoidi of Madrid. His paternal grandparents were Juan Manuel Lanz de Casafonda of Alfaro and Mariana Pascual of Pamplona. His maternal grandparents were Miguel de Ozcoidi of Rocaforte, Navarre, and Manuela Gutiérrez of Villaluenga, Palencia.

Lanz was admitted to practice law and entered the lawyers' guild in Madrid in 1748. He knew both Greek and Hebrew and established a reputation as an author, particularly of tracts on points of law.

As a result of his success as an author, the Crown named Lanz *fiscal* for New Spain to replace Bernardo Cavallero* on August 23, 1766. When the Council was expanded in 1773, he was named on July 29 to one of the two new posts of minister *togado*. On February 26, 1776, he was promoted to the Cámara, where he served until his death.

Lanz became a pensioned *caballero* of the Order of Charles III in 1772.

SOURCES: AGS, XXIII, 13–8–401, 2–57–300; AGI, Indiferente 871, 869, *expediente* Lanz de Casafonda; Vignau, *Carlos III*, p. 95; Sempere y Guarinos, *Ensayo*, II, 144–51; Lanz de Casafonda, *Diálogos*, pp. 17–19.

Lardizábal y Elorza, Martín de (c. 1696–October 23, 1743)

Lardizábal was born in Segura, Alava. His parents were Francisco de Lardizábal and Josepha de Elorza. His paternal grandparents were Martín de Lardizábal and Magdalena de Urquía. His maternal grandparents were Francisco de Elorza and Luisa de Larzanguren. His older brother Juan Antonio became the bishop of Puebla. A younger relative, Joseph de Lardizábal y Vicuña, also from Segura, went to New Spain with Martín's brother Juan Antonio. Subsequently he served on Spanish audiencias, ultimately reaching the Council of Hacienda.

Lardizábal entered the *colegio mayor* of San Bartolomé in 1713 and received the licentiate in civil law in 1716. Rector of his *colegio* in 1714 and again in 1719–20, he gained the chair of *Institutes* in 1725 and then advanced to that of *Código* at the University of Salamanca. On October 19, 1726, he was named *alcalde del crimen* of the Audiencia of Zaragoza, a post he had to delay entering while he found the means to pay the appointment tax (*media anata*). At the proposal of the Caracas Company, in 1732 he was sent to Caracas, Venezuela, as inspector-commandant. To reward him for fulfilling the commission, the king named Lardizábal a supernumerary *alcalde de casa y corte* in 1733 with the stipulation that he could not serve until the Venezuelan responsibilities were completed. Back in Spain, on May 22, 1740, Lardizábal was named a minister *togado* to replace José de Valdivieso.* His appointment met an objective the Caracas Company had set forth several years earlier.

SOURCES: AGS, XXIII, 13–9–433; Gracia y Justicia, 138, 139, 140; AHN, Consejos 17957, 13643; Ordenes Militares (Santiago), *expediente* 4319, *pruebas* of Francisco Xavier de Lardizábal de Arza; AGI, Indiferente 869, *expediente* Lardizábal; Roxas y Contreras, *Historia*, II, 608–9, 650–52, 1001; Hussey, *Caracas Company*, pp. 68, 105.

Laysequilla y Palacios y Aguilar, José de (Variants: Layssequilla, Laisequilla, La Isequilla) (March 17, 1677–September 18, 1755)

Laysequilla was born in Madrid. His father, Santiago de Laysequilla y Palacios, a native of Valle de Liendo in the mountains and Archbishopric of Burgos was official representative (*procurador general*) for *hidalgos*, *corregidor* of Orense and Ponferrada, and *relator*. His mother was *madrileña* Antonia Francisca de Aguilar. His paternal grandparents were Juan de Laysequilla y Martínez de Bolde and Francisca de Palacio y del Hoyo, both from Valle de Liendo. Jeronimo de Aguilar and María de Tovar, both from Madrid, were his maternal grandparents. Both his father and mother married twice. By his father's first wife, Filemón de la Mota y Rojas, Laysequilla had half sisters Josepha and Agustina. By his mother's first husband, Juan de Castro y Araujo, he had a half brother, José de Castro y Araujo, who served in audiencias in Spain and, from 1713 to 1739, on the Council of Castile. He also had a brother, Juan, who attended the University of Salamanca with him and became an attorney, and three sisters: Juana, Baltasara, and Teresa.

Laysequilla studied canon law at the University of Salamanca. He was licensed as an attorney to practice before the Royal Council in 1698. On November 22, 1704, he was named *oidor* of the Audiencia of Santo Domingo. He took the *residencia* of the departing governor in 1705. Subsequently, he was named to Quito as *oidor*, a post he assumed between December 1709 and October 1712, and served until the court's suppression in 1718. He remained in Quito executing commissions for the government until named *oidor* of Santa Fe de Bogotá on April 16, 1719. He went to Spain in mid–1722 after scarcely more than a year and a half in Bogotá. The following year, on September 23, he was named *fiscal* of the Council of the Indies for the Secretariat of Peru, receiving honors of minister on July 8, 1727. With the expansion of the Council in 1738 he was named to one of the two new posts of *ministro togado* on February 8 and to the Cámara as well. He received permission to attend only when he wanted in 1741. He died as the senior *ministro togado* of the Council.

Laysequilla married Mariana Pérez Dardón y Lazcano, who predeceased him. The couple had three daughters: Manuela Antonia, Micaela, and María Josefa. Manuela married the Marqués de la Vera. Micaela married Alonso Muñiz Caso y Osorio, Marqués del Campo de Villar, an audiencia minister in Spain who subsequently served from 1748 until his death in 1765 as secretary of state for grace and justice. María married Rodrigo de Hoces Torquemada y Córdoba. Laysequilla became a member of the Order of Santiago in 1728.

SOURCES: AGI, Indiferente 866, 870, 894, 897, 867; Lima 475; Quito 128; AGS, XXIII, 24–174–222; 2–18–92; AHN, Ordenes Militares (Santiago), *expediente* 4149, *pruebas* of José de la Ysequilla y de Aguilar; AUS, Libro 397; Restrepo, *Mandatarios*, p. 341; "Indice de documentos del volumen de 1714," p. 51; "Real Cédula de 31 de diciembre de 1704," p. 45; *Gazeta de Madrid*, September 30, 1755; Mejía Ricart, *Historia*, VI, 320; Escudero, *Los secretarios*, III, 729.

León y Escandón, Pedro de (1708–June 9, 1770)

León was born in Madrid. His parents were José de León y Espinosa, a knight of Santiago and native of Medina del Campo, and María Luisa Escandón. His paternal grandparents were Alonso de León y Espinosa, also from the *villa* of Medina del Campo, and Ana Luisa López Heredero of the *villa* of Catalapiedra. His uncle, Francisco Antonio Escandón, was named archbishop of Lima and took young Pedro with him to Peru.

In Lima León studied at the Jesuit *colegio* of San Martín from 1724 to 1733. Having studied canon law at the University of Salamanca earlier, he received a licentiate and doctorate from the University of San Marcos in 1721. Admitted to practice law by the Audiencia of Lima, Léon substituted in a chair of canon law at the University of San Marcos in 1733 and served as an attorney for prisoners of the Inquisition in the same year. His uncle also provided him with patronage appointments in the Church.

On October 8, 1735, León was named protector of the Indians for the Audiencia of Lima. Named oidor of the Chancellery of Valladolid in 1743, he requested remaining in Lima as a supernumerary *oidor* instead of returning to Spain. His petition was refused, however, and he served first in Valladolid and then, with an appointment of March 22, 1752, as a minister *togado* of the Council of the Indies. He served from March 23 until he joined the Council of Castile on September 1, 1766. León advanced to the Cámara of Castile on March 7, 1770. He served there until he died as a poor bachelor.

SOURCES: AGS, XXIII, 2–30–208, 13–8–554; Gracia y Justicia, 149; AGI, Lima 983, 401, *relación* of 1734; Indiferente 894, 899; AHN, Estado 6380(2); Ordenes

Militares (Santiago), *expediente* 4443, *pruebas* of José de León y Espinosa; *Gazeta de Madrid*, June 19, 1770; Mendiburu, *Diccionario*, VI, 429.

López Lisperguer, Francisco (1750–March 16, 1823)

López was born in the city of La Plata, present Bolivia. His parents were José López Lisperguer, a native of Santiago, Chile, who served for more than two decades as an *oidor* of the Audiencia of Charcas, and Ana María Nieto y Quintana of Buenos Aires. His paternal grandparents were Millán López Martínez, a militia commander (*maestre de campo*) and native of Cabrejas del Pinar, Soria, and María Lisperguer y Aguirre, a native of Santiago, Chile. His maternal grandparents were Francisco García Nieto, a native of Zamora who died in 1736 at the hands of the Portuguese as *sargento mayor* of the *plaza* (garrison) of Buenos Aires, and María Ana Quintana y Esquivel of Buenos Aires.

López studied philosophy and law in La Plata before journeying to Spain in 1770. There he also studied at the University of Valladolid. Received as an attorney by the Royal Council in 1776, he was named an *alcalde mayor* of Navalcarnero in 1782. After spending sixteen years in provincial administration, in early 1799 he was appointed to serve as *fiscal* of the *sala de alcaldes de casa y corte*, the criminal chamber of the Council of Castile, in the absences of the regular *fiscal*, Juan Meléndez Valdés. The following year Meléndez was retired and López assumed the regular position. On June 25, 1804, he was named a supernumerary *alcalde de casa y corte* and on March 9, 1806, he moved into a regular position. On April 1, 1807, he was named a minister *togado* of the Council of the Indies to replace José Agustín Castaño.* López served as a temporary (*suplente*) deputy for Buenos Aires at the Cortes of Cádiz. His position on the Council disappearing as the Council itself was temporarily abolished during Spain's War for Independence against the French, López was formally retired with half-salary on July 2, 1814, after the Council was restored. Although his political conduct had been unacceptable to Ferdinand VII, three weeks later his compensation was increased to full salary.

López married Antonia Arjona y Lecuona, a native of Real de Nobita, in the province of Chocó in present Colombia. Her father, Colonel Pedro Arjona, was a native of Cartagena, Murcia. Her mother, Francisca Lecuona y Alberto, was born in Guayaquil, Ecuador. The couple had five children. The four daughters were Petra, María, Manuela, and Evarista. Evarista married Fernando de Sada y Montaner, the Marqués de Campo Real. Son Ambrosio was a second lieutenant in the royal guards in 1818.

SOURCES: AGI, Indiferente 888, 892, 869, *expediente* López Lisperguer; AHN, Estado 6379(1); Hacienda 2051, *expediente* 8; 528, *expediente* 17; Consejos 13644; AGS, Gracia y Justicia 163; *Gazeta de Madrid*, March 3, 1799; Bernard, *Secrétariat*, p. 227; Burkholder and Chandler, *Biographical Dictionary*, pp. 184–85.

López Quintana, Antonio (December 6, 1739–August 26, 1814)

López, an only child, was born in the *lugar* of Orzales, Archbishopric of Burgos. Although baptized Domingo Antonio, he used only Antonio. His parents were Pedro López Quintana of Orazales, who died before Antonio reached the age of two, and Juana Teresa Fernandez Ruiz of the *lugar* of Villapaderne, who died before he turned nine. His paternal grandparents were Francisco Antonio López Quintana of the *lugar* of Monegro and Phelipa Gutiérrez of Orzales. His maternal grandparents were Francisco Fernández Ruiz of Villapaderne and Josefa Fernández Fontecha of the *lugar* of Somballe. His family for generations had made their living by raising cattle.

López was a student in the Colegio de Nuestra Señora de la Concepción de Huerfanos at the University of Salamanca. After studying philosophy, he advanced to the study of civil and canon law in 1755. Following additional study, he was received as an attorney by the Council of Castile in 1764.

In 1769 López went to the Canary Islands and was admitted to practice law there. While on Gran Canaria he served as interim *fiscal* of the audiencia for a period of four months. Returning to Madrid, in 1771 he began to obtain a series of prominent clients, including the cathedrals of Ciudad-Rodrigo and Seville, and nobles such as the Conde de Benavente, Duque de Gandía, Duque de Santisteban, Marqués de Valdecarzana, and Conde de Amayuelas.

On March 5, 1779, López was named criminal *fiscal* of the Audiencia of Guadalajara, but before he could leave for the New World he was asked in August to serve *ad interim* as *fiscal* of the Audiencia of the House of Trade in Cádiz, where he remained until 1783. López assumed his position in Guadalajara on November 28, 1783. Advanced on October 17, 1786, as *oidor decano regente* (combining the functions of senior judge and regent) of the new Audiencia of Caracas, he took over the post on June 25, 1787. While serving in Caracas, López was admitted to the Order of Charles III in 1791 and given honors of the Council of the Indies in 1798. Although appointed regent of the Audiencia of Santa Fe on May 17, 1804, he never served. On August 13 of the following year he was named *ministro togado* of the Council of the Indies to replace Escobedo.* War with England, however, delayed his departure. Still in Caracas in March 1809, in September López was ordered to assume his post. Some Venezuelans regarded him as sympathetic to their hopes in 1808 of establishing their own governing Junta in the king's name. In Caracas he was the first director of the Academy of Spanish and Public Law, which was created in 1790. He taught law there and left some distinguished students. After serving on the short-lived Supreme Tribunal of Justice in Spain, he was named to the restored Council of the Indies in 1814 but died soon afterward.

López married Manuela López de Fresnena of Segovia. Their daughter María, born in 1788, married Andrés Moreno in Caracas. Following his death in the 1812 earthquake that struck Caracas, she married Francisco de Saavedra, treasurer of the offices of Puerto Cabello. López's son Manuel was killed fighting the French in the Battle of Río Seco in Spain's War of Independence. Nine other children died in infancy. His wife died before López left Caracas.

SOURCES: AGI, Guadalajara 304, *relacíon* of 1776; Caracas 40, *relacíon* of 1796; Indiferente 866, 888, 869; Chile 258; Ultramar 862; AGS, XXIII, 2–63–17; 2–70–224; 2–82–165; 2–88–102; AHN, Estado (Carlos III), *expediente* 520, *pruebas* of Domingo López Quintana; AHPM, Protocolos 23734; Garcia Chuecos, *Estudios*, II, 9, 14; Instituto, *Conjuración*, pp. 12, 113, 118.

Luján y Silva, Fernando (1682–July 8, 1736)

Luján was born in Madrid. His parents were *madrileño* Fernando de Luján y Osorio, a professional soldier who became the first Conde de Castroponce, and Antonia de Silva Toledo y Vicentelo, whose father was the Marqués de Montemayor. His paternal grandparents were Diego de Luján, a knight of Santiago and attendant of Philip IV, and Leonor Osorio de Guzmán. His maternal grandparents were Francisco de Silva, the sixth Marqués de Montemayor, and María Vicentelo. His older brother José Nicolás became the second Conde de Castroponce and Duque del Arco.

Luján secured a university education and entered the prestigious *colegio mayor* of San Bartolomé at the University of Salamanca in 1700.

By a decree of April 24, 1709, that called attention to Luján's "quality and merits," he was named a supernumerary *oidor* of the Chancellery of Valladolid. Four years later he advanced to the Council of Orders. In 1715 he suffered from eye problems and related that reading books made them worse. As he expressed it, he was suffering "great unrest and fatigue of the mind." To ease his lot, he asked for an appointment as *mayordomo* or a *capa y espada* minister on the Council of Hacienda or the Council of the Indies. Named *mayordomo* in 1721 for the future King Luis I, he also served after 1730 as *aposentador mayor* of the palace. Also in 1721, by a decree of March 30, Philip V named him a minister *de capa y espada* of the Council of the Indies. Luján served as *mayordomo* for the future Ferdinand VI after the death of Luis I in 1724. He also remained on the Council until his death.

Luján, a knight of Alcántara, married Ana Antonia Góngora y Avilés, the daughter of Pedro Góngora y de los Rios, Marqués de Almodóvar, and María Catalina Avilés y Bañuelos, Condesa de Canalejas. As a result of his marriage, Luján shared the title Marqués de Almodóvar with his wife. Their son Pedro Francisco, born in Madrid in 1727, later inherited the title Marqués de Almodóvar and served as Spanish ambassador to Portugal and England. Their daughter Raphaela married the Marqués de Nules y Quirna. After Luján's death, his wife remarried Pedro de Chaves, a lieutenant general of the Royal Army.

SOURCES: AGS, XXIII, 13–8–462; AHN, Consejos 13537; Estado 1687, *expediente* 24; Alvarez y Baena, *Hijos de Madrid*, II, 68; Roxas y Contreras, *Historia*, II, 597–603, 976; Bernard, *Secrétariat*, p. 216; Ballesteros Robles, *Diccionario*, pp. 402–3.

M

Machado, Gonzalo (?–December 29, 1732)

Prior to his first appointment to the Council of the Indies, Machado served as an *oidor* on the Council of Santa Clara in Naples. After five years of imprisonment during the War of the Spanish Succession, he was named a minister *togado* of the Council on September 26, 1713. He took his oath of office two days later. In the reorganization of November 10, 1713, he was named the third of three presidents of the Council. Reappointed a minister *togado* on August 5, 1715, he survived still another reform to be named to the Council as reorganized on January 20, 1717. He subsequently advanced to the Cámara when it was reestablished on December 22, 1721. Granted permission to serve at his pleasure on February 15, 1732, he remained on the Cámara the duration of his life.

SOURCES: AGI, Indiferente 866, 867, 871; AHN, Estado 6380 (1); AGS, XXIII, 13–9–627, 631, 633; Bernard, *Secrétariat*, p. 215.

Machado Fiesco, Francisco Xavier (December 3, 1730–October 17, 1808)

Machado was born in San Cristóbal de la Laguna, Tenerife, Canary Islands. His parents, both from Tenerife, were Alvaro Machado Fiesco y González and María Eufemia Yáñez Felipe. His paternal grandparents were Lieutenant Colonel Juan Machado Fiesco and Ana González Pereira, both from Tenerife. His maternal grandparents, also from Tenerife, were Juan Yáñez Felipe and Ana Rodríguez Texera. Machado was probably the fifth of six children. His siblings were Domingo, a captain; Pedro Andrés, a canon of the Cathedral in Cuenca; Ana who married Lieutenant Colonel Gabriel Román Manrique de Lara; Beatriz de San Juan Baptista, who entered a convent in Laguna; and Agustín, a canon of the Cathedral in Cuenca.

Machado began his service in 1744 as a cadet in the infantry regiment of Guimat in the Canaries. He subsequently advanced to captain. In 1755 he went to Madrid, where he remained for years, as deputy general for the Canaries.

In 1765 Machado was named to serve as secretary to the general visitation of New Spain led by José de Gálvez.* After returning to Spain, he was named intendant of Cuenca in September, 1774. On September 12, 1777, he was named chief accountant (*contador general*) and minister *de capa y espada* of the Council of the Indies to replace Tomás Ortiz de Landazuri.* Advanced to the Cámara on October 5, 1790, on April 16, 1797, he was given the privilege of attending the Council at his pleasure. Retired with full pay on August 15, 1802, he was subsequently ordered to leave Madrid.

Machado received a license on January 27, 1779, to marry María Manuela Salcedo y Burgos of Cádiz. She was the daughter of *madrileños* Domingo Joaquín Salcedo y Castellanos, a knight of Santiago and lieutenant general, and Isabel Burgos y del Hoyo. Her paternal grandfather was Manuel Jacinto Salcedo.* The couple's son Justo Germán, born in Madrid, became a *caballero* of the Order of Charles III in 1807.

Machado was a hereditary alderman of La Laguna and, from 1774, a pensioned *caballero* of the Order of Charles III.

SOURCES: AGS, XXIII, 13–9–121, 13–9–555, 13–9–525; AGI, Indiferente 871, *expediente* Machado; AHN, Estado (Carlos III), *expediente* 1345, *pruebas* of Justo Germán de Machado Fiesco. Guerra, *Diario*, I, 137; Vignau, *Carlos III*, p. 106; García Carraffa, *Enciclopedia*, III, 121–2.

Magallón y Andrés, Fernando de (May 29, 1724, baptism–December 14, 1781)

Magallón was born in Tarazona. His parents were Melchor Baltasar Magallón y de la Peña, a hereditary alderman of his native city of Tarazona, and Felipa Juliana Escárroz, a native of Cintruénigo. His paternal grandparents were Marco Magallón y Navarro of Tudela and Isabel Peña y Corella of Tarazona. His maternal grandparents were Tomás Andrés Escárroz of Cintruénigo and Juana María Monreal de Sarría of Falces. His uncles Juan Mauricio and Pablo Antonio Magallón were canons in Tarazona.

Magallón followed a career in the Ministry of State. For ten years he served as secretary to the Spanish ambassador in Paris. For two years he was in the Secretariat of State for Foreign Affairs in Madrid. In 1766 he was named to the Committee for Commerce and Money. Granted honors of minister of the Council of the Indies on June 24, 1773, he was named a supernumerary minister *de capa y espada* on July 29, 1773, but ordered to continue to work with the Conde de Aranda in Paris on resolving Navarre's boundary with France. By early 1775 the boundary question had been resolved and Magallón was granted permission to tour and take the waters in England and Holland. Five years later, on April 25, 1780, he was given the commission of serving as a minister plenipotentiary to the duke of Parma. He died in Parma not long after arriving.

Magallón belonged to the Order of San Juan from 1767. He was a member of the Royal Academy of San Fernando and the Royal Academies of History, Spanish, and Fine Arts. He died a bachelor, leaving his nephews as heirs.

SOURCES: AGS, XXIII, 2–58–183; AGI, Indiferente 894, 871, *expediente* Magallón; AHN, Ordenes Militares (San Juan), *expediente* 24, 475, *pruebas* of Fernando Magallón y Andrés; Estado 3427, *expediente* 2; Bernard, *Secrétariat*, p. 221; *Armería*, III, 38–40.

Maldonado Sánchez Romero, Tomás de (December 26, 1686–May 17, 1765)

Maldonado was born in the *villa* of Agüimes in the Canary Islands. His parents were Sebastián Suárez Arías y Maldonado and María Calva Balboa, both *vecinos* of Agüimes. Maldonado attended the University of Granada for five years, studied canon and civil law, and received a baccalaureate in canon law in 1708. Short on funds, he found a position as a tutor for the household of a judge on the Chancellery of Granada. Benefiting from this association and his practicum with Félix de Herrera, he soon emerged as a highly regarded attorney before the Chancellery.

On May 5, 1741, Maldonado was named *fiscal* of the Chancellery of Granada. Seven years later, on September 16, 1748, he advanced to the court's civil chamber as an *oidor*. Almost immediately, on December 11 of the same year, he was promoted to Madrid as *fiscal* for the *sala de alcaldes de casa y corte*, the criminal chamber of the Council of Castile. On March 22, 1752, he was appointed fiscal for New Spain on the Council of the Indies to allow Manuel Pablo de Salcedo* to restrict his activities to the *fiscalía* for Peru. Advanced to the Council of Castile as a minister *togado* on December 18, 1760, a post he held from January 7, 1761, until his death, Maldonado also served on the Council of War.

SOURCES: AGS, XXIII, 13–8–668, 13–8–670; Gracia y Justicia 147, 150; AGI, Indiferente 894, 166, *relación* of 1734; 871, *expediente* Maldonado; AHN, Consejos 13520, *expedientes* 34, 44; ACRG, *cabina* 321, *legajo* 4292, *pieza* 4.

Mangino Fernández de Lima, Fernando José (October 7, 1731–May 1, 1806)

Mangino, an eldest son, was born in Seville. His parents were Antonio Mangino y Urceso from Genoa and Juana Fernández de Lima from Lisbon. His paternal grandparents were Benito Mangino y Noveta from Neriz, Genoa, and María Urcesi of Pieve de Saulo, Genoa. His paternal grandparents were Manuel Fernández de Lima from Santiago de Couro, Portugal, and Antonia Teresa Freitas from Lisbon. His brother Rafael, born in Madrid, was a *caballero* of the Order of Charles III. He also had a sister named María Ignacia.

Mangino was educated at the University of Alcalá and received a baccalaureate in canon law there which he subsequently incorporated at the University of Bologna.

On July 6, 1762, Mangino was named *corregidor* of Zacatlán de las Manzanas in New Spain. Subsequently, on July 18, 1775, he was appointed an accountant for tribute and mercury for New Spain. In the following year, on March 12, he was named superintendent of the mint for New Spain. Further advancement came in 1787 when he was named New Spain's intendant of the army, superintendent of the treasury, and *corregidor* of Mexico City. At the same time he was given honors of minister of the Council of the Indies. On January 16, 1788, he was appointed to the Council as a minister *de capa y espada*. Having received honors of the Cámara on August 8, 1798, he entered it with an appointment of October 26, 1800, to replace Antúnez* and served until his death in Madrid.

Mangino, a *caballero* of the Order of Charles III from 1791, married with a license granted in 1789 Josefa María Panes Soto Avilés, the widow of Lieutenant Colonel Santiago Spelungue. Her parents were Lieutenant Colonel Diego Panes Abellán and Beatriz Soto Avilés Hurtado de Mendoza. The couple apparently had no children for Josefa was Mangino's sole heir.

SOURCES: AGS, XXIII, 13–9–534, 13–9–529, 13–9–534, 13–9–507; AGI, Indiferente 885, 894, 871, *expediente* Mangino and *relación* of 1793; AHN, Estado (Carlos III), *expediente* 500, *pruebas* of Fernando Mangino; Hacienda 507, *expediente* 984; AHPM, Protocolo 22433; *Gazeta de Madrid*, June 24, 1806; García Carraffa, *Enciclopedia*, LIII, 72; *Enciclopedia Universal Ilustrada*, XXXII, 820.

Márquez de la Plata y Orozco, Fernando (September 3, 1740–December 17, 1818)

Márquez de la Plata was born in Seville to Rodrigo Márquez de la Plata, a native of the *villa* of Quesada, Valencia, and an *oidor* of the Audiencia of Sevilla and *caballero* of Charles III, and *sevillana* Luisa de Orozco y Martel. His paternal grandparents were Fernando Márquez de la Plata of Villanueva de las Cruzes and Manuela García de Celis of Madrid. His maternal grandparents, both from Seville, were Francisco Orozco, a lieutenant in the cavalry regiment of Seville, and María de Martel. He had two sisters, María de la Merced and Francisca de Paula, both unmarried in 1783. His cousin was José Márquez de la Plata, an audiencia minister in the Indies.

Márquez received his education in Seville at the College of Santo Tomás and subsequently at the University of Seville, from which he received the baccalaureate, licentiate, and doctorate.

Márquez went to America as *auditor de guerra* for the Cevallos expedition and then was named protector of the Indians for the Audiencia of Charcas on February 19, 1776, a position that gained him reclassification as *fiscal del crimen* on March 27 when the protectorship was ended. As *fiscal* he was active in pacifying La Paz and other cities during the Túpac Amaru Revolt. Advancement to Lima as *alcalde del crimen* followed on July 23, 1781, with possession on December 20, 1782. Appointed intendant of Huancavelica on November 21, 1783, he could not halt the mine's decline and, when it collapsed, tried to disguise the extent of the damage. Viceroy Teodoro de Croix decided he should be replaced and the collapse of the mercury mine fully investigated. As *alcalde*, Márquez took the *residencia* of Viceroy Manuel de Guirior. Named *oidor* of Lima on March 1, 1789, the case was not resolved when he was advanced to Quito as regent on July 12, 1796. In the same year he entered the Order of Charles III. Named regent of Chile on April 24, 1801, he assumed the post on April 28, 1803. Although named to the Council of the Indies in mid-1806 to replace Cortines,* he refused the appointment and remained in Chile, save for emigration to Mendoza in 1814, until his death. Juan Rodríguez Ballesteros, however, replaced him as regent.

Márquez was one of four audiencia ministers to marry a daughter of the Marqués de Villapalma and Margarita Recabarren y Pardo Figueroa when he wed Antonia Calvo Encalada in Santiago in 1786. One of his brothers-in-law was Cerdán*; another was Gorvea.* Marquez's son Fernando served as a deputy in the Chilean Congress.

SOURCES: AGI, Chile 173, Lima 876; AGS, 2–60–6, 2–60–54, 2–65–34, 2–73–50, 2–80–135, 2–85–46, AHN, Estado (Carlos III), *expediente* 955, *pruebas* of Fernando Márquez de la Plata; Espejo, *Nobiliario*, 561; Lohmann Villena, *Ministros*, pp. 64–65; Vargas Ugarte, *Historia*, V, 82; Udaondo, *Diccionario*, p. 555; Fisher, *Government*, pp. 37, 143, 244; *Gazeta de Madrid*, July 11, 1806.

Martínez Carvajal, Manuel (June 18, 1676, baptism–April 28, 1742)

Martínez was born in Segovia. His father, Andrés Martínez Rodríguez, was a native of Peñafiel, Valladolid, and served as a *familiar* for the Inquisition. His mother, Teresa Domínguez Carvajal, was a native of Segovia and previously married to Juan Alonso Sánchez. Martínez' paternal grandparents were Andrés Martínez and María Rodríguez, both from Peñafiel. His maternal grandparents were José Domínguez Navarro and Elena de Carvajal, both from Segovia.

Martínez was a student at the University of Salamanca and by 1704 had received a doctorate in civil law. Unassociated with a *colegio mayor* (a *manteista*), Martínez ultimately became the first professor of civil law at Salamanca, the pinnacle of his twenty-six years there.

On February 7, 1720, Martínez was named the *fiscal del crimen* of the Chancellery of Valladolid. Advanced to the Council of Orders as *fiscal* on November 17, 1725, he then moved to the Council of the Indies as *fiscal* for New Spain to replace Tomás de Sola* on March 28, 1726. Given honors and seniority as a councilor of Castile on March 8, 1734, he was granted equal treatment with its ministers *togados* on April 15, 1736. In 1738 he assumed a position on the Council of Castile which he served until his death.

Martínez married Catalina Tamayo y Martínez, a native of Alba de Tormes, Valladolid, in 1714. Her parents were Pedro Tamayo Téllez, a native of the province, hereditary alderman of Salamanca and a provincial administrator (*corregidor*) of Alba de Tormes, and María Martínez Cornejo. Their son Manuel, born in Salamanca, became a knight of Alcántara in 1728.

Martínez was a knight of the Order of Santiago from 1725.

SOURCES: AGS, XXIII, 13–8–450; AGI, Indiferente 871, *expediente* Martínez Carvajal; AUS, Libros 401, 409; García Carraffa, *Enciclopedia*, LIV, 112–13; Larios, *Nobiliario*, III, 243–44.

Mata Linares y Vázquez, Benito María de la (December 28, 1749–?)

Mata was born in Madrid. His father, *vallisoletano* Francisco de la Mata Linares, was a knight of Alcántara, señor of the *villa* Vallecillo de los Jantares, and of the *lugar* of Roza in the Valley of Peñarrubia, and a member of the Council and Cámara of Castile. His mother was Ana Vázquez Dávila y Arce, born in Tordesillas. Fernando Ventura Mata Linares, a native of the *villa* of San Vicente de la Barquesa in the Archbishopric of Burgos and an *oidor* of the Chancellery of Valladolid, was his paternal grandfather. His paternal grandmother was *vallisoletana* Fausta Jacinta Calderón de la Barca. His maternal grandparents were Jose Vázquez Dávila y Arce of Tordesillas and María de Jesus Vázquez Dávila y Arce of the *villa* of Colmenar de Oreja in the Archbishopric of Toledo. Benito had five brothers. Juan de Sahagún de la Mata Linares, Conde del Carpio and Marqués de la Solana, a knight of Calatrava, ended his career on the Council of Orders. Francisco de Paula, the second son, also a knight of Calatrava, ultimately became a general in the army. Pedro Regalado, the third son, was a lieutenant colonel in 1787 and a knight of Calatrava. José Eugenio was a student at the University of Alcalá in 1776. Enrique Camilo was an infantry captain in 1776 and became a *caballero* of Charles III in 1790. Benito, the fourth of the six sons, also had three sisters: María del Rosario, Francisca Xaviera, who married Miguel María Panes, Marqués de Villapanes, and Marta Margarita.

Mata began his university experience at Alcalá and received the baccalaureate of canon law in 1767. He then won a fellowship at the *colegio mayor* of San Bartolomé at the University of Salamanca where he assumed residence in 1768 and became rector in 1771. At Salamanca he incorporated the baccalaureate in canon law in 1770, and received a baccalaureate in civil law later in the same year and the licentiate in the same faculty in 1772.

On June 16, 1776, Mata was named *oidor* of the Audiencia of Chile, a post he assumed on April 15, 1777. While there he served as appeals judge for commercial cases, judge for land disputes, and legal adviser for the tobacco monopoly. He was advanced to Lima as *oidor*, with an appointment of November 26, 1778. In the wake of the Túpac Amaru Revolt, Mata accompanied Visitor General José Antonio de Areche* to Cuzco in 1781 and shared his view of emphasizing economy over preparedness. He served as the visitor's principal henchman in Cuzco and presided over the trials of Túpac Amaru II and Diego Cristóbal Túpac Amaru. He was one of the officials to sign the execution order for Túpac Amaru II and his family.

On August 18, 1783, Jorge Escobedo* named Mata subdelegate in Cuzco for the *visita* and subsequently intendant of Cuzco, a post he formally assumed in 1784. Suspicious that the local clergy of Cuzco had cooperated in the Túpac Amaru Revolt and supported the local creole elite against the royal government, he was antipathetic toward Bishop Juan Manuel Moscoso y Peralta, whom he suspected of sympathy toward the Túpac Amaru uprising, and advocated that all bishops and two-thirds of the lower clergy should be peninsulares. He supported the establishment of an audiencia in Cuzco as part of a broader effort to reinvigorate the city. He sought to increase the exportation of cochineal and obtained new tribute lists in Cuzco and, following reassessment, increased the tributaries by 50 percent. At the urging of Viceroy Teodoro de Croix and to calm a tense political situation in Cuzco where he had shown himself uncompromising in his hatred of Peruvians, Mata was advanced to Buenos Aires as regent of the audiencia, with an appointment of March 4, 1787, taking possession on June 23, 1788. In Buenos Aires he was a bitter enemy of Martín de Alzaga and the city council. The cabildo in turn denounced him from 1791, succeeding in obtaining a royal reprimand for the regent. He also continued his clashes with Viceroy Marqués de Avilés, clashes that dated back to the men's service in Cuzco. Mata's abilities and intellect were beyond doubt, but contemporaries questioned his judgment and partisan behavior. Viceroy Joaquín del Pino accused him of having ties to a notorious contraband trader. Given honors of the Council of the Indies on October 5, 1802, Mata was named to the body to replace Alvarez de Acevedo* on March 5, 1803. On September 3, 1807, he was advanced to the Cámara. He was still serving at the time of the French invasion in 1808, but was no longer listed as a member in September 1809. Upon the death of his older brother, the Conde del Carpio, he inherited the family patrimony.

In 1771 Mata entered the Basque Society of Friends of the Country. He was known as a cultural light in Buenos Aires. In 1787 he became a *caballero* of Charles III.

SOURCES: AGI, Charcas 510, *relación* of 1774; Buenos Aires 14, *relación* of 1793; Lima 877; Chile 258; Indiferente 871, 887; AGS, 2–60–134, 2–62–217, 2–71–46, 13–9–66, 13–9–57; AHN, Ordenes Militares (Calatrava), *expediente* 1552, *pruebas* of Benito de la Mata Linares; *Gazeta de Madrid*, October 4, 1808; Medina, *Diccionario*, p. 517; Hamnett, *Revolución*, pp. 183–84, 192; Campbell, *Military and Society*, pp. 121, 135, 156; Lohmann Villena, *Ministros*, pp. 67–68; Vargas Ugarte, *Historia*, V, 58, 62, 74; Gandia, *Orígenes*, p. 94; Mariluz Urquijo, *Avilés*, pp. 18, 320, 322–24; Fisher, *Government*, pp. 32, 46, 48–49, 112, 127, 244–45; Lohmann Villena, "Relaciones," p. 351 n.62.

Mendoza Caamaño, Mauro Fernando de (March 3, 1708–November 29, 1764)

Mendoza was the second son of Antonio José Mendoza Caamaño y Sotomayor, a native of the town of Las Vegas de Matute, Segovia, the third Marqués de Villa García, a knight of Santiago, and the viceroy of Peru from 1736 to 1745. His mother was Clara Benita Barrionuevo y Monroy. His paternal grandparents were Antonio Domingo Mendoza Caamaño y Sotomayor, the second Marqués de Villa García, a knight of Santiago, ambassador to Venice, and a member of the Council of War. His brother Rodrigo inherited his father's title.

Mendoza received an appointment as a minister *de capa y espada* of the Council of the Indies on February 23, 1735. The appointment, awarded for the merit of his father, went unfilled for years, for Mendoza accompanied his father to Peru and did not return to Spain until about 1747. Even after then, however, he served rarely if ever on the council. Attendance lists to 1758 do not reveal his presence. A member of the Order of San Juan, Mendoza left no direct heirs.

SOURCES: AGS, XXIII, 13–8–437; AGI, Indiferente 898, 899, 900; Alvarez y Baena, *Hijos de Madrid*, IV, 100–101; Bernard, *Secrétariat*, p. 217; *Armería*, IV, 248–9.

Mérida, Juan de (March 30, 1709–?)

Mérida was born in Cádiz. His parents were Nicolás de Mérida, a native of Antequera and agent (*familiar*) of the Inquisition, and Petronila Beyi de Cisneros. He attended the University of Granada. After he completed a practicum with José Manuel de Rojas* the Chancellery of Granada approved him to practice law on November 18, 1734.

Mérida served a variety of positions in Cádiz. He was a judge advocate for the naval office, a legal adviser for the military base, a local administrator (*alcalde mayor*), and a legal adviser to the merchant guild. He was named an interim *procurador* for the House of Trade on January 1, 1765, and served briefly. An *asesor de marina* in 1770, he was named an *oidor* of the House of Trade on February 8 of that year. The senior *oidor* and interim president when the Council of the Indies was expanded in 1776, Mérida was appointed a minister *togado* on March 18. Although he turned down the advancement, alleging Madrid would be disastrous for his health, he was allowed to retain honors of councilor.

Mérida married Josefa Segura. Their son Nicolás, a native of Cádiz, was named an *oidor* of the Audiencia of Chile in 1777, in part, at least, as a reward for his father's services.

SOURCES: AGS, XXIII, 2–55–356, 2–60–117; AGI, Indiferente 870, 1980; ACRG, 321/4293; Bernard, "Casa," pp. 31, 33; Burkholder and Chandler, *Biographical Dictionary*, p. 210.

Miraval y Espinola, Martín José de (c. 1655–September 20, 1720)

Miraval was born in Jerez de la Frontera to Juan Francisco Miraval y Lobatón, a knight of Alcántara, and María Luisa Espinola y Morales, both natives of the town. His grandparents were Juan Francisco de Miraval y Orihuela and María de Lobatón y Sarmiento, both from Jerez, on the paternal side, and Francisco de Espinola of Jerez and Beatriz de Morales of Alcalá de los Gazules on the maternal side. Martín's brother Juan Francisco was a knight of Calatrava. Brother Luis Félix became a councilor and for eight years governor of Castile and the first Marqués de Miraval.

Miraval studied canon law at the Universities of Seville and Salamanca in the 1670s. He became a *colegial* in the *colegio mayor* of Cuenca in 1684, received his licentiate and doctorate in canon law from Salamanca in 1701, and held a succession of chairs concluding with the first (*prima*) chair of canon law in 1701.

On March 15, 1705, Miraval was named an *oidor* of the Audiencia of Seville. Almost immediately moved to the Chancellery of Granada with an appointment of November 8, 1706, he was subsequently transferred to Valencia as an *oidor* on its short-lived chancellery. After being named to the Council of the Exchequer as a minister *togado*, on March 5, 1709, he was designated president of the House of Trade. Appointed the sole *fiscal* of the Council of the Indies on March 18, 1714, he was later, on August 5, 1715, given responsibility for Peru when the office was divided. On January 20, 1717, he was named a minister *togado* of the Council, a post he served from February 11, 1717, until his death.

SOURCES: AGS, XXIII 13–8–470, 13–8–472, 13–8–473; AHN, Consejos 13531, 13501, 13519; AGI, Indiferente 844; AUS, Libros 379, 387, 397, 401, 2309; AUSE, Libro 483; Esperabé, *Universidad de Salamanca*, II, 581; García Carraffa, *Enciclopedia*, LVII, 158; Bernard, "Casa," p. 276.

Mon y Velarde, Juan Antonio (August 1747–September 1, 1791)

Mon was born in the *lugarejo* of Mon in Asturias. His parents were Fernando Manuel Mon y Valledor, *señor* of a number of places in Oviedo, and Francisca Velarde y Cienfuegos. His brothers Arias and José Antonio, the Conde del Pinar, reached the Council of Castile, and Arias ultimately became a *camarista*. Brother Romualdo Antonio was a canon in Córdoba in 1791. Juan Antonio Velarde y Cienfuegos, a councilor of Castile and a member of the Order of Montesa, was his uncle.

Mon studied arts at the University of Oviedo and received from it a bachelor's degree in canon law in 1761. He incorporated the degree at Salamanca, where he received the baccalaureate in civil law in 1764. In the same year he entered its *colegio mayor* of Oviedo. By 1773 he had completed fifteen years of higher studies, been deputy for his college, and substituted in academic chairs.

Named *oidor* of the Audiencia of Guadalajara on June 12, 1774, Mon took possession on May 13, 1775. Appointed to the same office for the court of Santa Fe in 1778, he assumed the position on October 30, 1781. From mid–1785 to August 1788 he served as visitor of Antioquia, where he established public order and improved administration. Among other things, he advocated the creation of a bishopric for the province, an action taken years later. He also encouraged improvement in mining, agriculture, commerce, and public education, establishing schools in Medellín and Antioquia. His actions won applause from contemporaries and some later historians, although his reforms can be seen as responding to rather than initiating the region's recovery. Advanced to Quito as president regent with an appointment of November 21, 1789, he entered the post on April 29, 1790 and served until March 5, 1791. Named to the Council of the Indies as a *ministro togado* to replace Huerta* on April 25, 1790, he died in Cádiz without serving.

Mon was a bachelor in 1773 and apparently never married.

SOURCES: AGI, Lima 876; Guatemala 409; Guadalajara 304; Indiferente 866, 871 *expediente* Mon; Mexico 1161; Charcas 500, *títulos* of 1772; AGS, 2–58–220, 2–73–267, 13–8–62; AHN, Hacienda 527; Restrepo, *Mandatarios*, pp. 368–79; Castillo, *Gobernadores*, pp. 271, 275; Twinam, "Enterprise and Elites," p. 450.

Moñino, Francisco (c. early 1740s–c. 1798)

Moñino was born in Murcia, Bishopric of Cartagena, to José Moñino Gómez, a notary, and Francisca Redondo Bermejo. He was the youngest of five children. The eldest, José, became best known as Conde de Floridablanca, the powerful minister of Charles III and Charles IV. His brother Fulgencio became a priest and *racionero* in the Cathedral of Murcia, where he died in 1778. His sister Gregoria married

Antonio Robles Vives, an attorney who in 1779 became a minister *togado* on the Council of Hacienda. His sister Manuela married Carlos Salinas.

Moñino's career was closely tied to the fortunes of his brother. After he had completed a practicum with Francisco Ortuño Fernández in Madrid, the Royal Council admitted Francisco to practice law in 1762. He began his royal service soon afterward. In 1778 he was intendant of the province of Soria when named on December 24 to replace Casimiro Osorio* as minister *de capa y espada* on the Council of the Indies. He entered the post on March 13, 1779. On October 22, 1781, he was appointed as extraordinary minister plenipotentiary to the grand duke of Tuscany with retention of his seat on the Council. In 1785 he was named extraordinary ambassador to the Republic of Venice. Subsequently named ambassador to Portugal, also with retention of his seat, Moñino never assumed the post. Instead he was named governor of the Council to replace José de Gálvez* on July 15, 1787. He entered the post on August 7 but repeatedly received licenses to take leave in order to recover his health. On March 19, 1792, less than three weeks after his brother had been dismissed as first secretary to Charles IV, Moñino was removed from office allegedly because of his ill health and inability to attend Council meetings. He was given twenty-four hours to leave Madrid and ordered to go to his father-in-law's residence near the *villa* of Daymiel. Three years later he was given a generous pension of 60,000 *reales de vellón*, but was forbidden to go to Madrid or any of the royal palaces.

With a license granted December 12, 1786, Moñino married Mariana Pontejos, daughter of the Marqués de Casa Pontejos.

SOURCES: AGS, XXIII, 13–9–553, 13–9–533; AGI, Indiferente 894, 885, 886, 902, 871, *expediente* Moñino; AHN, Hacienda 506, *expediente* 874; Estado 3162, 4430, *expediente* 5; Consejos 12122; Bernard, *Secrétariat*, p. 212; Hernández Franco, *La gestión político*, pp. 28–30.

Moreno Hurtado, José Domingo (Variant: Moreno Guerrero) (1702–April 3, 1778)

Moreno was born in Lucena, Córdoba, to Jerónimo Gregorio Moreno y Hurtado and Margarita Paula Guerrero, both of Lucena. His paternal grandparents were Francisco Moreno de Arroyo y Cózar and Isabel Hurtado.

Moreno attended the University of Granada and the University of Salamanca. After taking a practicum in Madrid, he was admitted as an attorney by the Chancellery of Granada. Prior to beginning his career in the courts, he competed unsuccessfully for a benefice at the cathedral in Toledo.

On May 5, 1732, Moreno was named a judge on the Audiencia of the Canaries. Moved to the Audiencia of Valencia as an *oidor* on May 16, 1736, he subsequently advanced to Madrid with an appointment to enter the first vacant position of *alcalde de casa y corte*. On March 22, 1752 he was named a minister *togado* of the Council of the Indies, a post he held for a little over a decade. His final promotion came on August 8, 1763, when he was named a minister *togado* of the Council of Castile. On August 12, 1777, he was given the privilege of attending the Council at his pleasure. The governor of the Council of Castile, Manuel Ventura de Figueroa, considered him an honest, hardworking, and able minister.

Moreno married three times. His first wife was Rita Roca y Pascual of Valencia. She was the daughter of Joanes Roca y Pascual of Valencia and María Manuela Pascual y Martínez de Mesa of Alicante. The couple had two sons, Gerónimo and Vicente. Gerónimo secured an education in law, ultimately inherited the family *mayorazgo*, and tried unsuccessfully to follow his father with a career on the Spanish courts. Both sons became knights of the Order of Montesa in 1783. Moreno's second wife was Antonia Tejada. His third wife, *madrileña* Micaela Daoiz y Parcero, was the daughter of a minister of the Council of the Exchequer, Saturnino Daoiz, a native of Miranda de Agar, Navarre, and Josefa Parcero of Granada. The couple had three sons, Tomás, Pantaleón, José, and a daughter, María. José and Pantaleón followed military careers. José and Tomás became knights of Santiago in 1793.

SOURCES: AGS, XXIII, 13–8–191; Gracia y Justicia 146, 158, 159, 820; AGI, Indiferente 871, *expediente* Moreno Hurtado; AHN, Ordenes Militares (Santiago), *pruebas* of José Moreno y Daoiz; *Gazeta de Madrid*, April 7, 1778.

Mosquera y Pimentel Quintanilla, Luis Francisco (1719–April 29, 1778)

Mosquera was born in Pontevedra, the son of Gaspar Mosquera, Marqués de Aranda, *capitán de granaderos* of the *tercio* of Tuy in the War of the Spanish Succession. His maternal grandfather Francisco de Aranda Quintanilla, Marqués de Aranda and knight of Santiago, was named to the Council of the Indies in 1697 before advancing to the Council of Castile. His cousin, the Marqués de Guimares, left him an entailed estate (*mayorazgo*) in Galicia.

Educated at the University of Salamanca, Mosquera was a member of the *colegio mayor* of Oviedo. He claimed seventeen years of higher studies. The University of Avila conferred upon him the baccalaureate of civil law, which he then incorporated at the University of Salamanca, where he received the baccalaureate in canon law. At Salamanca he competed for academic chairs without success.

Ferdinand VI appointed Mosquera *fiscal del crimen* of the Audiencia of Mexico on May 17, 1748. He took up the post in 1749 and served until advanced to the civil *fiscalía* on February 15, 1755. With the death of his father in 1760, Mosquera gave up his post in Mexico, which he did not like, to return to Spain. Named *fiscal* of the Council of the Indies for New Spain to replace Maldonado* on July 19, 1761, he was elevated to the position of *ministro togado* of the Council to replace Cornejo* on February 3, 1765. Nearly deaf and blind, he retired on January 17, 1774, with half salary. While on the Council he served on the General Committee for Commerce, Money, and Mines (*Junta General de Comercio, Moneda y Minas*).

Mosquera married Francisca de Paula Moscoso. The couple had at least two sons, Mariano and Luis Mosquera y Moscoso, both of whom served in the Walloon Guards, and one daughter. Heir to the titles Marqués de Aranda and Marqués de Guimares,

Mosquera became a *caballero* of the Order of Charles III, with pension, in 1778, the year in which he died in Barcelona. His wife outlived him.

SOURCES: AGI, Indiferente, 894, 1519, 870A; AGS, 2–36–258, 2–41–112, 13–8–414, 13–8–405, 2–58–6; *Gazeta de Madrid*, No. 42, September 29, 1778; Vignau, *Indice de pruebas*, p. 17; Hamnett, "Mexican Bureaucracy," p. 25; Fayard, *Conseil*, p. 559.

Munive y Tello, Gabriel de (Variant: Munibe) (c. 1709–May 3, 1793)

Munive was born in Huamanga, Peru. He was the son of *limeño* Francisco Javier Munive y Garavito of Lima, the third Marqués de Valdelirios, and Teresa Tello y Espinosa of Huamanga. His paternal grandparents were Lope Antonio de Munive y Aspe, knight of Alcántara and president of the Audiencia of Quito, and Leonor María de León Garavito. His maternal grandparents, both from Huamanga, were José Tello de Contreras and Josefa Ortiz de Espinosa. Munive's nephew the Marqués de Feria inherited the title Marqués de Valdelirios from him.

Already a field marshal (*mariscal de campo*) in the Royal Army, on July 5, 1750, Munive was named a minister *de capa y espada* on the Council of the Indies to replace José de la Quintana.* His appointment specifically referred to his understanding of American affairs as an important qualification. Ferdinand VI named Munive, in September 1751, the commissioner to handle the question between Portugal and Spain over the boundary between their respective empires in South America. After spending nearly a decade in South America, on July 1, 1761, Munive returned to Spain. On October 19, 1777, he was made a gentleman of the royal chamber. Although from September 13, 1781, he was allowed to attend Council meetings at his pleasure, on August 14, 1785, he was named to the Cámara to replace Felipe de Arco.* Ill since 1786, on December 10, 1792, he received honors of the Council of State in order to increase his pay.

Munive held the title fourth Marqués de Valdelirios. He died a bachelor, or as he expressed it, "free and single."

SOURCES: AGS, XXIII, 13–8–422, 13–8–356; Gracia y Justicia 922; AGI, Indiferente 873, *expediente* Marqués de Valdelirios; AHN, Estado 879, *expediente* 67; AHPM, Protocolo 18195; Mendiburu, *Diccionario*, XI, 141; Lohmann Villena, *Americanos*, II, 305; Vargas Ugarte, *Títulos*, p. 67; Lohmann Villena, *Ministros*, pp. 182–83.

Muñoz de la Torre, Pedro (February 8, 1721–?)

Muñoz was born in the *villa* of Colmenar, Málaga, to José Miguel Muñoz de la Peña and Isabel Ruiz, both natives of Colmenar. His paternal grandparents, also from Colmenar, were Antonio Muñoz Palomo and Catalina Pérez Rodríguez. His maternal grandparents, Alonso de la Torre and Clara Ruiz, were also from Colmenar. He had five siblings: Catalina, Clara, María, Josefa, and Antonio.

Muñoz received his education at the University of Granada. The Royal Council admitted him to practice law in 1745, and he joined the lawyers' guild in Madrid the following year.

Muñoz spent many years as a *relator*, preparing briefs for use in court. He held the post for the Council of War from 1756 to 1763 and for the Royal Delegation of Caballería from 1763 to his appointment on March 15, 1775 as *alcalde de casa y corte*. During José de Gálvez's* visitation to New Spain, Muñoz served as his attorney at court. On April 13, 1777, he was named a minister *togado* to replace Domingo de Trespalacios* on the Council of the Indies. Advanced to the Cámara on December 4, 1785, to replace Manuel Lanz de Casafonda,* he received the right to attend at his pleasure on November 26, 1808. The following March he secured a license to take the waters at Sacedón for three months.

Muñoz, a pensioned *caballero* of Charles III from 1785, married Lorenza Tuñón, his niece and second wife, with a license granted in 1766. Their son Ramón, born in Madrid in 1769, became an attorney in 1795 and a pensioned *caballero* of Charles III the following year. The couple had two other children.

SOURCES: AGS, XXIII, 13–8–525, 13–8–533; Gracia y Justicia 161; AHN, Consejos 13644; Hacienda 504, *expediente* 230; Estado (Carlos III), *expediente* 230, *pruebas* of Pedro Muñoz de la Torre; AGI, Indiferente 886, 892, 871, *expediente* Muñoz de la Torre; Vignau, *Carlos III*, p. 121; García Carraffa, *Enciclopedia*, LX, 104.

Mutiloa y Lodosa, Juan José (Variant: Mutiloa y Andueza) (1668–August 1, 1743)

Mutiloa was born in Tudela to Juan José Mutiloa and Margarita Lodosa. His paternal grandparents were Juan de Mutiloa and Petronila Torres. His maternal grandparents were Fermín de Lodosa y Andueza and Catalina Oquendo.

After receiving a baccalaureate degree in civil law from the University of Huesca in 1687, Mutiloa was admitted to the *colegio mayor* of San Bartolomé at the University of Salamanca on May 18, 1690. He received the licentiate in civil law from the university in 1695, was rector of his *colegio* in 1691–92 and 1694–95, and held the chairs of *Institutes*, *Código*, and *Volumen* from 1701 to 1707.

On August 3, 1707, Mutiloa was appointed *oidor* of the Audiencia of Seville. Three years later, on October 13, 1710, he was named an *alcalde de casa y corte* with the commission to go to Buenos Aires. He continued in his position upon return from the New World and then advanced to the Council of Hacienda as a minister *togado* in 1723. On November 20, 1725, Mutiloa was named a minister *togado* of the Council of the Indies to replace Antonio Valcárcel.* He served until 1730 when he advanced on April 26 to the Council of Castile as a minister *togado*. Mutiloa never married.

SOURCES: AGS, XXIII, 13–8–238; Gracia y Justicia 136, 138, 140; AHN, Consejos, 13501, 13643, 13385, *expediente* 81; Estado 6380(2), 6400(2); García Carraffa, *Enciclopedia*, LX, 207–8; Ibarra, *Navarros*, III, 219–20; Roxas y Contreras, *Historia*, II, 562–3, 1000.

Múzquiz y Aldunate, Luis Antonio de (August 25, 1760–October 31, 1828)

Múzquiz, the youngest of three children, was born in Viana, Navarre. His parents were Fermín Múzquiz and Martina Aldunate, both from Viana. His paternal grandparents were Martín de Múzquiz of Yrujo and María la Torre of the *lugar* of

Villanueva. His maternal grandparents were José Aldunate of the *villa* of Peralta and Teresa García Villaciain. Rafael Múzquiz y Aldunate, a cleric in attendance in the royal chapel, confessor to the queen, and a *caballero* of Charles III in 1788 was his brother. His sister Ynés de Múzquiz in 1770 married Felipe de Aldunate, a clerk (*oficial*) in the Secretariat of the Council of the Indies for New Spain.

Múzquiz received the licentiate and doctorate in civil law from the University of Alcalá, finishing in 1786. He also had a doctorate in canon law. The following year he was incorporated by the Royal Council.

Charles IV named Múzquiz legal adviser (*teniente asesor*) to the governor of Yucatán on March 6, 1790, but then on September 21, 1791, advanced him to *oidor* of the Audiencia of Guadalajara. He served there from December 17, 1792, until promoted to the position of supernumerary *alcalde* of the *sala de casa y corte*, in Madrid, by decree of September 18, 1793. Named a minister *togado* of the Council of the Indies on May 21, 1798, Múzquiz served until the tribunal was abolished by the Cortes of Cádiz. After reestablishing the Council in 1814, Ferdinand VII named him to its Cámara on July 23. He was dispossessed and exiled to Málaga on July 22, 1822. Ferdinand subsequently reappointed him in 1823, and Múzquiz was the senior member of the Council when he died.

Múzquiz was admitted to the Order of Charles III in 1792 and received the title Conde de Torre Múzquiz on August 30, 1795. Undoubtedly while in Mexico Múzquiz married María Josefa Martín de Chaves, a native of Mexico City and the daughter of José Martín de Chaves of the Archbishopric of Seville and Manuela Antonia Reyes González of Oaxaca, Mexico. The couple's son Nicolás was born in Madrid in 1802. He received a license to marry *murciana* Juana Cutillas y Lozano in 1811 but may not have used it. In January 1816, he married María Candido López del Hoyo, a native of Viana, and the widow of Juan José Solano, a military officer. She survived him.

SOURCES: AGI, Indiferente 825, 887, 888, 872, 873, 892; Guadalajara 304; AHN, Consejos, *Inventario de Abogados*, No. 4985; Libro de Plazas 740, pp. 143, 181; Estado (Carlos III), *expediente* 593, *pruebas* of Luis Antonio Múzquiz; Hacienda 529, *expediente* 31; AGS, 2–74–38, 2–75–174; Atienza, *Nobiliario*, p. 979.

O

Omulryan, Ignacio (var. Omul-Rian, Omulerian, Omulrrian) (January 19, 1752–February 3, 1836)

Omulryan was born in the *villa* of Arén, Benabarre, Huesca. His parents were José Omul-Rian and María Rourera y Pallás, both of Arén. His paternal grandparents were Guillermo Omul-Rian of Thurles, Ireland, a soldier (*sargento mayor*) and Antonia Berart y Cortiada of Barcelona. His maternal grandparents were Francisco Rourera y Grau of Arén and Rosa Pallás y Bonet of Lugar de Betesa, Benabarre, Huesca. He had three siblings: Manuel, Francisco, and José.

Omulryan began his royal service in 1774. Prior to 1788 he held an appointment as royal administrator for the postal service of Pamplona. In 1788 he was the chief accountant for the highway department. Later the general director of the postal monopoly, he was named intendant of Léon in 1797, "by the intrigue and despotism of Don Manuel Godoy," but never served. He was appointed a supernumerary minister *de capa y espada* of the Council of the Indies on September 15, 1798. Omulryan survived the Spanish War of Independence, received a vote in the Cámara on March 28, 1815, and was still on the Council serving as its senior minister (*decano*) in 1832.

A pensioned *caballero* of the Order of Charles III from 1792, Omulryan received a license in 1788 to marry Jacinta Cevallos Vera, a lady-in-waiting of the Infanta María Luisa. Eight years later, in 1796, he married *limeña* Manuela Zini Darcourt, a lady-in-waiting to Queen María Luisa. His wife's parents were Antonio Zini of Puigcerdá, Gerona, and Catalina Darcourt of Ciudad Rodrigo, Salamanca. The couple had three sons, including Carlos Luis who became a *caballero* of Charles III in 1827. In 1831 Omulryan was given the Large Cross of Isabel the Catholic. He died in Madrid.

SOURCES: AGS, XXIII, 13–9–140; AGI, Indiferente 825, 871, *expediente* Olmurrian (sic); AHN, Estado (Carlos III), *expediente* 648, *pruebas* of Ignacio Omul-Rian; Estado 878, *expediente* 116; Hacienda 2051, *expediente* 85; 529, *expediente* 32; 507, *expediente* 941; García Carraffa, *Enciclopedia*, LXIV, 138–9; Vignau, *Carlos III*, p. 128.

Orrantia, Domingo José de (December 23, 1728–April 7, 1780)

Orrantia was born in Lima, Peru. His father, Juan José Orrantia y Ortiz de Azqueta, was a native of Abando, Vizcaya, a knight of Santiago, and prior of the merchant guild of Lima. His mother was the *limeña* María Josefa Leandra Albero y Ortega. His paternal grandparents were Juan Bautista de Orrantia y Ortiz of Orrantia, Burgos, and María Concepción de Garay y Olaso of Baracaldo. His maternal grandparents were Tomás de Albero y Ortega of San Sebastián, Guipúzcoa, and *limeña* Eugenia Jacoba de Marieluz.

Orrantia received his education at the College of San Martín in Lima, which he entered in 1741. He received the licentiate and doctorate from the University of San Marcos in 1745. A competitor for chairs at San Marcos, he was admitted to practice law before the Audiencia of Lima in 1747.

Orrantia left soon for Spain and in 1749 paid 47,500 pesos for an appointment as a supernumerary *oidor* in Lima and dispensations for being a minor, to marry a native, and to own property in the district. The sum was the highest paid by any purchaser of an American audiencia appointment. Taking possession the following year on December 5, he served as a supernumerary for years, becoming *de número* only in 1767. Along with fellow *oidor* Juan José de la Puente e Ibáñez, he oversaw the expulsion of the Jesuits from the College of San Pablo in Lima. Having returned to Spain, on October 10, 1774, he was named a councilor of the Indies. He held the post until his death.

Orrantia had at least two brothers, Juan José, a knight of Santiago, and Tomás, a canon in the cathedral chapter of Lima and rector of the University of San Marcos in 1791. Orrantia was admitted as a member by the Economic Society of Madrid and the Royal Academy of History. He died in Rome, apparently unmarried.

SOURCES: AGI, Lima 597; 615; Indiferente 894, 871 (*expediente Orrantia*); AGS, 2–37–101, 2–58–285; Mendiburu, *Diccionario*, VIII, 268; Lohmann Villena, *Americanos* I, 294; Lohmann Villena, *Ministros*, p. 87; Vargas Ugarte, *Historia*, IV, 312.

Ortiz de Landazuri, Tomás (December 22, 1722, baptism–August 13, 1777)

Ortiz de Landazuri was born in the *lugar* of Nuvilla, Vitoria, Alava, to Domingo Ortiz de Landazuri of Nuvilla and Antonia Arriaga y Basave of Lezama, Alava. His paternal grandparents were Felipe Ortiz de Landazuri and Magdalena de Montoya, both from Nuvilla. His maternal grandparents were Juan de Arriaga and María Tomasa de Basave, both from Lezama, Alava. His brother Bartolomé was a priest in Lezama. In addition, he had four sisters: Agueda, María, Lorenza, and Josepha.

As a young man Ortiz de Landazuri went to New Spain where he served in the secretariat of Viceroy Conde de Fuenclara from 1741 to 1743. In the latter year he moved to Guadalajara, where he held the post of secretary to the governor and captain general. From 1747 to 1749 he was the *corregidor*, mining judge, and lieutenant of the captain general in the mining town of Zacatecas. Elected a magistrate (*alcalde ordinario*) of the city of Guadalajara in 1756, he also served as an alderman (*regidor*) and representative (*procurador*) of the city.

On January 19, 1765, Ortiz de Landazuri was named chief accountant (*contador general*) for the Council of the Indies. Two years later, on March 18, 1767, he was given honors of the Council of the Indies. A full position of minister *de capa y espada* followed on May 9, 1767. He remained as *contador general* and councilor of the Indies until his death.

Ortiz de Landazuri, a knight of Santiago from 1761, married Josefa de Sierra, a daughter of Manuel de la Sierra, an alderman of Guadalajara, Mexico, and secretary of the cámara of the audiencia located there. His wife presumably predeceased him for on October 14, 1773, he received a license to marry Juana María Pontoja y Canal, a student in Madrid. Ortiz de Landazuri had daughters Isidora Josefa Paula and Ignacia Josefa by his first wife and María Ramona and María Eustaquia by his second.

SOURCES: AGS, XXIII, 2–51–53, 13–8–666, 13–8–665; AGI, Indiferente 158, *relación* of 1759, 902, 871, *expediente* Ortiz de Landazuri; AHN, Ordenes Militares (Santiago) *expediente* 6037, *pruebas* of Tomás Ortiz Landazuri; Hacienda 504, *expediente* 99; *Gazeta de Madrid*, August 26, 1777; García Carraffa, *Enciclopedia*, LXV, 249.

Orueta y Yrusta, Andrés de (c. 1665–December 2, 1733)

Orueta was born in Bilbao. His parents were Juan Bautista Orueta and Teresa de Yrusta. His paternal grandparents were Andrés de Orueta and Juana de Zezeyaga. His maternal grandparents were Diego de Yrusta and Angela de Aldape. His cousin Juan Bautista de Orueta y Yrusta was an audiencia minister in America.

Orueta received a baccalaureate in canon law from the University of Oñate in 1685. He subsequently studied at the University of Salamanca, receiving both a baccalaureate and licentiate in civil law in 1694. At Salamanca, Orueta was a *colegial* of the *colegio mayor* of San Bartolomé and held a succession of academic chairs.

On May 31, 1717, Orueta was named an *oidor* of the Audiencia of Seville. Promoted to the Chancellery of Granada as an *oidor* on August 13, 1725, he was immediately named to Valladolid as an *oidor* on December 3 of the same year. An appointment as regent of the Audiencia of Zaragoza followed on April 6, 1729. His final post was that of minister *togado* of the Council of the Indies, a position received on January 16, 1733. He held the post until his death.

SOURCES: AHN, Consejos 13386, 13501, 13531, 13519, 17954, 17955; AGS, Gracia y Justicia 133, 138, 140, 142; AUS, Libro 397; Roxas y Contreras, *Historia*, II, 565–66.

Osorio Rubín de Celis, Casimiro (1688–November 29, 1778)

Osorio was probably born in León. He was related to Juan Pizarro y Aragón* and was the uncle of the Marquesa de Mortara.

After an appointment to the Council of Hacienda, Osorio was named on April 4, 1741, a supernumerary minister *de capa y espada* of the Council of the Indies.

He advanced into a regular post with full salary on March 1, 1746. By the early 1760s Osorio was nearly deaf and rarely attended the Council. When he did, his infirmity embarrassed both him and his colleagues. Consequently, when Pizarro became president of the Council in February 1763, he almost immediately took steps to have his wife's relative decorously allowed to keep his salary without attending meetings. On May 2, 1763, Osorio received *preeminencias* that permitted him to attend the Council at his pleasure.

A gentleman of the royal chamber, Osorio was a hereditary alderman for the city of León and a deputy for the province of León. He died a bachelor.

SOURCES: AGS, XXIII, 13–9–441; AGI, Indiferente 885, 894, 871, *expediente* Osorio; *Gazeta de Madrid*, December 18, 1778; Bernard, *Secrétariat*, p. 218.

P

Palacios, Prudencio Antonio de (May 3, 1682–June 13, 1755)

Palacios was born in the city of Logroño, La Rioja, Bishopric of Calahorra, to Manuel de Palacios of Nájera and María de Santander of Logroño. His paternal grandparents were Mateo de Palacios y Carranza of Briviesca, Burgos, and Isabel Herreros y García of Arenzana de Arribas, Logroño. His maternal grandparents were Lázaro Santander from Ladero and María Pérez Fernández of Logroño.

Educated at the Universities of Huesca and Salamanca, Palacios attained the bachelor's degree in canon law at Salamanca in 1704. The Royal Council licensed him to practice law in 1708.

After fighting for Philip V in the War of the Spanish Succession, on February 27, 1713 Palacios was appointed deputy to the governor of Havana (*teniente gobernador*) and judge advocate (*auditor de guerra*) and at the same time made a supernumerary *oidor* of the Audiencia of Santo Domingo, the appointment to take effect after his tour as deputy. Several days later, on March 5, he was commissioned to prosecute the treasury officials of Havana for allowing fraud in their accounts. In 1716 the king sent him to New Spain as a special visitor of the royal treasury and promised him the post of *oidor* on the Council of Hacienda when he finished. Palacios's actions as visitor were approved in 1719, and he was given the post of *oidor* of Guadalajara on March 16, 1720, a position he assumed on January 9, 1721. Advanced to the civil *fiscalía* of the Audiencia of Mexico on May 26, 1723, he served in the post about a decade. In 1732 the king allowed Palacios to assume the seat on the Council of Hacienda promised sixteen years earlier.

As a result of Palacios' upright service in Mexico, and his visitation there years before, Philip V named him *fiscal* of the Council of the Indies for Peru to replace Laysequilla* on February 2, 1738. On November 4, 1741, he was promised the first vacant seat as *ministro togado* on the Council. In due course the vacancy occurred with the death of Lardizábal,* and Palacios, named to the post on March 3, 1744, served until his death.

Palacios married Ana López de Cangas of Cádiz in Cuba in 1722. She brought a dowry valued at 14,000 pesos. Her parents were Mateo López de Cangas, a native of Villafranca del Bierzo and a military officer in Cuba, and María Antonia Martín de Gavilanes, a native of Valencia. Palacios died leaving four sons: Vicente Manuel, a treasury official and *caballero* of the Order of Charles III; Prudencio José; Manuel; and José; and eight daughters: Francisca Plácida, María Antonia, Ana María, Juliana, Barbara, Joaquina, Ricarda, and Agustina. Francisca was the first wife of Pedro Joseph Pérez Valiente, who culminated his career on the Cámara of Castile and fathered by his second wife José María Pérez Valiente, who was on the Council of Orders in 1806. Palacios' grandson Joseph Prudencio Palacios y León served on the Audiencia of Galicia. In 1738 Palacios became a knight of Calatrava.

SOURCES: AGI, Indiferente 871, 898, 1508, *relación* of 1743; Mexico 452, *relación* of 1721; Guatemala 429, *relación* of Joseph Prudencio Palacios y León; AGS, 2–13–106, 2–29–2; 2–13–107, 2–18–215, 2–21–124, 13–8–559, 13–8–557; AHN, Consejos 12114; Estado (Carlos III), *expediente* 898, *pruebas* of Vicente Palacios and *expediente* 200, *pruebas* of Josef María Perez Valiente.

Patiño, Manuel (Variant: Cobelo Patiño) (c. 1701–September 18, 1767)

Patiño was born in Valladolid and educated at its university, earning a baccalaureate in civil law in 1721 and in canon law in 1727. He subsequently received licentiate and doctorate degrees in law in 1759. Admitted to practice law by the Chancellery of Valladolid in 1725, he also pursued a career within the university, rising to hold the chair of *Decreto*.

Considered an outstanding attorney in Valladolid, Patiño trained in his office a number of men who had strikingly successful careers. Among them were Manuel Ventura de Figueroa, governor of the Council of Castile; Jacinto Miguel de Castro*; Pedro González de Mena*; and Cristóbal de la Mata y Bujedo, also a councilor of Castile. Patiño was selected on April 11, 1761, as *fiscal* for the Chancellery of Granada. On January 24, 1764, he was named *fiscal* for Peru on the Council of the Indies to replace Manuel Pablo de Salcedo.* His tenure was brief, however. He served from February 4, 1764, until he entered the Council of Castile on June 1, 1767, as a minister *togado*. He served on the Council of Castile until his death in the town of Arganda.

SOURCES: AGS, XXIII, 13–8–407; Gracia y Justicia 158, 159; AHN, Consejos 13520; AGI, Indiferente 865; ARCV, Secretaría del Acuerdo, *caja* 16, 17; AHPUV, Libros 200, 229; Alcocer, *Universidad de Valladolid*, III, 401.

Pedrosa y Guerrero, Antonio Ignacio de la (c. 1660–June 28, 1733)

Pedrosa was born in Seville. His father was Andrés de la Pedrosa. After legal studies at the University of Salamanca, Pedrosa was appointed a protector of the Indians for the Audiencia of Santa Fe de Bogotá in 1684. Subsequently named an *alcalde de casa y corte* in 1706, he served as superintendent general of Murcia from 1711 to 1713. Named a minister *togado* of the Council of Hacienda in 1713, he lost the position later in the year as a result of reform. In the reorganization decreed on January 20, 1717, he was named a minister *togado* of the Council of the Indies, a post he entered on February 13, 1717. Given a commission to establish the viceroyalty of New Granada, he reached Santa Fe de Bogotá at midnight on June 7, 1718. His stay in Bogotá was brief, however, for he was back in Cádiz in December, 1720. He remained on the Council of the Indies until his death.

Pedrosa was *senor* of the town of Bujes.

SOURCES: AGS, Gracia y Justicia 133; AGI, Indiferente 844, 870A, *expediente* Alvarez de Abreu; AUS, Libro 383; Bernard, *Secrétariat*, p. 215; Garrido Conde, "Creación," pp. 24, 37, 79.

Pérez de Araciel, Alonso (?–January 5, 1718)

Pérez de Araciel was born in Alfaro in the Bishopric of Tarazona. His parents were Alvaro Pérez de Araciel and Barbara de Rada. His paternal grandparents were Alonso Pérez de Araciel and Isabel de Valdivieso. His uncle García Pérez de Araciel served on the Council of Castile. The future councilor was the third of five children. His oldest brother, García, was a knight of Santiago and councilor of Castile. Manuel, his next older brother, became archbishop of Zaragoza. His younger brother León entered the Carmelite order. Vicente, his youngest brother, became a knight of Alcántara and minister of the Council of Orders.

Pérez de Araciel studied canon and civil law at the University of Salamanca beginning about 1662 and became a *colegial* in the *colegio mayor* of San Bartolomé.

On March 17, 1683, Pérez de Araciel was named an *alcalde del crimen* of the Council of Navarre. An advancement to *oidor* followed on February 25, 1685. The following year he was named *lugarteniente* of the viceroyalty of Naples. Given honors of the Council of the Indies on August 23, 1700, he remained in his post in Naples until named to the Council with an appointment of July 13, 1702. Almost immediately, however, Philip V designated him president of the Council of Santa Clara in Naples. On November 10, 1713, Pérez de Araciel was named the second of three presidents of the Council of the Indies as part of the reform of that year. When the Council was reorganized on January 20, 1717, he was appointed a minister *togado*. He served until his death.

SOURCES: AGI, Indiferente 826, 866; AGS, XXIII, 13–9–379, 13–9–390; AUS, Libros 371, 375, 381; AHN, Libros de Plazas 730, 732; Roxas y Contreras, *Historia*, II, 474–75; Fayard, *Miembros*, pp. 89, 241.

Pérez Gamoneda Casco Villademoros, Juan Antonio (April 16, 1726–October 11, 1768)

Pérez was born in the *villa* of Luarca, Oviedo. His parents were Santiago Pérez Gamoneda and Francisca Casco Villademoros, both from Luarca. His paternal grandparents were Alonso Pérez Gamoneda of Luarca and María Fernández of the *lugar* of Paredes, Oviedo. His maternal grandparents, both from Luarca, were

Francisco Casco Villademoros and María Fernández Rochel. He had three brothers: Sebastián, Javier, and Juan.

Pérez spent fifteen years serving as secretary to the Queen Mother. As a reward for this service, on December 20, 1759, Charles III named him minister *de capa y espada* of the Council of the Indies and simultaneously appointed him to the Cámara, positions he held until his death.

Pérez married Agustina Correa Quiñones y Benavente. The couple had two children, María del Rosario and Josepha. Pérez held the title Marqués de Gamoneda and was a knight of Santiago from 1755. Enjoying honors of the Council of State, he was a gentleman of the chamber of the king of the Two Sicilies.

SOURCES: AHN, Ordenes Militares (Santiago), *expediente* 6370, *pruebas* of Juan Antonio Pérez Gamoneda y Casco; AGI, Indiferente 870, 894; *Gazeta de Madrid*, October 25, 1768; Vignau, *Santiago*, p. 271; Bernard, *Secrétariat*, p. 220.

Pez y Malzarraga, Andrés Matías de (c. 1657–March 7, 1723)

Pez was born in Cádiz. His father Andrés de Pez was a naval officer who had been born in Sopuerta, Vizcaya. His mother was Marina de Malzarraga, the widow of Martín de Revelle. His paternal grandparents were Juan de Pez and María de Capetillo, both of Sopuerta. His maternal grandparents were Francisco Malzarraga and Antonia de Adoro, both from the valley of Orozco, Vizcaya. He had an elder brother who along with his father was killed in the Battle of Palermo.

Pez entered the navy as a youth, probably in 1673. For eight years he was a sailor. About 1681 he transferred to the windward squadron (Armada de Barlovento) as an ensign (*alferez*) and began some thirty years of intermittent service in the New World. Quickly he made a reputation for his valor in encounters with buccaneers. In the mid and late 1680s he led three expeditions in search of René Robert Cavalier, Sieur de La Salle, along the coast of the Gulf of Mexico. Convinced that Pensacola Bay should be settled and fortified, he became the foremost advocate for doing so. By the early 1690s he was an admiral of the windward squadron. Accused of cowardice in 1697 as a result of an encounter with buccaneers, his reputation was not cleared until 1701; consequently he was unable to participate in founding a settlement at Pensacola Bay. Pez won the favor of Philip V, however, and was again given positions of great responsibility. In 1710 he was the commander of the fleet sent to the Indies. From 1712 to 1714 he was engaged in suppressing the Catalonians as the War of the Spanish Succession came to a close. Named to the Council of War in 1715, he was designated governor of the Council of the Indies in the reorganization of January 20, 1717. In this capacity he was important in transferring the House of Trade to Cádiz from Seville. In January 1721 he was appointed secretary of state for the navy to replace Fernández Durán.* After his death Sopeña* replaced him as secretary.

Pez was married to Bernarda de Aguila y Roxas, who outlived him. He entered the Order of Santiago in 1690.

SOURCES: AGI, Indiferente 865, 871; Bernard, *Secrétariat*, p. 211; Leonard, *Spanish Approach*, pp. 20–22; Weddle, *Wilderness Manhunt*, passim; Escudero, *Los orígenes*, I, 59, 64, 65; García Carraffa, *Enciclopedia*, LXXI, 163.

Piña y Mazo, Pedro de (May 31, 1716–July 4, 1777)

Piña was born in the *villa* of Astudillo in the Bishopric of Palencia. His parents were Pedro Piña Aguado, a native of Astudillo and an attorney authorized to practice by the Chancellery of Valladolid, and his second wife Manuela Mazo Villazán. His paternal grandparents were Luis de Piña y Hermosa, a native of the *villa* of Hitero de la Vega, a member of the Royal Guards of Castile, and an illegitimate son of Antonio Piña y Hermoso who died *electo* president of the Council of Castile, and Anastasia Aguado of Astudillo. His maternal grandparents were Pedro Mazo Alvarez and Ana Villazán, both from Astudillo. He had a half brother, Antonio, and three full siblings: José, an attorney who held the post of *fiscal* for the *juzgado de obras y bosques* in Madrid, Ana, and Luis, a cleric.

Piña began his higher education in 1731. Receiving a baccalaureate in canon law from the University of Valladolid in 1739, he secured a baccalaureate in civil law there in 1750. He incorporated a degree at Salamanca in 1753 and held a succession of chairs at the University of Valladolid. The Royal Council admitted Piña to practice law in 1743 and he joined the lawyers' guilds in both Madrid and Valladolid. An attorney for the poor in the city from 1751 to 1753, Piña held a variety of law-related appointments in Valladolid. He was a practicing attorney with clients that included various religious orders and grandees. Among the men who clerked with him was Gabriel de Achútegui, who ultimately reached the Council of Castile. In 1766 Piña published a *Memorial a Su Magestad en defensa de su Real Patrimonio. . . .*

On December 17, 1766, Charles III named Piña *fiscal* of the Audiencia of Asturias. Six years later, on June 22, 1772, he replaced Pedro González de Mena* as *fiscal* for Peru on the Council of the Indies. He entered the post on August 26, 1772. Named a pensioned *caballero* of Charles III in 1774, he received a vote in the Cámara on May 21, 1777, just before his death.

Piña married María Manuela Cacho y Calderón, also a native of Astudillo. She brought a dowry valued at 62,140 *reales de vellón*. The couple had at least two sons, Pedro Joaquín and Tadeo, and four daughters: Manuela, Petra, Raphaela, and Cordula María Ursula. One son served in the navy and another in the army.

SOURCES: AGS, XXIII, 13–8–537, 13–9–534; Dirección General del Tesoro, Inventario 39, legajo 13; AGI, Indiferente 871, RMS of 1764, *expediente* Piña; AHN, Estado (Carlos III), *expediente* 12, *pruebas* of Pedro de Piña y Mazo; ARCV, Secretaría del Acuerdo, *caja* 18; AHPM, Protocolo 19826; *Gazeta de Madrid*, July 15, 1777; Vignau, *Carlos III*, p. 139.

Pineda Capdevila, Antonio José de (February 20, 1681 baptism–August 25, 1743)

Pineda was born in the city of Lérida, Catalonia, to Francisco de Pineda and Paula de Pineda y Capdevila, both of Lérida. His paternal grandparents were Pedro Ramos de Pineda, a native of the *villa* of Cilleros in the Bishopric of Soria and a *sargento mayor*, and Theresa Pineda y Mateu. His maternal grandparents were Tomás

Capdevila, a deputy of Catalonia, and Elvira Baiona. His brother Francisco was a member of the cathedral chapter of Lérida. He also had a sister named Paula.

Pineda received a doctorate in civil law from the University of Lérida in 1702 and served as a professor of *Institutes* at the same university. On April 18, 1709, he was named a supernumerary *oidor* of the Chancellery of Granada. In January, 1719, he was transferred to Madrid to serve as *alcalde de casa y corte*. Advanced to the Council of the Indies as a minister *togado* to replace Antonio de la Pedrosa* on July 24, 1734, simultaneously he was also assigned to serve as a minister *togado* on the Council of the *Cruzada*. In 1736 he received responsibility for the *juzgado de tierras y multas* for the Indies.

Pineda married Teresa Rita Tavares de Barrios of Gibraltar. Their son José, born in Madrid, served on the Audiencia of Guatemala and the Chancellery of Granada. The couple had at least four other children, among whom were two military officers.

SOURCES: AGS, XXIII, 13–9–363; Gracia y Justicia 143; AGI, Indiferente 870B, *expedientes* Contreras and Pineda; AHN, Ordenes Militares (Santiago), *expediente* 6489, *pruebas* of José Alfonso de Pineda y Tavares; Burkholder and Chandler, *Biographical Dictionary*, pp. 263–64.

Pizarro y Aragón, Juan (December 14, 1697–January 18, 1771)

Pizarro was born in Madrid. His father, variously referred to as Juan or Francisco Pizarro y Mendoza, was a native of Romangordo, Cáceres, the first Marqués de San Juan de Piedras Albas, a knight of Calatrava, and the *mayordomo* and first equerry (*primer caballerizo*) for the queen in 1727. His mother was Isabel Rubín de Celis. His paternal grandparents were Juan Pizarro y Aragón, a native of Truxillo and knight of Calatrava, and María de Mendoza of the *Villa* of Casa Rubios del Monte. Pizarro was named minister *de capa y espada* of the Council of the Indies on February 28, 1728, as a result of a representation in his behalf by his father. Subsequently named to the Cámara, Pizarro was named president of the Council on February 20, 1763, a post he held until his death.

Pizarro inherited the title of Marqués de San Juan de Piedras Albas, was a grandee, belonged to the Order of San Genaro, and was a gentleman of the royal chamber. He also served as *sumiller de corps* and first equerry for Philip V and, until he resigned on March 25, 1748, for Ferdinand VI. He married Juana Josefa de Herrera Ayala y Roxas. Their only child, Florentina Pizarro, married Pasqual Benito Belvis de Moncada, Marqués de Belgida. Subsequently Pizarro married Francisca Osorio del Aguila, a relative, perhaps a sister, of Casimiro Osorio.*

SOURCES: AGS, 13–8–232; Gracia y Justicia 922; AGI, Indiferente 894, 871, *expediente* Osorio; AHN, Estado 6380(1); AHPM, Protocolos 18188, 18212; Bernard, *Secrétariat*, p. 212; Atienza, *Nobiliario*, p. 1629; Vignau, *Calatrava*, p. 133; García Carraffa, *Enciclopedia*, LXXII, 129; Ozanam, *La diplomacia*, pp. 152, n. 2, 303, n. 1.

Porcel, Antonio (June 14, 1755–?)

Porcel was born in the *lugar* of Mairena in the Archbishopric of Granada. His parents were Juan Porcel of the *lugar* of Mecina de Alfahar and Ana María Ruiz del Pino of Mairena. His paternal grandparents were Matías Porcel and Magdalena

Fernández Ballesteros, both of Mecina. His maternal grandparents were Mateo Ruiz Román of Mayrena and Catalina Ruiz del Pino of the *lugar* of Berchules. He had two brothers, José and Juan, and was probably the youngest of the three.

A man noted for his religiosity, Porcel was a career bureaucrat who, beginning in 1784, progressed through ever higher ranks as clerk (*oficial*) in the Secretariat of the Ministry of the Indies. Assigned to the Ministry for Grace and Justice for the Indies on February 3, 1789, he became its chief clerk (*oficial mayor*) on February 19, 1791. On November 27, 1798, he was named secretary for New Spain of the Council of the Indies. On August 15, 1802, he was appointed a minister *de capa y espada* to replace Francisco Xavier Machado.* The following month he was told to continue as secretary but with a vote in the Cámara.

On July 17, 1809, Porcel managed to escape Madrid and French domination. The Junta Central ordered him to Seville on August 4. Retired from his post as secretary of the Council in July 1813, he reassumed the office under Ferdinand VII but was retired again in 1817. The Liberals named him secretary of state for overseas affairs (*Ultramar*) in early 1820. How long he served and his subsequent career are unknown. He was still alive in 1830.

With a license granted in 1787, Porcel presumably married María Manuela Rubio y Ambiela. Fifteen years later he married Isabel Lobo Velasco y Mendieta, a native of Ronda. Her parents were Joaquín Lobo Velasco, a native and permanent alderman of Ronda, and *sevillana* María de las Mercedes Velasco y Mendieta. By 1809 he had four children, the eldest six years of age, by his "young wife." Two daughters, Isabel and Josefa, began drawing a pension in 1842. Porcel entered the Order of Charles III in 1791.

SOURCES: AHN, Estado 29G; Hacienda 2051, *expediente* 101; 506, *expediente* 873; 513, *expediente* 2530; Estado (Carlos III), *expediente* 493, *pruebas* of Antonio Porcel; AGI, Indiferente 825, 870, 887, 888; Bernard, *Secrétariat*, p. 226; Magdaleno, *Catálogo XX*, pp. 30, 80, 81, 82.

Porlier, Antonio de (April 16, 1722–February 7, 1813)

Porlier was born in La Laguna, Canary Islands, to Esteban Porlier y Durath, a Parisian, member of the Order of San Lázaro, and consul general for France in the Canaries, and Rita de la Luz Dutari Sopranis, a native of La Laguna. His paternal grandparents, both natives of Paris, were Juan Porlier Pagnon and Maria Durrut. His maternal grandparents, both *vecinos* of La Laguna, were Juan de la Luz Dutari and Jacobina de la Haya Sopranis. His brother José was a naval captain who died fighting to defend the *Thetis*. He had four other siblings: María, who married Luis del Hoyo Solórzano y Benítez de Lugo, the third Marqués de la Florida; Felipa Magdalena, who married Pedro de Nava; Juan Antonio; and Esteban Joseph.

Porlier studied in the Convent of Santo Domingo in La Laguna for six years, but the absence of a university in the Islands forced him to go to Spain to study law. In 1745 Porlier received the bachelor's degree in canon law from the University of Toledo after five years of study. He incorporated the degree in the University of Salamanca, from which he received the baccalaureate of civil law in 1748. In 1749 he received the licentiate and doctorate in canon law from the University of Avila. Porlier both competed for and substituted in chairs of laws at Salamanca. After participating in law academies at Salamanca and after spending two years in a practicum with Lázaro de Otaola, in 1752 he was admitted to practice law by the Royal Council.

Porlier's career in the bureaucracy began with an appointment on February 3, 1757, as protector of the Indians for the Audiencia of Charcas. Promotion to *oidor* of that court on April 30, 1765, was followed by a move to Lima as *fiscal del crimen* on December 7, 1766. Porlier occupied this post from October 9, 1769, to January 31, 1775, when he returned to Spain to serve as *fiscal* of the Council of the Indies for the affairs of New Spain with an appointment recommended by the Cámara on October 8, 1773. He assumed his post on September 9, 1775. On June 12, 1780, Porlier was given a vote in the Cámara of the Indies, and on July 8, 1787, he became the secretary of state for grace and justice for the Indies. In January 1789 he joined the Council of State. With the reorganization of April 25, 1790, he became secretary of state for grace and justice for Spain and the Indies. Replaced as secretary, on July 28, 1792, he returned to the Council of the Indies as its governor, a post he held until after the Napoleonic invasion of Spain. As a result of following the *rey intruso* José Napoleon I, Porlier's property was ordered sequestered by the Junta Central in 1809.

While in Charcas in 1765, Porlier married a native of Salta, Tucumán, María Josefa de Asteguieta. Her dowry enabled him to pay off his creditors for debts incurred by his appointment as protector of the Indians. Her father, Juan Manuel de Asteguieta y Cortázar, was a native of Legarda, Alava, who held an appointment as governor of Salta. Her mother, a native of San Andrés de Pica, was Josefa Sebastiana de Iribarren. Porlier and his wife had at least three sons: Esteban, born in La Plata in 1768, a page at court, an army officer, and knight of Santiago; Rosendo José Antonio, born in Lima in 1771, a naval officer and knight of Santiago; and Antonio Domingo, born in Lima in 1772, a pensioned *caballero* of Charles III in 1789, and an *oficial* of the Secretariat of Grace and Justice for the Indies beginning that year. They also had a daughter named Juana María. Porlier's nephew Francisco de Nava Grimón, son of the Marqués de Villanueva del Prado, served on the Audiencia of Guadalajara.

In 1753 Porlier was named an honorary member of the Royal Academy of History; he was also an honorary member of the Royal Spanish Academy. A *caballero* of the Order of Charles III, he received the title of Marqués de Bajamar in 1791 and the *gran cruz* of the Order in 1792. He died in Madrid.

SOURCES: AGI, Charcas 195, *relación* of 1754; Guadalajara 304, *relación* of Francisco de Nava; Indiferente 870B *expediente* Cerdá, 871 *expediente* Porlier, 901B, 824, 894, 892; AHN, Estado 2839 (1), 3449(2); Ordenes Militares (Santiago), *expediente* 6601, *pruebas* of Esteban Porlier; Estado (Carlos III), *expediente* 2473, *pruebas* of Donato de Porlier; AGS, 2–43–6; 2–49–61; 2–50–170, 2–50–217, 13–9–348, 13–9–335; Vignau, *Indice*, p. 140; *Gazeta de Madrid*, January 16, 1789, March 15, 1791, April 24, 1792; Lohmann Villena, *Americanos*, I, 332–33, II, 402;

Magdaleno, *Catálogo XX*, p. 82; Millares, *Escritores*, p. 423; Primo de la Guerra, *Diario*, II, 167; Escudero, *Los orígenes*, I, 505–9.

Portilla y Gálvez, José de la (July 21, 1736–c. 1809)

Portilla was born in the *villa* of La Rambla, Córdoba, to Ambrosio de la Portilla y Gálvez and Catalina Josefa del Río y Mariscal. His maternal grandfather was Alonso del Río. His older brother Juan was admitted to practice law by the Chancellery of Granada in 1758.

Portilla received the baccalaureate, licentiate, and doctorate in civil law from the University of Granada. After a four-year practicum with Manuel de Ortega y Espinosa, the Chancellery of Granada admitted him to practice law; he also joined the College of Attorneys at court.

Without seeking the appointment, in 1779 Portilla was named legal adviser (*asesor general*) for the viceroy of Peru, a post he assumed on February 24, 1781, while Viceroy Agustín de Jáuregui was in office. Given honors of *alcalde del crimen* on August 25, 1784, Portilla was named *oidor* of Lima on November 16, 1785, and took possession on May 12, 1786. In Lima Father Juan Rico, in trouble with the Inquisition for reading prohibited literature, considered Portilla his protector. Portilla advanced to Cuzco as regent and intendant on May 3, 1787. While there he initiated the repair of roads from Cuzco to Lima. Portilla served as intendant until 1791 and continued as regent until his appointment as a councilor of the Indies on July 31, 1804, to replace Manuel de Soto. In 1792–93 and 1803 he served as temporary president of Cuzco. Fisher considers him a "conservative peninsular bureaucrat." War made his return to Spain difficult, but on November 1, 1805, Portilla received permission to embark from Río de Janeiro in a Portuguese ship. He was listed as absent in the *Guía de Forasteros* for 1808 and was not on the Council in July 1808. He may never have served.

Since he was moving to Cuzco, in November 1787 Portilla was given a license to marry Francisca González de la Fuente, daughter of José González Gutiérrez, a native of Villavelayos, knight of Santiago, colonel of the army, first Conde de Fuentes González, and Rosa de la Fuente y Argandona, Condesa de la Villa de Fuentes, a native of Lima. The marriage never took place, however.

SOURCES: AGI, Lima 617; Cuzco 15; Indiferente 871 *expediente* Portilla; 892; AGS, 2–68–139, 2–69–244, 2–71–111, 2–88–172; ACRG, *cabina* 321, *legajo* 4296, *pieza* 4; Lohmann Villena, *Ministros*, pp. 104–5; Mendiburu, *Diccionario*, IX, 203; Vargas Ugarte, *Historia*, V, 148; Fisher, *Government*, pp. 147, 246; Fisher, "Royalism," p. 239.

Portocarrero de Guzmán Luna, Cristóbal Gregorio (April 12, 1692–June 21, 1763)

Portocarrero was the son of Cristóbal Portocarrero de Guzmán Enríquez y Luna, a native of Montijo, Badajoz, and fourth Conde de Montijo, Conde de Fuentidueña, Marqués de la Algaba y Valderrábano, *mayordomo* of the king, knight of Santiago, and, from 1697, a grandee of Spain. His mother was María Regalado de Villalpando,

Marquesa de Osera. His paternal grandparents were Cristóbal Portocarrero Luna of Montijo, Marqués de Valderrábano, and Inés de Guzmán y Córdoba, a native of the *villa* of Teba, Málaga. His maternal grandparents were Francisco de Villalpando and María Leonor de Monroy.

Portocarrero began his royal service in 1730. From 1732 to December 1735 he was the Spanish ambassador to England. Although the English considered him troublesome while there, Benjamin Keene, the English ambassador to Spain, regarded him in the late 1730s as "the most reasonable and most instructed person I meet with." Soon after his return to Spain, Portocarrero was named president of the Council of the Indies, on June 18, 1737. From 1742 to 1744 he was in Frankfurt, where he participated with Carvajal* in the election of Charles VII as Holy Roman Emperor. He retired as president of the Council on January 27, 1748.

Portocarrero, who inherited the title Conde de Montijo, was a knight of the Golden Fleece, San Genaro, San Miguel, and Sancti Spiritus. He also held the titles Conde de Fuentidueña, Marqués de la Algaba, de Valderrábano, and de Osera. A grandee of Spain first class, he was a gentleman of the royal chamber. He also served as first equerry (*caballerizo mayor*) and *mayordomo* for Queen Isabel Farnese from 1745 to 1747.

Portocarrero married María Dominga Fernández de Córdoba, his niece. Her parents were Antonio Fernández de Córdoba and Catalina Portocarrero, Condes de Teba. Their son Cristóbal inherited the family titles.

SOURCES: AGI, Indiferente 865, *Gazeta de Madrid*, June 21, 1763; Bernard, *Secrétariat*, p. 211; McLachlan, *Trade and Peace*, p. 101; Hildner, "Role", p. 332; García Carraffa, *Enciclopedia*, LXXIV, 51–52; Ozanam, *La diplomacia*, p. 273, n. 1.

Posada y Soto, Ramón de (January 3, 1746–?)

Posada, the third of four sons, was born in the *lugar* of Onao, Diocese of Oviedo, to Joaquín de Posada y Rivero of the *villa* of Llanes and Josefa de Soto y Posada of the *lugar* of Labra, "descendants of the first nobility of that region," according to his résumé. His paternal grandparents were Captain José de Posada Yntriago, a native of the *lugar* of Celorio, and Lucía de Rivero Cienfuegos of Llanes. His maternal grandparents were Felipe de Soto Yntriago of Labra and Francisca de Posada Velarde of Llanes. His brother Joaquín was a governor of Perote, Mexico, a colonel, and a knight of Santiago. Another brother, Felipe, held a benefice in the Cathedral of Avila. Sebastián, his eldest brother, inherited the family entail and married Juana de Jovellanos Ramírez Miranda. He had three sisters. Lucia and Rosa entered the convent of San Pelayo in Ovieda; his other sister, Josepha Casada, married José Cortés y Noriega. In addition, he had an illegitimate half brother named Sebastián who was sent to the Indies, probably at a young age.

After studying three years of philosophy in the Benedictine convent of San Salvador in Celorio, Posada began to study law at the University of Valladolid in 1762. He received the baccalaureate in civil law from the University of Burgo del Osma and the licentiate in civil and canon law from the University of Avila. He then incorporated the civil law degree in the University of Valladolid in 1767. At

Valladolid he competed for several chairs and substituted in three chairs of law. After Posada had participated in several practicums in law, the Council of Castile accepted him as an attorney in 1773. During his youth he became interested in drawing and proved so capable that in 1774 he was made an honorary member of the Royal Academy of San Fernando.

Posada's first audiencia appointment came on July 8, 1774, when Charles III named him an *oidor* of the Audiencia of Guatemala, a post he assumed on December 22, 1774. Present during the rebuilding of Guatemala City, he was responsible for obtaining Indian labor for construction projects and for overseeing the construction of the customs house, various churches, and the maintenance of streets and roads. Although named an *alcalde del crimen* of the court in Lima on June 6, 1779, the appointment was superseded on October 25 with one as the first *fiscal de hacienda* for the Audiencia of Mexico, a post he assumed on January 30, 1781, and one in which he distinguished himself for his expeditious handling of thousands of official documents and legal cases. Viceroys Martín de Mayorga, Manuel Antonio Florez, and the Conde de Revillagigedo II praised his services as *fiscal* and in the commissions he served.

Posada had caught the attention of José de Gálvez* while in Guatemala because of his excellent reports and good judgment in the choice of his wife, and the secretary secured him membership in the Order of Charles III in 1785. Posada favored more open and free commerce for the Indies and attacked the "royal monopoly" in supplying wheat to Cuba in 1781 on the grounds that it hampered private trade. A follower of Melchor de Jovellanos's ideas on agrarian reform and influenced by physiocratic thought, he considered agriculture and industry, not bullion, to be true wealth. He encouraged interprovincial trade and local industry.

In 1787 Posada started soliciting his return to Spain. Repeated pleas brought a promotion to the Council of the Indies as *fiscal* for New Spain to replace Uruñuela Aransay* on July 11, 1793, a post he assumed on October 26, 1794. In 1796 he was commissioned along with the Conde de Campomanes and Viana y Zavala* to report on direct commerce between the Philippines Company and India and China. He continued to work with the company until 1815. Posada received the right to vote in the Cámara in 1798 and was made a *ministro togado* on February 9, 1803. When the Council was reestablished in 1814, he declined an appointment to it and received retirement with full salary.

In Guatemala on November 22, 1778, Posada married Ana Fernández de Córdoba, a native of the *villa* of Canillas de Albayda, Málaga, niece of Ana de Zayas, wife of the viceroy of Mexico, Matías de Gálvez, and sister of Francisco Fernández de Córdoba. Her parents were Josef Fernández and Dorotea Zayas y Ramos of Ysnate. Their son, Vicente de Posada Fernández de Córdoba, began a career of audiencia service with an appointment to the court in Manila in 1811. The couple had six other children: María Buensuceso, who died in 1799, María Guadalupe, Ana, María, Ramón, and María de la Concepción. Posada's wife died February 2, 1799, perhaps of complications resulting from María de la Concepción's birth six weeks earlier. In March 1800, Posada married María Magdalena López Cabrejas y Gómez, a native of the *lugar* of La Laguna, Bishopric of Cuenca. Her parents were Miguel López Cabrejas and Catalina Gómez. The couple had two daughters, Eusebia and Juana.

Posada was "a remarkably intelligent and enlightened public servant" and a staunch supporter of the intendancies and other policies of José de Gálvez. A member of the Basque Economic Society, he was one of the stellar lights of the Enlightenment in Mexico. He was one of the officials most knowledgeable about economic affairs in Mexico and regarded as an active supporter of the Natural History Museum and Botanical Garden in Mexico. Posada wrote "Sobre el comercio libre de las harinas" and "Discurso pronunciado con motivo de la instalación del Supremo Tribunal de Justicia" (Cádiz, 1812). Goya painted his portrait in 1794, and it can be found in the Young Memorial Gallery in San Francisco.

SOURCES: AGI, Lima 876; Guatemala 556, 409; Indiferente 865, 886, 887, 871, *expediente* Posada, *relación* of 1789 and *relación* of 1797; AGS, 2–58–241, 2–63–76, 2–63–132, 13–8–595, 13–8–59, 13–9–280; AHN, Estado (Carlos III), *expediente* 225, *pruebas* of Ramón de Posada y Soto; Hacienda, 2051, *expediente* 10; 512, *expediente* 2325; AHPUV, Libros 80, 212; AHPM, Protocolo 22537; Brading, *Miners*, pp. 57–58, 75; Miranda, *Humboldt y México*, pp. 26, 32; Shafer, *Economic Societies*, p. 134; Arcila Farías, *El siglo ilustrado*, pp. 13–16; Luque Alcaide, *Sociedad económica*, p. 343; Calderón Quijano, *Los virreyes . . . Carlos III*, II, 123–26; Stoetzer, *Scholastic Roots*, p. 83; Pérez Valenzuela, *Nueva Guatemala*, p. 126; Beristain, *Biblioteca*, 2nd ed., II, 444–45; Rodríguez García, "Posada," passim.

Q

Quintana, José de la (?–May 22, 1750)

Quintana was descended from a branch of the family that had settled in Bilbao. He was named minister *de capa y espada* of the Council of the Indies on January 10, 1737, after service in the chief accounting office (*contaduría mayor de cuentas*) and committee for commerce and money (*junta de comercio y moneda*). Appointed along with Abaría* in January 1739 a plenipotentiary to work out with the English commissaries the issues of Georgia's boundary and depredations in the Caribbean after the Convention of Pardo, on March 7, 1739, Quintana was named secretary of state for the Indies. Two years later, on October 24, 1741, he was appointed to the Cámara where he served until his death.

Quintana married Josefa de Lezama. On December 11, 1737, he received a pension of 1,500 escudos for the life of his wife and himself. Josefa became Quintana's sole heir, for the couple had no children.

SOURCES: AGS, XXIII, 13–8–221, 13–8–210; AGI, Indiferente 894, 897, 871, *expediente* Quintana; Bernard, *Secrétariat*, p. 217; García Carraffa, *Enciclopedia*, LXXVI, 21; Lanning, *Diplomatic History*, pp. 148–49.

R

Rada, Pedro de (?–December 8, 1782)

Rada was born in the *villa* of Castro-Urdiales in the Bishopric of Santander. His parents were Francisco de Rada and Francisca de Aguirre. He began his royal service in the early 1740s. His career included service in provincial tax offices (*rentas provinciales*), the central treasury (*tesorería mayor*), the Ministry of the Navy (*marina*), and from 1764 as a clerk (*oficial*) in the Ministry of the Indies. Rada served a commission as secretary of the cámara for the viceroy of New Spain, to which he had been appointed in 1766, perhaps largely to keep an eye on Gálvez* for Secretary of State for the Indies Julián de Arriaga. Rada was allowed to return to Madrid in 1769, a consequence of his desire to leave Mexico, where he had become an enemy of both Gálvez and Viceroy Marqués de Croix. He was the chief clerk (*oficial primero*) of the Ministry of the Indies when a decree of April 12, 1776, named him to fill the first vacancy as minister *de capa y espada* of the Council of the Indies. On September 2, 1776, he replaced José Banfi.*

Rada, a pensioned *caballero* of the Order of Charles III from 1772, received a pension of 1,000 pesos on February 16, 1776, drawn on the treasury of Mexico as an indemnity for the expenses and losses he had incurred while in New Spain. He served on the Council until his death. Rada died a bachelor and left Francisco Santivañés as his sole heir.

SOURCES: AGS, XXIII, 13–8–536; AGI, Indiferente 866, 871, 894, 872, *expediente* Rada; Vignau, *Carlos III*, p. 145; Priestley, *Gálvez*, pp. 229–30; Magdaleno, *Catálogo XX*, pp. 79, 102.

Remírez de Baquedano, Gonzalo (var. Ramírez) (June 8, 1662, baptism–December 29, 1730)

Remírez was born in the *lugar* of San Martín, Navarre, the second son of Diego Remírez de Baquedano, Marqués de San Martín de Amescua, and María Alvarez de Eulate. His paternal grandparents were José Remírez de Baquedano, a native of San Martín and *señor* of the *palacios* of Ecala, San Martín, and Baquedano, and María de Arcaya of the *villa* of Torres. His maternal grandparents were Juan de Eulate of San Martín, *señor* of the *palacio* of Eulate, a *maestre de campo*, and a knight of Santiago, and María de Albizu, also of San Martín. His brother Juan, Marqués de Andia and a knight of Calatrava, was a councilor of Castile. His brother Diego Phelipe, a knight of Santiago, was on the Council of Orders. His brother Fernando, the oldest son, was a captain and knight of Calatrava.

Remírez studied at the College of the Holy Spirit of the University of Oñate, entering it in 1683 and continuing until 1689 when he left with a licentiate. He also spent time at the Universities of Valladolid and Salamanca, where he substituted in academic chairs.

Considered on October 3, 1689, for the post of *fiscal* in Quito, on January 19, 1690, Remírez was named *fiscal* of the Audiencia of Chile, a post he used to increase the collection of Crown revenues. Advanced to Lima as *oidor* on June 24, 1702, he assumed the post in 1704. He paid 2,000 *doblones* in 1711 for a *futura* as *fiscal* of the Council of the Indies. In 1714 he was also serving as superintendent of the mint in Potosí. Continuing in Lima until his *residencia* was completed, he went to Spain in 1716 and was named a councilor of the Indies by a decree of February 8, 1718. Two years later he received a license to become a cleric. Remírez, a knight of Santiago, died in Madrid.

In 1705 Remírez married *limeña* María Rosa Castro y Oyague, daughter of Gerónimo de Castro Gallegos, knight of Calatrava, and chief accountant of the Tribunal of Accounts of Lima, and Francisca de Oyague y Londoño. Her dowry was nearly 60,000 pesos.

SOURCES: AGI, Lima 345, 401, *títulos* of 1689; Quito 4; Indiferente 866, 867; AGS, 24–171–118, 24–123–115; AHN, Ordenes Militares (Santiago), *expediente* 6910, *pruebas* of Gonzalo Remírez Vaquedano y Eulate; Tovar Velarde, "La audiencia," pp. 387–89, 392; Lohmann Villena, *Ministros*, pp. LXXXI, 113–14; Vargas Ugarte, *Historia*, IV, 100; Vargas Ugarte, *Impresos*, IX, 36.

Requena y Herrera, Francisco de (January 26, 1743–February 11, 1824)

Requena, probably the younger of two sons, was born in Oran to Francisco Requena y Molina, a native of the *villa* of Río, Córdoba, and the *ayudante contralor* of artillery for the military post in Oran, and María de Herrera y Cabellón of Málaga. His paternal grandparents were Francisco Ruiz de Requena of Río and Francisca Molina y Beleña of Montoro, Córdoba. His maternal grandparents were Salvador Valentín de Herrera and Mariana Cabellón, both of Málaga.

At the age of about fifteen, Requena embarked upon a military career that would lead him to spend some thirty years in the Indies. He was a lieutenant in the engineering corps in Panama in 1766–67. By 1773 he was in Guayaquil, present Ecuador, as an engineer for the army. He also served as the governor of the province of Mainas. In 1779 he made a map of the audiencia district of Quito. By 1798 he had reached the rank of brigadier general in the army. On January 12 of that year he was named a minister *de capa y espada* of the Council of the Indies. Made a field marshal by 1803, in 1805 he was commissioned to direct the construction of a canal from Reus to the Mediterranean port of Salou. By 1810 he held the rank of lieutenant general. On October 28, 1810, he was named to the Cámara to replace Salcedo.* When the Cortes of Cádiz established a new Council of State in 1812, it appointed Requena to serve on it. Ferdinand VII subsequently named him to the restored Council of the Indies in 1814 and again, following the Liberal *trienio*, in 1823.

In 1772 Requena married María Luisa Santisteban y Ruiz Cano, a native of Guayaquil. Her parents, both from Guayaquil, were Domingo Santisteban y Morón de Butrón and María Jacinta Ruiz Cano y Ramírez de Arellano. The couple had at least four children. Francisco followed a military career and entered the Order of Charles III. María entered a religious order in Spain. Rafaela married Brigadier Antonio García de los Ríos in Spain. Teresa Josefa married Francisco Cortázar, an audiencia minister in America. After the death of his first wife, Requena married Teresa Fraga in 1810 with a special dispensation that entitled her to draw a pension after his death despite his being over sixty years of age when they married. Her parents were Antonio Fraga of Barcelona and Teresa Garcés of the *villa* of Reus in the Bishopric of Tarazona. The couple had a daughter, María de las Mercedes, born in Madrid in 1814.

Requena received the Large Cross of the Order of San Hermenegildo and also belonged to the Order of Isabel the Catholic.

SOURCES: AGS, XXIII, 13–9–508, 2–92–309; AGI, Indiferente 825, 866, 887, 888, 872, *expediente* Requena; AHN, Estado 879; Estado (Carlos III), *expediente* 1194, *pruebas* of Francisco María Herrera; Hacienda 529, *expediente* 30; García Carraffa, *Enciclopedia*, LXXVII, 190–91; Burkholder and Chandler, *Biographical Dictionary*, pp. 93–94.

Riva Agüero y Baso, Fulgencio de la (January 16, 1753–December 4, 1838)

Riva Agüero was born in the city of Cartagena, Spain, the son of Manuel Riva Agüero, a native of Ajo and a reviewing officer (*comisario de guerra*) and accountant (*contador*) in Cartagena, and Francisca Baso of Cartagena. His paternal grandparents were José de la Riva Agüero of Ajo and Manuela de Noja. His maternal grandparents were Bartolomé del Baso, a sea captain (*capitán del mar*) and María Antonia Boagno, both born in Marquesado del Final. His brother José served as the director of the tobacco monopoly in Peru. His brother Juan was the chief accountant for tribute in New Spain. Both were *caballeros* of the Order of Charles III.

In 1769 Riva Agüero went to Madrid to work in the home of the secretary of state for the Indies and the Navy, Julián de Arriaga, as a *page de bolsa*. Not surprisingly, several years later, in 1773, he began to serve in the Secretariat of the Ministry of the Navy. He progressed through the ranks of clerk (*oficial*), reaching that of first clerk (*oficial primero*) by 1793. Through the influence of the royal favorite Manuel Godoy, on November 1, 1793, he was named a supernumerary minister *de capa y espada* of the Council of the Indies. A normal advancement would have been as intendant of the naval base in El Ferrol. A regular position came on September 10, 1794. Until the following July 27, however, he continued in the Ministry of the Navy because of the war with France. On that date he was relieved of further service in the Ministry as a result of a long illness resulting from his excessive work. A *caballero* of the Order of Charles III from 1783, Riva Agüero eventually secured retirement from his Council position.

In 1776 Riva Agüero received a license to marry Josefa Clavijo. Subsequently, with a license granted in 1786, he married Gertrudis de Llano, a niece of the Marqués de Llano and of the Conde de Sanafe. She was a sister-in-law of General Winthuysen. The couple had two children. Manuel, born in 1787, entered the Walloon Guards as a cadet in 1803. Xaviera, born in 1789, was educated in the convent of Las Salesas.

SOURCES: AGS, XXIII, 13–9–514; AGI, Indiferente 825, 866, 888, 870A, *expediente* Acedo; 872, *expediente* Riva Agüero; AHN, Estado (Carlos III), *expediente* 177, *pruebas* of Fulgencio de la Riva Agüero; Hacienda 506, *expediente* 839; 505, *expediente* 497; 2051, *expediente* 16; Vignau, *Carlos III*, 149; Bernard, *Secrétariat*, p. 225.

Rivera y Peña, Ramón (c. 1730–July 13, 1789)

Rivera was born and baptized in the *villa* of Ares, Archbishopric of Santiago, Galicia, to Miguel Teodoro Rivera y Peña and María Manuela de la Carrera. His only brother was a priest.

Rivera studied in the University of Santiago and completed baccalaureates in civil law in 1750 and in canon law in 1756. He entered the *colegio mayor* of Fonseca in 1756 and served as its rector in 1759. Two months after entering Fonseca, he received the licentiate and doctorate in canon law. Rivera took his practicum in law with Diego Antonio Cornide y Saavedra, an attorney of the Audiencia of Galicia who later was named to that court. The Audiencia of Galicia admitted him to practice law in 1753, but Rivera devoted most of his early professional years to university service, ultimately becoming professor of *Institutes* at the University of Santiago. During these years he also competed for ecclesiastical benefices.

On April 23, 1767, Rivera was named a supernumerary *oidor* of the Audiencia of Charcas, a post he assumed on December 5, 1768. Promoted to Lima as an *alcalde del crimen* on January 26, 1777, he assumed the post on June 5, 1778. He advanced to *oidor* on November 26, 1778, and then returned to Spain with an appointment of May 31, 1781, as *oidor* of the House of Trade. Six years later, on October 4, he became the *fiscal* for New Spain of the Council of the Indies, a post he served from November 16, 1787, until his death in Ares.

In the 1770s Rivera married María Antonia Herboso y Arburúa, a native of Lima or La Plata. She was the daughter of José Herboso y Figueroa, an accountant in the Tribunal of Accounts in Lima, and Josefa Arburúa y Vicuña, and the niece of the Bishop of La Plata Francisco Ramón de Herboso y Figueroa. She brought a dowry of 35,781 pesos. The couple had three children: Domingo, María, and Juana.

SOURCES: AGI, Indiferente 865, 894, 1980, 872, *expediente* Rivera y Peña, 1509, *relación* of 1774; Lima 829; Charcas 423; AGS, 2–51–71, 2–61–5, 2–62–221, 2–65–21, 13–8–596; AHN, Consejos 20344; Lohmann Villena, *Ministros*, pp. LXXXII, 118.

Rojas, José Manuel de (April 10, 1678–September 15, 1755)

Rojas was born in the city of Jaén. His father was Francisco López de Rojas y Almansa, a native of Andújar. His mother was María Ortiz Navarro Santaella of the *villa* of Luque, Córdoba.

The Chancellery of Granada admitted Rojas to practice law in 1703. A highly regarded attorney in Granada, he was named an *oidor* of the Chancellery of Valladolid on September 6, 1734. On March 28, 1744, he advanced to the Council of the Indies to replace Prudencio Antonio de Palacios* as *fiscal* for Peru. He served several years before being promoted to the Council of Castile as a minister *togado* on November 22, 1748.

In May 1704, Rojas married Beatriz de Doblas of Granada. Her parents were Juan de Doblas and Josepha María de la Cueva. The couple had six children: Miguel José served on the audiencias of Guadalajara and Mexico; José Francisco held ecclesiastical positions; Ana married Anastasio Francisco de Aguayo, *alcalde mayor* of Trujillo in 1754; Josepha married José Calvo y Villalba; María Teresa entered a Franciscan convent; Angela's fate is unknown. Just prior to his death Rojas published a work on entailed estates useful for audiencias. He ordered an entailed estate be established upon his death.

SOURCES: AGS, XXIII, 13–8–204; Gracia y Justicia 149, 150; AHN, Consejos 13532, Estado 6380 (2); ACRG, *cabina* 321, *legajo* 4298, *piezas* 2 and 3; AGI, Indiferente 872, 885, 894, 898; AHPM, Protocolo 18544; *Gazeta de Madrid*, September 23, 1755. Burkholder and Chandler, *Biographical Dictionary*, p. 298, which this entry supersedes concerning José Manuel de Rojas.

Rojas y Contreras, José Simeón de (October 28, 1702–July 30, 1770)

Rojas was born in Valladolid, the son of Diego de Rojas y Ortega* and María de Contreras y Contreras. See his father's entry for grandparents and siblings.

After receiving baccalaureate degrees in canon and civil law from the University of Valladolid, Rojas transferred to the University of Salamanca. There he received a licentiate in civil law and in 1719 entered the *colegio mayor* of San Bartolomé. He substituted in the professoriat at Salamanca.

On May 4, 1733, Rojas was named an *alcalde de la quadra* of the Audiencia of Seville. Advanced to the civil chamber in Seville on January 9, 1736, he was subsequently promoted to *alcalde de casa y corte* on April 27, 1750. An appointment as minister *togado* on the Council of the Indies followed on March 15, 1752. On December 18, 1763, he was named to the Cámara, where he served from February 4, 1764, until his death.

Rojas was a knight of Calatrava from 1712. Charles III granted him the title Marqués de Alventos in 1761. Rojas, an alderman of Seville (*veintiquatro*), earned the lasting gratitude of contemporary *colegiales* and later historians with his *Historia del colegio viejo de San Bartolomé.*

Rojas married María Prieto of Valencia. She was the daughter of Cayo Prieto who died as a minister *togado* of the Council of Orders and *sevillana* Teresa Claudia Morel. They had three sons and two daughters living in 1768. José was the eldest. Antonio María, a knight of Calatrava, served as a royal page. Manuel entered the *colegio mayor* of Cuenca at the University of Salamanca and became a knight of Calatrava in 1761. The daughters were named María Josepha and María Lorenza.

SOURCES: AGS, XXIII, 13–8–193; 13–8–409; Gracia y Justicia 140, 144, 151; AHN Ordenes Militares (Calatrava), *expediente* 2242, *pruebas* of José de Rojas y Contreras; AGI, Indiferente 885, 899, 894; *Gazeta de Madrid*, August 21, 1770, February 3, 1761; Rezabal, *Biblioteca*, p. 313; García Carraffa, *Enciclopedia*, LXXIX, 208; Roxas y Contreras, *Historia*, II, 694–709.

Rojas y Hierro, José de (February 6, 1748–?)

Rojas was born in Toledo. His parents were *vallisoletano* Bernardo de Rojas y Contreras, a knight of Calatrava, intendant of the province of Murcia, and member of the Royal Junta of Commerce and Money, and his second wife María Josepha de Hierro y Arriaga, a native of Guadalajara. His paternal grandfather was Diego de Rojas y Ortega.* His maternal grandparents were José de Hierro y Herrera, Vizconde de Palazuelos, a native of Guadalajara and a member of the Council of Hacienda, and María Teresa de Arriaga, who was born in Avila when her father was *corregidor* there. María Teresa's brother was Julián de Arriaga, the secretary of state for the Indies from 1754 to 1776. Rojas had five siblings. His older brother Francisco Javier, born in 1742, was a naval officer and a knight of Calatrava. His other siblings were María Antonia, María Teresa, Manuela, and Fernando.

After service as governor of the mercury mines in Almadén, Rojas was named a minister *de capa y espada* of the Council of the Indies on August 4, 1800. He retained the position when, after a brief interruption in its existence during the Spanish War of Independence, the Council was reestablished in 1814. He retired almost immediately, however, with half salary on July 2, 1814. Following a fire that destroyed his house on April 17, 1815, he secured an increase in his pension to full salary as minister.

Rojas, a knight of Calatrava from 1761, received a license in 1801 to marry Isidra Justiani y Pereda, daughter of the Marqués de Peñaflorida.

SOURCES: AHN, Hacienda 512, *expediente* 2440; Universidades 670, *expediente* 46; Ordenes Militares (Calatrava), *expediente* 2245, *pruebas* of Francisco Javier de Rojas y Hierro; AGS, XXIII, 13–8–1; Dirección General del Tesoro, Inventario 39, *legajo* 16; AGI, Indiferente 888, 872, *expediente* Rojas; Vignau, *Calatrava*, p. 145.

Rojas y Ortega, Diego de (September 11, 1659–June 13, 1734)

Rojas was born in Antequera. His father was Alonso de Rojas y Boza of La Pizarra, Málaga, an agent (*familiar*) of the Inquisition, knight of Santiago, and *senor* of the town of Rincón de Herrera y Alinas. His mother was María Antonia de Rojas Padilla of Antequera. Rojas's paternal grandparents were Juan de Rojas Trillo of Antequera and Leonor Boza y Figueroa of La Pizarra. His maternal grandparents were Diego de Ortega, a native of Loja who served as an alderman of the city and as a *familiar* of the Inquisition, and Marina de Zea y Porras, also from Loja. By his father's first wife, María de Padilla, Rojas had a half brother, Gerónimo, a knight of Calatrava, alderman in perpetuity (*regidor perpetuo*) of Antequera, and *senor* of the *Villa* of Alimaros, and a half sister, Leonor María who married Pedro Rosales y Luna. He also had an older brother, Juan de Rojas y Ortega, a knight of Calatrava, *colegial* at the University of Salamanca, and *familiar* of the Inquisition, and three sisters: Jacinta María, María Magdalena, and Gerónima. An aunt married Bernardino Castejón, a minister of the Council of Orders.

Rojas was a *colegial* in the *colegio mayor* of Cuenca at the University of Salamanca. He also taught canon law at the university, holding the second (*vísperas*) chair. By a *consulta* of October 23, 1697, he was named an *alcalde de los hijosdalgo* of the Chancellery of Valladolid. Although named an oidor of the Chancellery of Granada in February, 1704, he succeeded in getting the appointment changed for one of *oidor* to Valladolid. Advanced to the Council of Orders as *fiscal* in 1706, he was appointed minister *togado* of the Council of the Indies in the reorganization of November 10, 1713, and survived the reorganization of January 20, 1717. He served the final appointment from July 27, 1717, until his death.

Rojas, a knight of Calatrava from 1706, married María de Contreras y Contreras, a native of Valladolid and the Marquesa de Villanueva del Duero. Her parents were Pedro Romualdo de Contreras of Madrid and María Ventura Contreras of Jaén. Her father had been an *oidor* of the Chancellery of Valladolid and was *senor* of Villanueva del Duero and Villamarciel. Rojas and his wife had seven children. Son José Simeón de Rojas y Contreras* also served on the Council of the Indies. Diego Fernando, a knight of Calatrava, became governor of the Council of Castile. Bernardo Luis was a knight of Calatrava, an alderman of Toledo, an intendant, and ultimately a minister *de capa y espada* on the Council of the Exchequer. The other children were Pedro José, the eldest son, who became a knight of Calatrava and inherited the title Marqués de Villanueva del Duero, Antonio Joachín, María Joachina, and Ysabel María.

SOURCES: AHN, Ordenes Militares (Calatrava), *expediente* 2245, *pruebas* of Francisco Xavier de Rojas y Hierro; *expediente* 2250, *pruebas* of Diego de Rojas y Ortega; Consejos 13531; AGS, XXIII, 13–9–479; AGI, Indiferente 844; Bernard, *Secrétariat*, p. 215; García Carraffa, Enciclopedia, LXXIX, p. 203–8.

Romay Armada y Sotomayor, Antonio Jacinto (c. 1698–November 8, 1760)

Romay was born in Galicia to Juan Antonio Romay and Isabel Rosa Armada y Mondragón. His paternal grandparents were Theodosio Romay y Sotomayor and Jacinta de Lis Saabedra. His maternal grandparents were Pedro Manuel Armada, a knight of Santiago, and Isabel Salgado y Mondragón. His maternal uncle, Ignacio de Armada, Marqués de Santa Cruz de Rivadulla, left his entailed properties (*mayorazgos*) to Romay.

Romay attended the University of Santiago, where he received the baccalaureate and then, in 1735, the licentiate and doctorate in canon law. He belonged to the *colegio mayor* of Fonseca from 1723, served as its rector in 1727, and held chairs, including, by 1735, that of first chair (*prima*) of canon law.

Romay secured his appointment as a minister *togado* to replace Luis Fernando de Isla* on October 13, 1743. His appointment was the direct result of his marriage to Josefa Antonio de Ahumada. She had received on September 16, 1741, a decree granting her a dowry of a seat on the Council of the Indies for whomever she married who was judged qualified for the position. This dowry was a reward for the services of her father, the Marqués de Montealto, as *corregidor* of Madrid. After an investigation of his qualifications, Romay married Josefa and received the appointment. He served until his death. Her subsequent request to have the dowry continue was denied.

SOURCES: AGS, XXIII, 13–9–360; Gracia y Justicia 148 and *relacíon* of 1735 located there; AGI, Indiferente 898, 894, 872, *expediente* Romay; *Gazeta de Madrid*, February 10, 1761; Cabeza de León, *Universidad de Santiago*, p. 175.

Romero y Alesón, Manuel (1718–October 22, 1798)

Romero was born in the *villa* of Sotés in the province of La Rioja. His parents were Francisco Romero and Coloma Alesón, both from Sotés. His brother Santiago was *senor* of the *villa* of Bobadilla.

Romero received his baccalaureate in civil law from the University of Valladolid in 1743. Subsequently, he spent nine years, from 1751 to 1760, as a judge advocate for naval forces at Cartagena, Spain. On June 30, 1760, he was given honors of *oidor* of the Audiencia of Santa Fe de Bogotá as an appropriate accompaniment for his appointment as legal adviser (*asesor general*) for the viceroy of New Granada, Pedro Mesía de la Cerda, who had selected him. Romero served from 1761 to 1765. Returning to Spain, he was appointed on September 9, 1773, an *oidor* of the House of Trade. With the expansion of the Council of the Indies in 1776, he was named on May 4 to replace Juan de Mérida,* who had declined one of the new positions. Granted the right to attend the Council at his pleasure on April 16, 1797, Romero received honors of the Cámara the following August 23.

Romero was a bachelor in 1772 and probably never married, for he left as heirs his neices Teresa and Isabel Corral y Romero.

SOURCES: AGS, XXIII, 2–44–187, 2–57–198, 13–8–388, 13–8–323; AGI, Indiferente 894, 1980, 870B, *expediente* Cerda, 872, *expediente* Romero; Santa Fe 535; AHPUV, Libro 201; Restrepo, *Mandatarios*, p. 527.

S

Saavedra y Carvajal, Francisco de (c. 1738–April 3, 1809)

Saavedra was born in the *lugar* of San Esteban de Loentia, Galicia, to Francisco Saavedra and Hermenegilda de Carvajal y la Barrera. His paternal grandparents were Francisco Saavedra y Sotomayor and Elena Freyre. His maternal grandparents were Antonio López Carvajal and Catalina Carvallido de la Barrera.

Saavedra studied in the University of Santiago where he gained the baccalaureate in canon law in 1760. In 1762 he received the baccalaureate in civil law from the University of Valladolid and incorporated it at the University of Salamanca. In July 1763 he took the licentiate and doctorate in canon law from the University of Avila. At Valladolid Saavedra was a substitute in the chair of *Sexto* in 1761 and competed unsuccessfully for the first chair of canon law in 1763. In 1762 he joined the law academy at Salamanca, serving as president. He studied law at Salamanca with Antonio Gamarra from 1760 to 1764 and subsequently with future Councilor of Castile Pedro Carrasco in Madrid. Saavedra went to Madrid in 1764, the Council of Castile accepted him as an attorney in 1765, and he joined the College of Attorneys of the court.

Charles III named Saavedra *fiscal* of the Audiencia of Guatemala on August 20, 1775, and he entered the post on February 15, 1776. He brought with him from Spain as a *criado* Juan López Cancelada, the future editor of the *Gazeta de México* and an infamous creole baiter and polemicist. After 1776 Saavedra was *fiscal de lo civil.* He distinguished himself in the Indian uprising of 1783. Named *alcalde del crimen* of the Audiencia of Mexico on December 13, 1787, he remained in the South for a time as governor and intendant of Chiapas, a post to which he was named on September 20, 1786. He assumed his duties in Mexico City on May 18, 1789. Advanced as regent of the Audiencia of Manila on November 11, 1789, he refused the post for reasons of health. When named regent of the Audiencia of Guadalajara on December 14, 1794, however, he accepted and assumed the position on June 6, 1795. Saavedra was given honors of the Council of the Indies on September 15, 1798, and named to replace Gutiérrez de Piñeres* as a minister *togado* on March 5, 1803. His departure in leaving Mexico was delayed, however, by the outbreak of yellow fever that killed Cerdán.* He finally left Veracruz on January 11, 1804, and, after a stop in Havana, reached La Coruña on March 17, 1804. He was still serving on the Council at the time of the French invasion in 1808.

Saavedra was a member of the Economic Society of Santiago de Compostela, Galicia.

SOURCES: AGS, 2–59–100, 2–78–182, 2–73–260, 2–82–166, 13–9–122, AGI, Lima 876; Mexico 1642, *relación* of 1784; Guadalajara 304; Filipinas 364; Indiferente 872, 887; AUAV, Registro de Grados, 1763; Navarro García, *Intendencias*, p. 50; Núñez y Domínguez, *La virreina*, p. 81n.; Samayoa Guevara, *Los gremios*, p. 60; Toreno, *Historia*, p. 242; *Diario curioso*, May 18, 1789 (courtesy of Linda Arnold); *Gazeta de Madrid*, July 24, 1808.

Salcedo, José (1748–October 25, 1810)

Salcedo began his career at the age of fifteen as a cadet in the royal artillery corps. He spent twenty-one years in the army reaching the rank of captain in the engineering corps. Turning to civil administration, he was the chief clerk (*oficial mayor primero*) in the Secretariat of the Ministry of the Exchequer by 1794. Having received honors of a minister on April 14, 1794, on October 31 of that year he was named a supernumerary minister *de capa y espada* of the Council of the Indies. He replaced Hermosilla* in a regular position upon his death and on September 21, 1810, was named to the Cámara. His brother Manuel was an archdeacon of the cathedral in Valladolid, Michoacán.

Salcedo was married, but his wife's name is unknown. Their only son died in 1802.

SOURCES: AGS, XXIII, 13–8–42, 13–8–35, 2–92–281; AGI, Indiferente 824, 886, 887, 872, *expediente* Salcedo.

Salcedo, Manuel Jacinto de (September 12, 1682, baptism–June 30, 1747)

Salcedo was born in the *villa* of Castro-Urdiales, Santander. His parents were Juan Francisco de Sierralta y Salcedo of the *villa* of Balmaseda, Vizcaya, a knight of Santiago, and Clara de Rado y Mena of Castro-Urdiales. His paternal grandparents were Francisco Hurtado de Salcedo, a knight of Calatrava and a native of Balmaseda, and Michaela de Sierralta of the *villa* of Otañes in the jurisdiction of Castro-Urdiales. His maternal grandparents were Juan de Rado y Bedia, a knight of Santiago, native of Balmaseda, and alderman of Castro-Urdiales, and Ana María de Mena of Castro-Urdiales. He had at least three brothers: Miguel Fernando, a knight of San Juan and a district administrator (*alcalde mayor*) of Castro-Urdiales; Lorenzo, a knight of Calatrava; and Francisco Antonio.

Salcedo began his career, probably as a cadet, in 1698. After progressing up several military ranks, on December 5, 1734, he was named governor and captain general of the province of Yucatán. Authorities in Madrid considered him to be doing a good job in 1741. Already holding the rank of brigadier in the Royal Army, on June 10, 1745, he was granted an appointment as minister *de capa y espada* of the Council of the Indies in return for a secret payment of 9,000 pesos of fifteen *reales de vellón* each. While sales of audiencia appointments were numerous in the 1740s, this is the only sale yet revealed of a seat on the Council at that time. Salcedo assumed his post on June 25, 1745, and served until his death in Madrid.

Salcedo, a knight of Santiago, married *madrileña* Francisca Castellanos. Her parents were Alfonso Castellanos, a native of the city of Logroño and a councilor of Castile, and María Sáez of the villa of Budia. The couple had four sons. Domingo became a knight of Santiago in 1757; his daughter María Manuela married Francisco Xavier Machado Fiesco.* The other sons were Manuel José, Joachín, and Francisco Vicente.

SOURCES: AHN, Ordenes Militares (Santiago), *expediente* 7477, *pruebas* of Manuel Jacinto de Salcedo y Sierralta; Estado 2330; (Carlos III), *expediente* 1345, *pruebas* of Justo Germán de Machado Fiesco; AGS, XXIII, 13–8–425; AGI, Indiferente 866, 894, 872; *Gazeta de Madrid*, July 11, 1747.

Salcedo, Manuel Pablo de (Variant: Alfonso de Salcedo) (1700–January 25, 1773)

Salcedo was born in the *villa* of Anguciana in the province of Logroño. His parents were Antonio Alfonso de Salcedo y Ugarte, eleventh *señor* of Anguciana, and Rosa Josepha Ortes de Velasco y Luyando. His paternal grandparents were Manuel Alfonso de Salcedo y Eguiluz and María Francisca de Ugarte. His maternal grandparents were Francisco Antonio Ortes de Velasco and Feliciana de Luyando. Upon the death of his elder brother Antonio Ignacio, Manuel became the thirteenth *señor* of Anguciana. A sister was named María Nicasia.

Salcedo entered the *colegio mayor* of San Bartolomé at the University of Salamanca in 1727, received a licentiate in 1730, and competed for academic chairs.

On April 14, 1739, Salcedo was named *fiscal del crimen* of the Audiencia of Valencia. He subsequently made the routine move into the civil *fiscalía*. On February 2, 1749, he was named *fiscal* for Peru on the Council of the Indies to replace José Manuel de Rojas.* The following year he temporarily assumed the *fiscalía* for New Spain as well, an assignment that would last until 1752. Probably as a reward for this service, on March 15, 1752, Salcedo was granted honors of councilor of Castile. On December 18, 1763 he advanced to the Cámara, where he served from February 4, 1764, until his death. His contemporary Rojas y Contreras* considered him extremely able and well informed in affairs pertaining to the Indies.

While in Valencia, Salcedo married María Thomasa Aliaga, daughter of Martín de Aliaga and Mariana Martínez de Larraga. Their daughter María Antonia married Miguel José de Uztáriz y Arroyabe, Marqués de Echandia. Another daughter, María Francisca de Paula, married Manuel Duque de Estrada, Conde de la Vega de Sella. Salcedo's nephew Iñigo Ortes de Velasco served on the Chancellery of Granada.

Salcedo was named a pensioned *caballero* of the Order of Charles III, but died before professing.

SOURCES: AGS, XXIII, 13–8–408; Hacienda 119; Gracia y Justicia 820; AGI, Indiferente 865, 894, 872, *expediente* Salcedo; AHN, Estado, Libro 114; *Gazeta de Madrid*, February 9, 1773; Roxas y Contreras, *Historia*, II, 763–66.

Santelices y Venero, Ventura de (c. 1698–December 20, 1763)

Santelices was born in Escalante, Santander, to Manuel de Santelices Carredaño, a native of Escalante and *colegial* of San Bartolomé at the University of Salamanca, and María Antonia de Venero of the *lugar* of Castillo, Santoña. His paternal grandparents were Francisco Antonio de Santelices y Rugama, *señor* of Santelices and a native of Escalante, and María Carredaño of the *lugar* of Güemes, Santoña. His maternal grandparents were Juan Antonio de Venero, *señor* of Casa de Venero in the *lugar* of Castillo, and Francisca Pelegrín. His brother Antonio married Antonia de Venero.

An eldest son, Santelices received a baccalaureate in canon law from the University of Hirache in 1719 and incorporated it at the University of Valladolid in 1721. The same year he received the baccalaureate in civil law at Valladolid. He entered the *colegio mayor* of San Bartolomé at the University of Salamanca in 1723. While affiliated with Salamanca, he received a licentiate degree and held chairs in canon law.

On June 9, 1746, Santelices was named an *oidor* of the House of Trade. Later named *corregidor* and superintendent of mines for Potosí, Peru, he was named a minister *togado* of the Council of the Indies by a decree of July 20, 1760. The title of appointment followed on November 4, 1763. Having reached Cádiz on August 2, 1763, Santelices replaced José Moreno Hurtado* on November 24, 1763. His service was extraordinarily brief, however, for he died later in the year.

Santelices probably never married. His nephew Juan Antonio Santelices was his heir.

SOURCES: AGS, XXIII, 2–35–143, 13–9–426; AGI, Indiferente 885, 894, 1980, 872, *expediente* Santelices; AHPUV, Libro 200; Bernard, *Secrétariat*, p. 220; García Carraffa, *Enciclopedia*, LXXXIII, 19; Roxas y Contreras, *Historia*, II, 735–42.

Santos de San Pedro, Juan Francisco (c. 1661–February 9, 1726)

Santos was born in Valladolid. His parents were Juan Santos de San Pedro, a native of the *lugar* of Santa Erbas de la Vega in the Bishopric of León and an *oidor* on the Chancellery of Valladolid, and Juana María Velázquez of Madrid. His paternal grandparents were Alonso Santos de San Pedro of Santa Erbas de la Vega and Antonia Escudero of the *lugar* of San Martín, León. His maternal grandparents were Francisco Velázquez, a native of Madrid, knight of Santiago, and equerry (*cavallerizo*) for the Queen Mother, and Catalina de Busto who had been born in Seville *de paso* when her father was serving as an *oidor* on its audiencia.

Santos received a baccalaureate in canon law in 1681 from the University of Valladolid and a licentiate in canon law from the University of Avila in 1685.

Elected to the *colegio mayor* of San Ildefonso at the University of Alcalá in 1685, he subsequently served as rector from 1688 to 1690 and held academic chairs beginning in 1698, reaching the chair of *Decreto* in 1702.

In 1704 Santos was named *oidor* of the Chancellery of Valladolid. Appointed governor of Asturias in 1707, he was subsequently given an option to the first vacancy on the Council of the Exchequer and an appointment as *alcalde de casa y corte*. He served on the Council of the Exchequer in 1713 and 1714, but lost his seat during the reform that shuffled many ministers out of the system, at least temporarily. Given a post as *corregidor* of Segovia, he followed that with an appointment as minister *togado* of the Council of the Indies on December 12, 1720, to replace Martín José de Miraval.* He served from December 20 until his death.

Santos entered the Order of Calatrava in 1694. He married María Josefa Ortiz, a lady-in-waiting (*camarista*) of the queen. Her dowry was his initial appointment in 1704. The couple had six children.

SOURCES: AGS, XXIII, 13–8–252; Gracia y Justicia 133, 135; AGI, Indiferente 866; AHN, Ordenes Militares (Calatrava), *expediente* 2411, *pruebas* of Juan Francisco Santos de San Pedro; Estado 6399 (1); Consejos 13537; Universidades, Libro 1147, f. 4–5, 25; AUAV, Registro de Grados, 1685; Rújula, *Indice*, p. 783; Vignau, *Calatrava*, pp. 154–55.

Santos Domínguez, Felipe (c. 1714–May 7, 1788)

Santos was born in the *villa* of Allariz in the Bishopric of Orense in Galicia. His parents were Pedro Santos Fernández of Villanueva, just outside Allariz, and María Gómez Domínguez of Allariz. He obtained baccalaureate, licentiate, and doctorate degrees at the University of Salamanca in 1733. He remained at the university for many years, ultimately becoming a professor.

Santos was named a *fiscal* of the Chancellery of Granada on March 17, 1764. Moved to Madrid as an *alcalde de casa y corte* on October 23, 1769, he advanced to the Council of the Indies on May 6, 1773, as a minister *togado* replacing Manuel Bernardo de Quiros.* On February 26, 1776, Santos was named to the Cámara. After serving there for nearly a decade and suffering from prolonged illness, on January 9, 1786, he was given the right to attend at his pleasure.

Santos married María Teresa Hoyos y Villegas of Allariz. Her parents were Juan Francisco de Hoyos of the *lugar* of Monnegro of the Archbishopric of Burgos and Thomasa Sierra de la Peña of Allariz. The couple had at least three children. Martín, born in 1755, received an appointment as *oidor* of the Audiencia of Guadalajara in 1786 as a result of his father's persistent lobbying. María Francisca married Galician Francisco Andrés de Losada. A second daughter was named Polonia. Santos' wife outlived him.

SOURCES: AGS, XXIII, 2–57–60, 13–9–559; AGI, Indiferente 865, 866, 894, 1626, 872, *expediente* Santos Domínguez; AHN, Consejos 12136, *expediente* 52; *Gazeta de Madrid*, May 20, 1778; Burkholder and Chandler, *Biographical Dictionary*, p. 319.

Silva Rivera, Manuel (?–January 2, 1746)

Silva, who held the title Marqués de Montemayor, was named a minister *de capa y espada* and given a seat on the Cámara of the Indies on March 13, 1725. He served from March 22, 1725 until excused from attendance on August 9, 1737.

SOURCES: AGS, XXIII, 13–8–454; AGI, Indiferente 866, 894; Bernard, *Secrétariat*, p. 216.

Silva y Meneses, Manuel de (?–May 11, 1743)

Silva was a military officer by profession. He began his military service in 1683 and rose to the rank of captain general of the Royal Army. From 1697 he was *general de mar*. Named a minister *de capa y espada* of the Council of the Indies on February 10, 1710, he took his oath of office on February 22. He survived the various reforms in the 1710s and was on the Council as reorganized on January 20, 1717. When the Cámara was reestablished in 1721, Silva was one of the two *capa y espada* ministers named to serve on it. On February 20, 1739, he received permission to attend the Cámara at his pleasure, which he did until his death.

SOURCES: AGS, XXIII, 13–8–457, 13–8–478; AHN, Estado 6380 (1); AGI, Indiferente 866, 872; Bernard, *Secrétariat*, p. 215.

Sola y Fuente, Gerónimo de (1691–February 13, 1767)

Sola was born in Alcalá de Henares where his father Tomás de Sola* was a professor. He attended the University of Alcalá, earning a baccalaureate in canon law in 1708 and a licentiate in 1712. He belonged to the *colegio* of Santa Catalina, also known as "Los Verdes." In 1721 he became a professor of *Institutes* at the university. He had advanced to the chair of *Decretales* by 1723.

On March 29, 1724, Sola was named an *alcalde de la quadra* for the Audiencia of Seville. Promoted to *oidor* of the tribunal on May 12, 1732, he was subsequently named superintendent general for the mercury mines of Huancavelica, Peru and given a simultaneous appointment as a minister *togado* of the Council of the Exchequer to add luster to his credentials. As superintendent general, Sola resorted to tinkering with rather than overhauling the mines' means of production. Output did increase by twenty percent, however, and the discovery of the mine's main vein while Sola was administrator earned him the title "Restorer of the Mine" from the miners. Although named a minister *togado* of the Council of the Indies on January 28, 1742, Sola remained in America until 1749. After years of service on the Council, he was named to the Cámara on December 18, 1763.

While Sola was in America, his family was in San Ildefonso in the service of the Queen Mother. Sola founded an entailed estate of property in Madrid. He left it to his sole heir, his nephew Gerónimo de Velarde y Sola who ultimately became a councilor of Castile.

SOURCES: AGS, XXIII, 2–30–81, 13–9–620, 13–9–617; Gracia y Justicia 140, 142; AHN, Consejos 13501, 18514; Universidades 46; AGI, Indiferente 885, 894, 899, 872, *expediente* Sola; *Gazeta de Madrid*, March 3, 1767; Rújula, *Indice*, p. 804; Whitaker, *Huancavelica Mercury Mine*, passim.

Sola y Soto, Tomás de (1655–October 14, 1726)

Sola was born in Loeches in the Bishopric of Toledo. He received a baccalaureate in canon law from the University of Alcalá in 1673, a licentiate in 1677, and a doctorate the following year. He served as a first (*prima*) professor of canon law in Alcalá.

On April 26, 1700, Sola was named an *oidor* of the Audiencia of Galicia. Advanced to the Chancellery of Valladolid on January 10, 1707, he was appointed *fiscal* (*abogado real*) of the *sala de alcaldes de casa y corte* in 1714. He also served as the *abogado general* for the Council of War. On January 27, 1718, he was designated *fiscal* for New Spain on the Council of the Indies to replace Antonio Valcárcel.* Sola received honors of councilor of Castile in 1721. Perhaps because he was "almost blind" he was named to the less onerous post of minister *togado* of the Council on March 28, 1726; he replaced Juan Francisco Santos de San Pedro.*

Sola was married to Gerónima de la Fuente and had six children. Not wealthy for a councilor, in 1723 he secured a grant of 2,000 pesos from the Crown to provide dowries for his daughters Tomasa and Josepha. His son Gerónimo de Sola y Fuente* would later serve on the Council of the Indies.

SOURCES: AGS, XXIII, 13–8–674, 13–8–673; Gracia y Justicia 133, 140; AHN, Consejos 13531, 13495; Universidades, Libro 455 F, Libro 1146F, f. 165; Estado 3149; AGI, Mexico 1951, Indiferente 1293, 872, *expediente* Sola; Fayard, *Miembros*, pp. 352, 421, 425, 433.

Soler Ruiz, Gaspar (September 4, 1715–March 24, 1799)

Soler was born in the *villa* of Elche, Valencia. His parents were Gaspar Soler and Guiomar Ruiz. He studied law at the University of Orihuela beginning in 1732, securing a baccalaureate in 1735 and a licentiate in 1742. The Royal Council admitted him to practice law in 1739.

Soler began his royal service in 1751, but in what position is unknown. In 1771 he held the position of *fiscal* of the general superintendency of mercury. The following year he was described as prudent and of good judgment, well versed in the affairs of the Indies, but hardly known in any tribunal except the Council of the Indies. At that time he was considered to be well off financially. He was the dean of the lawyers' guild in Madrid in 1772. Named governor and superintendent of the mines at Almadén in 1773, he received honors of *oidor* of the House of Trade in 1776 and of the Council of the Indies on September 10, 1779. Appointed to the Council as a minister *togado* to replace Marcos Jimeno* on February 2, 1782, he was later commissioned to return to Almadén as governor. He served in that capacity from June 4, 1786 to June 6, 1789. He was granted honors of the Cámara on November 14, 1798. He served on the Council until his death.

Soler married María de la Cruz Díaz de Arcaya y Lezama, a native of Betoño in the Bishopric of Calahorra, on April 6, 1751. Her parents were Juan Díaz de Arcaya and María de Lezama. The couple had two children, Gaspar María and María. In 1782 María received a license to marry Joaquín Cubells, an official of the House of

Trade in Cádiz. In 1794 Soler was seeking an appointment for his son as a supernumerary clerk (*oficial*) in one of the secretariats of a ministry.

SOURCES: AGS, XXIII, 13–9–616, 24–186–124, 2–82–214; Gracia y Justicia 160; AHN, Hacienda 505, *expediente* 379; AGI, Santa Fe 283, *relación* of 1745, Indiferente 872, *expediente* Soler; Bernard, "Casa," p. 32.

Sopeña y Mioño, Antonio de (1678–May 15, 1748)

Sopeño began his government service in the early to mid–1690s. A clerk (*oficial*) in the Secretariat of State, Sopeño was named secretary of state for the Navy and Indies on January 10, 1724. He served until early 1726. Appointed minister *de capa y espada* of the Council of the Indies on February 12, 1726, he subsequently advanced to the Cámara on October 24, 1741. He was the senior minister (*decano*) of the Council when he died.

SOURCES: AGS, XXIII, 13–9–369, 13–9–358; AGI, Indiferente 872, *expediente* Sopeña; *Gazeta de Madrid*, May 21, 1748; Escudero, *Los orígenes*, I, 64, 65n., 80, 81.

Soto, Manuel de (March 9, 1736–May 12, 1804)

Soto, an only son, was born in Baeza. His parents were Agustín Francisco Soto, a native of the *villa* of Villa-Carrillo and at the time of his death in 1777 the chief clerk (*oficial mayor*) of the royal income (*rentas*) for the province of Jaén, and María Francisca de la Cárcel of Baeza. The family was not well off when Soto was a youth. When his mother died in 1753 she did not even make a will because there was not enough property to worry about. His paternal grandparents were Luis Gallego Pérez de Soto, who was born in the *villa* of Cardela in Granada, and Lucia Gallego de Mora of Villa-Carrillo. His maternal grandparents, both from Baeza, were Juan Antonio de la Cárcel and María de Cozar. By his second wife, María del Arco, Soto's father had a daughter Isabel who was not yet aged twenty-five in 1777 when he died.

Soto attended the University of Granada, competing for and temporarily teaching in chairs there. The Chancellery of Granada admitted him to practice law in 1761.

In 1775 Soto was named *fiscal* of the *real alcaidía del Pardo*, a post that allowed him to expand his contacts in Madrid. Named *alcalde de hijosdalgo* of the Chancellery of Valladolid on January 24, 1789, he advanced to *oidor* of that tribunal on August 21, 1791. An appointment as regent of the Audiencia of Seville followed on July 7, 1794. On November 14, 1798, he was named a minister *togado* of the Council of the Indies to replace Manuel Romero.* He served from February 7, 1799, until his death in Madrid.

Soto married twice. His first wife was Rosalia Montemayor. In 1793 he married Juana de Urquijo y de Soto, the daughter of Francisco Policarpo de Urquijo, a member of the Cámara of Castile, and Ramona de Muga. At his death he left three children named Luis María, Matilde Yrene, and Francisco Policarpo de Soto y Urquijo. Soto became a pensioned *caballero* of the Order of Charles III in 1800.

SOURCES: AHN, Estado (Carlos III), *expediente* 1109, *pruebas* of Manuel de Soto; AGS, XXIII, 13–8–318; AGI, Indiferente 894, 866, 872, *expediente* Soto; Vignau, *Carlos III*, p. 164.

T

Torrero y Marzo, José (?–April 18, 1763)

Torrero was born in Zaragoza. His parents were José Torrero, also of Zaragoza, and Thomasa Marzo Cubel of Daroca, Aragon. His sister María Luisa married Joachín Mateo Díaz. When named a minister *de capa y espada* of the Council of the Indies on December 4, 1746, Torrero held an appointment as Spanish ambassador to Portugal. He assumed his position as councilor on December 19 and served sporadically. Named to the Cámera on September 7, 1762, he died the following year. He left his heirs an entailed estate and stocks in the Havana Company and companies in Zaragoza. His wife Mariana Monserrat survived him. The couple had no children so the entailed property went to Torrero's nephew Joaquín Mateo y Torrero. Torrero's high position in Aragonese society is revealed by the fact that he named the Conde de Aranda one of the executors of his estate.

SOURCES: AGS, XXIII, 13–8–202, 13–8–171; AGI, Indiferente 898, 899, 900; AHPM, Protocolo, 17012; Bernard, *Secrétariat*, p. 219.

Torres y Morales, Rodrígo (April 7, 1687, baptism–December 15, 1755)

Torres was born in Guadalajara, Archdiocese of Toledo, to Rodrígo de Torres y Mesía, a native of Guadalajara, knight of Calatrava and *señor* of *los términos* of Albatajar Mejorada, la Vieja, and El Canalizo, and Isabel María Morales y Zúpide of Madrid, *señora* of the *villas* of Romanones and Valdemorales. His paternal grandparents were Antonio Torres of Guadalajara and his second wife Juana Mesía of Hita. His maternal grandparents were Manuel Morales Calderón of the *villa* of Utande and Isabel Zúpide of Rome. He had two older brothers, José and Antonio.

Torres began his career on April 11, 1705, probably entering the navy at that time. By 1745 he was a lieutenant general in the navy. On March 14 of that year he was named a minister *de capa y espada* and given a place on the Cámara of the Indies. He served from March 24, 1745, until his death.

Torres became a *caballero* of the Order of San Juan in 1708 and received the title Marqués de Matallana de Val Madrigal in 1745. He married Isabel Cayetana Ruiz de Rivera, a Mexican, in Chiclana in 1735. Her parents were Pedro Ruiz de Castañeda y Pimentel, also from Mexico, and María de Rivera Benavente of Guadalajara, New Spain. Their second son, Miguel, born in Segovia in 1738, was a knight of the Order of Calatrava.

SOURCES: AHN, Ordenes Militares (Calatrava), *expediente* 2622, *pruebas* of Miguel de Torres Ruiz; (San Juan), *expediente* 23,612, *pruebas* of Rodrigo Torres Morales; AGS, XXIII, 13–8–602, 13–8–603; AGI, Indiferente 894, 898; *Gazeta de Madrid*, December 30, 1755; Larios, *Nobiliario*, V, 75.

Trespalacios y Escandón, Domingo de (August 12, 1706, baptism–February 5, 1777)

Trespalacios was born in the *lugar* of Allés, Oviedo, to Pedro de Trespalacios and Juliana Escandón, both of Allés. His paternal grandparents were Pedro de Trespalacios and María Díaz de Carabes, also from Allés. His maternal grandparents were Pedro de Escandón y Mier of Allés and María de la Torre from the *lugar* of Mier in the valley of Peñamellera. Trespalacios had four siblings: Francisco; María, who married Diego Guerra de Mier; Toribio; and María Ana, who married Antonio Basilio de Mier Villar. His uncle Luis Escandón was a *relator* of the Council of the Indies.

Trespalacios claimed twelve years of study at the University of Salamanca, where he gained the baccalaureate in canon law in 1729. He was a member of the Trilingual Academy at Salamanca and held minor orders in the Church. After a practicum with Andrés Vásquez, the Royal Council licensed him as an attorney.

Named *oidor* of the Audiencia of Santa Fe on March 14, 1738, Trespalacios was appointed *oidor* of the Audiencia of Guatemala the following June 8 but never served in that post either. Still in Spain when named *oidor* of the Audiencia of Mexico on August 2, 1741, he assumed this more desirable position on August 7, 1742, and served until March 10, 1764. Promoted to the Council of the Indies as a *ministro togado* by a royal order of December 22, 1762, he left Veracruz on April 25, 1764, and assumed the post on November 5, 1764. The trip cost 9,000 pesos. Advanced to the Cámara on April 14, 1767, he served until his death. From 1748 until his departure for Spain, Trespalacios was judge for the appointment tax (*media anata*) and judge superintendent for the revenues (*propios y rentas*) of Mexico City. From 1749 to 1764 he was protector and judge for the Shrine of Guadalupe and did an outstanding job. While serving as superintendent of the drainage project in the Valley of Mexico in 1754, he wrote a detailed history of the project from its beginning and helped to persuade the king to continue financial support for the operation.

Trespalacios received a license to marry a native of the audiencia district in 1741 and in 1757 married María Cecilia Rodríguez de Albuerne, daughter of Juan Rodríguez Gómez de Albuerne, an oidor of the Audiencia of Mexico, and Luisa Pérez de Tagle. They had a daughter, María Manuela, born on January 19, 1761, and a son, José Antonio. After his wife's death, Trespalacios obtained a license in 1769 to marry Francisca Antonia de Escandón y Enríquez. Trespalacios became a knight of Santiago in 1743.

SOURCES: AGI, Mexico 385, *relacíon* of 1734; Indiferente 866, 894, 872, 884, 901B; AGS, 2–31–182, 2–31–187, 2–33–44, 13–9–466, 13–9–465; AHN, Ordenes Militares (Santiago), *expediente* 8222, *pruebas* of Domingo Trespalacios y Escandón; *Gazeta de Madrid*, February 11, 1777; *Gazetas de México*, III, 261; Cooper, *Disease*, pp. 11–12; Martínez Cosío, *Caballeros*, p. 185; López Sarrelangue, *Una villa mexicana*, pp. 39, 40, 62, 108, 170.

U

Ubilla y Medina, Antonio Cristóbal de (November 28, 1643–October 16, 1726)

Ubilla was born in Madrid. His parents were Antonio de Ubilla, a native of Fuenterravia, Guipúzcoa and chief clerk (*oficial mayor*) of the Secretariat of State for Italian Affairs, and Antonia de Medina y Vega of Madrid.

Ubilla began his government service in 1661. Prior to joining the Council of the Indies, he was secretary of the Council of the *Cruzada*, of the Council of Orders, and of the Council of Milan. From July 13, 1695 to 1698 he was secretary for Peruvian affairs of the Council of the Indies. Named secretary of state for Italian affairs on June 1, 1698, he became secretary of state and *del Despacho* later in the year. On January 25, 1705, he was named a minister *de capa y espada* of the Council and War Committee (*Junta de Guerra*) of the Indies. Although suspended in 1706, he survived the changes in the Council during and immediately after the War of the Spanish Succession and was on the Council as reorganized on January 20, 1717. When the Cámara was reestablished on December 22, 1721, he was one of the two ministers *de capa y espada* named to serve on it.

Ubilla married three times. His first wife was Jerónima Calvo. The second wife was Ana María de Sobremonte. His third wife and widow was Ana María de Fernández de Mesa y Sousa. She maintained that her husband left her in poverty when he died.

In 1704 Ubilla published *Sucesión de D. Felipe V en la corona de España y diario de sus viajes*. He was a knight of Santiago and the first Marqués de Rivas.

SOURCES: AGS, XXIII, 13–9–393; AHN, Libro de Plazas 732; Alvarez y Baena, *Hijos de Madrid*, I, 174–76; Bernard, *Secrétariat*, p. 215; Escudero, *Los secretarios*, III, 724.

Urbina, Cayetano de (1762–January 28, 1834)

Urbina was born in the city of Antequera, Málaga. His parents were Cayetano Urbina, a native of Antequera and the Conde de Carbajal, and María de los Remedios Urbina. Urbina served as treasurer of the army in Catalonia in 1793. He had been intendant of Guadalajara since at least 1796 and was an intendant of the army in Valencia from at least 1802 and when named a minister *de capa y espada* of the Council of the Indies on October 27, 1807. On August 22, 1809, the Junta General granted him permission to go to Seville. Referred to as a former minister on April 23, 1814, he was later reinstated. He was retired on November 22, 1824.

In 1792 Urbina married María Manuela Daoiz y Niderist, a native of Barcelona and the daughter of field marshal (*mariscal de campo*) and Knight of Santiago Isidoro de Daoiz of Madrid and Luisa Teresa de Niderist of Palma, Mallorca. Prior to wedding, María served as a lady-in-waiting to Queen María Luisa. Their son Felipe, who was born in Madrid in 1797, was admitted to practice law by the Chancellery of Granada in 1820. The couple had six other children by 1809: María Luisa, Cayetano María, José Salvador, Manuel María, Juan Baptista, and María del Carmen.

SOURCES: AGS, XXIII, 13–9–67; AGI, Indiferente 825, 873, *expediente* Urbina; AHN, Estado 29G, *expediente* 249; Hacienda 528, *expediente* 22; ACRG, *cabina* 321, *legajo* 4301, *pieza* 4.

Urízar y Bolívar, José Antonio de (October 6, 1738–?)

Urízar was born in the *anteiglesia* of Castillo y Elexabeitia in the Bishopric of Calahorra, Vizcaya. He was the only son of Manuel de Urízar y Belaustegui of the *anteiglesia* of Galdácano and María Antonio de Bolívar y Avendaño of the *villa* of Villaro. His paternal grandparents, both from Galdácano, were Juan de Urízar y Belaustegui and Josefa de Belaustegui y Olaeche. His maternal grandparents were Pedro de Bolívar y Garay, a native of Villaro who was a notary (*escribano*) there, and María de Avendaño y Sarria, also from Villaro. His only sister, María Josefa, married Francisco Antonio de Arguinzoniz.

Educated at the University of Oñate, where he began to study law in 1756, Urízar incorporated his degrees from there at the University of Valladolid in 1758. The Royal Council licensed him as an attorney in 1762.

On June 20, 1766, the king named Urízar legal adviser (*teniente asesor*) and judge advocate (*auditor de guerra*) for the governor and captain general of Venezuela, a position he served until promoted to *oidor* of Santo Domingo on May 11, 1772. He moved to the Audiencia of Mexico when designated *alcalde del crimen* there on June 10, 1778. Three years later Urízar was elevated to the civil chamber with an appointment of September 23. He served as *oidor* until named regent of the Audiencia of Santo Domingo on November 17, 1787. In 1781 he successfully handled an Indian uprising in Izucar. Given honors of a minister of the Council of the Indies on August 31, 1792, on April 21, 1795 Urízar was elevated to the status of a *ministro togado* of that tribunal but ordered to continue as regent for four years before assuming his new post. He entered the Council in 1799 and was still serving in

1808. He was no longer listed as a member in September 1809. While on the Council he wrote a discourse on modifying slavery.

Urízar received a license to marry Rosa de Aristigueta, daughter of Miguel de Aristigueta, a knight of Santiago, and Josefa María Blanco, citizens of Caracas, in 1773. He was admitted to the Order of Charles III in 1792.

SOURCES: AGI, Santo Domingo 922; Quito 231; Indiferente 873, 887; AGS, 2–50–91, 2–56–57, 2–62–97, 2–65–55, 2–76–178, 13–8–35; AHN, Estado (Carlos III), *expediente* 634, *pruebas* of Josef Antonio de Urízar; AHPUV, Libro 314, 315; Calderón Quijano, *Los virreyes*, II, 168–74.

Urriza, Juan Ignacio de (?–December 14, 1792)

Urriza was born in Santisteban, Navarre. His father was Juan Thomas Urriza. He had a brother named Norberto who became his sole heir in 1792. Urriza was serving as *comisario ordenador de marina* and administrator of taxes (*rentas generales*) and the postal service of Havana when named a pensioned *caballero* of the Order of Charles III in 1772. He participated in the expedition against Mobile and Pensacola that were part of the Spanish effort to recapture Florida from the British. In Cuba, he led a vigorous campaign against contraband trade. His accomplishments as intendant of the army and exchequer were recognized on September 29, 1781, when he was given honors of minister *de capa y espada* on the Council of the Indies. A decade later, on December 18, 1791, he was named a supernumerary minister *de capa y espada*. He entered the position on January 2, 1792, and served until his death.

SOURCES: AGS, XXIII, 2–65–57, 13–8–56; AGI, Indiferente 894, 866, 873, *expediente* Urriza; Vignau, *Carlos III*, p. 172; Lewis, "Anglo-American entrepreneurs," p. 120.

Uruñuela Aransay, Juan Antonio (August 27, 1729–April 7, 1793)

Uruñuela was born in the *villa* of Santurde, Burgos. His parents were Lucas Felipe de Uruñuela Gómez and María Aransay Sancho, both of Santurde. His mother died in a tragic fire on January 3, 1748, in which a younger brother and sister of Juan Antonio's also perished. His paternal grandparents were Lucas de Uruñuela y Cañas and Ana Gómez, both from Santurdejo. His maternal grandparents were Juan de Aransay Larrea and María de Sancho Ortega. His younger brother Enrique, an administrator of royal revenues (*rentas*) in Toledo, married Alfonsa María Dávalos. Their son Apolinar was a page to the king and subsequently a *caballero* of Carlos III.

Educated at the Universities of Siguenza and Salamanca in the 1750s and 1760s, Uruñuela belonged to the *colegio mayor* of Oviedo at Salamanca and received the licentiate from the University of Avila. He competed for chairs in canon law at Salamanca and was rector of his college.

The king named Uruñuela a supernumerary *oidor* of the Audiencia of Manila on December 4, 1766, and he arrived there with 3,000 pesos and other property that he had friars declare was for missions in China to avoid paying duties. Simón de

Anda accused him of being in league with Manuel Galván in the aftermath of the controversy engendered by the expulsion of the Jesuits. Promoted to *alcalde del crimen* of the Audiencia of Mexico on February 27, 1777, Uruñuela advanced to the civil chamber on June 10, 1778 and was named regent of the Audiencia of Guatemala on June 9, 1782. While regent he was denounced for possessing prohibited books. At the end of that decade, on November 5, 1789, Uruñuela was designated *fiscal* for New Spain in the Council of the Indies to replace Rivera.* He held the post from February 5, 1791, until his death in Madrid. He was admitted to the Order of Charles III in 1789.

Uruñuela never married.

SOURCES: AGI, Indiferente 865, 885, 894, 873; AGS, 2–50–214, 2–61–17, 2–62–96, 2–66–58, 24–188–773; AHN, Estado (Carlos III), *expediente* 1939, *pruebas* of Apolinar Uruñuela; *expediente* 309, *pruebas* of Juan Antonio de Uruñuela; *Gazeta de Madrid*, no. 41, May 21, 1793; Nogaledo Alvárez, "El colegio menor," p. 120; Blair and Robertson, *Islands*, L, 301; Pérez-Marchand, *Dos etapas*, pp. 101, 166, 168.

V

Vadillo Estrada y Velasco, Manuel de (July 13, 1659–June 25, 1729)

Vadillo was born in Ciella, Valle de Mena, Santander. His parents were Juan de Vadillo Estrada, a native of the *lugar* of Quincoces in the Archbishopric of Burgos, and María Feliberta de Velasco. His paternal grandparents were Juan de Vadillo of Quincoces and María de Ayala of the *lugar* of Villota, Burgos. His maternal grandparents were Mauricio de Velasco of Ciella and María Ybañez de Ybarguen of the *lugar* of Valle, Burgos. When Vadillo was a young boy he was taken to Madrid by his relative Pedro Fernández del Campo.

Vadillo began his royal service in 1673. He started at the lowest-ranked desk in the Secretariat of the *Despacho Universal* and progressed to the first desk in addition to serving in the office of Italian affairs in the Secretariat of State. Subsequently, he served in the Secretariats of the Council of Orders, the Cámara of Castile, the Council of Italy, and *Real Patronato*. On October 6, 1706, he was named secretary of state *en gobierno*. On April 30, 1714, he advanced to secretary of the *Despacho Universal de lo Político*. Appointed secretary of state for grace and justice on November 30, 1714, he served until appointed a minister *de capa y espada* on January 28, 1717. Vadillo entered the Council on February 11, 1717 and served until his death.

A knight of Santiago in 1685, Vadillo was a *comendador* of Pozuela for the Order. He died leaving his widow Teresa Gorzey y Atayde with very little income.

SOURCES: AGS, XXIII, 13–8–471; Secretaría y Superintendencia de Hacienda, *legajo* 56; AGI, Indiferente 844; AHN Estado 6380(1), Ordenes Militares (Santiago), *expediente* 8395, *pruebas* of Manuel Vadillo; Escudero, *Los secretarios*, III, 664–66, 668–69, 729.

Valcárcel Dato, Juan de (?–November 25, 1730)

Valcárcel was born in Murcia. He began his career as an *oidor* of the Audiencia of Seville in 1695. Advanced to the Chancellery of Valladolid in 1704 as an *oidor*, he was subsequently sent to the short-lived Chancellery of Valencia on June 5, 1714, as president and then became the first regent when the court was changed to an audiencia in 1716. On December 26, 1718, Valcárcel was moved to Aragon as regent of the audiencia located in Zaragoza. Named *fiscal* of the Council of the Indies for Peru to replace Juan Cavallero y Soto* on October 8, 1720, he entered the post on October 12, 1720. Almost immediately, however, he was appointed, on April 21, 1721, president of the Chancellery of Valladolid. Valcárcel's final advancement came on December 4, 1724, when he was named a minister *togado* of the Council of Castile. He served the post until his death.

Valcárcel married María Theresa Gamez y Melgarejo in 1691. Her parents were Dr. D. Andrés Gamez and Francisca Melgarejo. She brought a dowry of 191,859 *reales de vellón*. He, in turn, provided *arras* of 4,000 *ducados de vellón*. Before her death in 1710, María Theresa bore six children: Pedro, Andrés, Diego, Joseph, Juan Joseph, and Francisca. Both Juan Joseph and Francisca entered religious orders. Andrés followed his father in a career on the courts and ultimately reached the Council of Castile. In 1714 Juan remarried María Theresa Ladrón de Guevara. Juan Valcárcel was a rich man at his death. His estate was worth almost nine hundred thousand *reales de vellón*. He owned property in Madrid, Murcia, and the *villa* of Roa.

SOURCES: AGS, XXIII, 24–171–132, 13–8–245; Gracia y Justicia 136, 138; AHN, Consejos 13531, 13536, 13501, 18213; Estado 6380(2); AGI, Indiferente 865; AHPM, Protocolo 16596; Fayard, *Miembros*, p. 213n; Tejera, *Biblioteca del murciano*, p. 811.

Valcárcel y Formento, Antonio Jacinto (February 28, 1663, baptism–February 2, 1737)

Valcárcel, a native of Madrid, was the son of Francisco Valcárcel y Velásquez, a native of Zamora, knight of Santiago and councilor of Castile, and Isabel Formento of Valladolid. His paternal grandparents were Lorenzo de Valcárcel, a native of Xerez de los Caballeros, Extremadura, and an *alcalde del crimen* of the Chancellery of Granada, and Luisa Velázquez of Medina de Rioseco. His maternal grandparents were Clemente Formento, a native of the Piedmont in the Duchy of Savoy who became a *vecino* and alderman (*regidor*) in Valladolid, and Angela de Renolis of Madrid. Valcárcel's brothers Francisco, Pedro, and Joseph Ignacio were knights of Santiago. Joseph followed a career in the Spanish courts and retired as an *oidor* of the Chancellery of Valladolid in 1680. His brother Lorenzo was a canon in the Cathedral of Granada. His sister Luisa entered a convent in Valladolid.

Valcárcel studied at the University of Salamanca, receiving a baccalaureate in canon law in 1684. The following year he entered the *colegio mayor* of Cuenca. While at Salamanca, he competed for academic chairs.

Valcárcel received his first appointment as an *oidor* of the Chancellery of Granada in 1695. Moved to Seville as regent of the court there in 1709, he was named a minister *togado* of the Council of the Indies on February 19, 1714. Subsequently appointed *fiscal* for New Spain on the Council on August 5, 1715, he was reappointed a minister *togado* on February 8, 1718. A final promotion as minister *togado* of the Council of Castile came on May 7, 1725.

A knight of Calatrava, Valcárcel married María Ignacia de Vaquerizo Pantoja y Carrión, a lady-in-waiting to Queen María. She was the daughter of Diego Ignacio Vaquerizo y Pantoja, a knight of Santiago and councilor of Castile, and Juliana de Carrión, a lady-in-waiting to Queen Mariana of Austria. After his first wife's death, Valcárcel married Isabel Francisca Teruel y Cepeda. The couple had three children. Valcárcel received 2,000 pesos from the Mexican account for the sale of offices in 1723 to provide a dowry for his daughter Rosa de San Joseph y Valcárcel. His son Domingo Valcárcel y Vaquerizo, a knight of Calatrava, served for many years on the Audiencia of Mexico and refused an informal offer of a post on the Council of the Indies. His son Vicente Valcárcel y Vaquerizo, Marqués de Pejas, died as a councilor of Castile.

SOURCES: AGS, XXIII, 13–9–380, 13–8–467; Gracia y Justicia 138; AHN, Estado 6380(2); Consejos 13386, *títulos* of 1694; Ordenes Militares (Santiago), *expediente* 8399, *pruebas* of Francisco Valcárcel y Formento; (Calatrava), *expediente* 1678, *pruebas* of Antonio Jacinto de Valcárcel y Velázquez; AGI, Indiferente 169, relación of Antonio Valcárcel Altamirano; 872, *expediente* Sola; 873, *expediente* Valcárcel, 892; Mexico 1951; Burkholder and Chandler, *Biographical Dictionary*, pp. 339–40; Alvarez y Baena, *Hijos de Madrid*, I, 176–77; Ballesteros Robles, *Diccionario*, p. 637.

Valdivieso, José de (Variant: Ruiz de Valdivieso) (c. 1672?–1739)

Valdivieso received a baccalaureate in canon law from the University of Salamanca in 1692. Following a practicum, he was admitted to practice law by the Royal Council in 1697.

Named an assistant to the civil *fiscal* (*agente fiscal*) of the Council of Castile in 1706, he was named *fiscal* of the Audiencia of the Canary Islands on March 26, 1710, but never served. From 1711 to 1715 Valdivieso was *alcalde mayor* of Cádiz. Named an *oidor* of the House of Trade on November 9, 1717, he replaced Gonzalo Remírez de Baquedano* as a minister *togado* of the Council of the Indies with an appointment of March 21, 1732. He served until January 11, 1739, but from 1737 had permission to attend at his pleasure as a result of health problems.

SOURCES: AGS, XXIII, 13–8–228; Gracia y Justicia 141; AGI, Indiferente 824, 866, 885; Bernard, "Casa," p. 281; Bernard, *Secrétariat*, p. 217.

Valencia y Sáenz del Pontón, Francisco de (November 25, 1742–July 17, 1806)

Valencia, a second son, was born into a prominent and powerful family in Popayán, present Colombia. His father, Pedro Agustín Valencia, also a native of Popayán, was the treasurer of the mint in Popayán. His mother was Jerónima Rosa Sáenz del

Pontón, a native of Bogotá. Francisco's paternal grandparents were Pedro Valencia of Málaga and Josefa Fernández del Castillo of Popayán. His maternal grandparents were Martín Carlos Sáenz del Pontón, a native of Santa Cruz de Mompós, secretary of the Cámara of the Audiencia of New Granada and superintendent of the province of Chocó, and María Luisa de Hurtado of Popayán. Francisco's brother Joaquín was an honorary member of the Council of the Exchequer (*Hacienda*) and superintendent of the mint in Popayán. Two other brothers were Pedro, a naval commander, and Tomás, a militia colonel in Popayán. His parents had seven children at home in 1787.

Valencia migrated to Spain as a young man. There he established a very important family relationship through his marriage to a daughter of a councilor of Castile. In late 1787, he was the second clerk (*oficial segundo*) of the Secretariat of State and Ministry of War and Finance for the Indies. Named director of the treasury and commissary of the Council of the Indies on June 29, 1790, with honors of the Council, he was advanced on December 23, 1794 to the position of chief accountant (*contador general*) of the Council and a position as minister *de capa y espada*. He entered the post on February 14, 1795, and served until his death.

On January 3, 1767, Valencia married María Josefa Codallos y Bernaldo de Palacio, a native of Seville. María was the daughter of Felipe Codallos y Rabala, a councilor of Castile, and *madrileña* Juliana Bernaldo de Palacio y Salinas. The couple had at least five daughters, Juana, Marcela, María Josepha, María Domingo, and Salvadora Bernardina, and a son, Pedro Felipe. The son succeeded his father in the family title and combined a military career with service in the Department of State. At one time he was the *chargé d'affairs* for the Spanish Embassy in Berlin.

Valencia was named a pensioned *caballero* of the Order of Charles III in 1787. On October 20, 1789 he was granted the title Conde de Casa Valencia.

SOURCES: AGI, Indiferente 875, 887, 894; AHN, Estado (Carlos III), *expediente* 263, *pruebas* of Francisco de Valencia; Hacienda 528, *expediente* 13; Bernard, *Secrétariat*, p. 224; Cadenas, *Caballeros*, pp. 91–92; Vignau, *Carlos III*, p. 175; Atienza, *Nobiliario*, p. 1429; Kuethe, *Military Reform*, pp. 71, 158; Lohmann Villena, *Americanos*, II, 441–43.

Valenzuela y Aguilar, Pedro Jacinto de (June 6, 1738, baptism–September 18, 1809)

Valenzuela was born in the *villa* of Martos, Jaén, Granada, to Manuel Silvestre de Valenzuela and Barbara de Aguilar. He studied philosophy at the Mercedarian Convent in Jaén, and was educated at the university there. After he had spent four years in the law office of Juan Francisco Perceval y Marín in Granada, the Chancellery of Granada licensed him to practice law in 1763. He was incorporated by the Royal Council in 1768.

Martos elected Valenzuela in 1767 to represent its interests, and he proceeded to the Chancellery of Granada to vent a variety of local concerns. In addition, he served as an attorney for the Duque de Albuquerque and the Duque de la Roca. Named legal adviser (*asesor general*) to the viceroy of New Spain on November 10, 1784, he occupied the post until July 13, 1789, when, already bedecked with honors of *alcalde del crimen* of the Audiencia of Mexico (conferred in 1788) to strengthen his prestige and authority, he was dispatched on commission to serve as interim *fiscal* of the Audiencia of Santo Domingo. With the completion of that assignment, Valenzuela was named *alcalde del crimen* of the Audiencia of Mexico on April 16, 1791, a post he assumed on July 18 of that year. Despite the judicial appointment, Valenzuela served on commission as temporary legal adviser (*asesor general*) to Viceroy Marqués de Branciforte with an appointment of November 19, 1795, and, again to bolster his position and to compensate him for his willingness to serve, he was given honors of the Council of the Indies at the same time. Valenzuela was instrumental in helping to bring about the use and acceptance of inoculation in Mexico City during the epidemic of 1797. His career was capped by an appointment to a proprietary position as supernumerary *ministro togado* of the Council of the Indies on November 27, 1798. He replaced Soler* in a regular position. Although suffering from ill health in early 1805, and allowed to take a leave of absence, he retained his post. He served on the Council until retired with two-thirds salary on March 7, 1806. He died in his natal village.

SOURCES: AGS, 2–68–208, 2–72–176, 2–73–183, 2–75–75, 2–79–259, 2–79–260, 24–188–43, 13–9–276; AGI, Quito 231, *relación* of 1768; Indiferente 866, 886, 887, 825, 1519, 873 *expediente* Valenzuela; AHN, Hacienda 528, *expediente* 14; ARCG, *cabina* 321, *legajo* 4302, *pieza* 1; *Gazeta de Mexico* IV, No. 38, July 26, 1791, p. 355; Beristain, *Biblioteca*, V, 83; Cooper, *Disease*, pp. 113–16.

Valiente y Bravo, José de Pablo (1740–October 28, 1817)

Valiente was born in Cumbres-Mayores in the province of Seville and was educated at the University of Seville, where he received the baccalaureate, licentiate, and doctorate of civil law. He was professor of civil law at the University of Seville from 1772 to 1778. The Audiencia of Seville licensed Valiente as a lawyer in 1773, and he joined the College of Attorneys in Seville later in the year. From 1773 to 1779 he was an attorney in Seville. The Royal Council incorporated him in 1779, and he subsequently joined the College of Attorneys at court and practiced law.

A legal opinion Valiente wrote caught the attention of José de Gálvez* and as a result Charles III named the attorney *oidor* of the Audiencia of Guatemala on July 14, 1782, a post he may not have assumed, and *fiscal del crimen* of the Audiencia of Mexico on November 10, 1784. Valiente assumed his post in Mexico on September 5, 1785, but was soon sent to Cuba as an interim intendant, a post he occupied from May 6, 1787 to November 6, 1788. He was sent back to Cuba as intendant with an appointment of November 3, 1791. On January 21, 1792, he received honors of the Council of the Indies. As intendant, a post he assumed on February 16, 1792, Valiente reportedly was "deliberately lax" in enforcing commercial statutes as he supported free trade for America. Remaining in Cuba until named a supernumerary *ministro togado* on March 8, 1799, he reached Cádiz in 1800 aboard the *Delfín*. Soon after his arrival an epidemic of yellow fever swept the port, and the populace considered him responsible. Held in Seville for several years while the origin of the epidemic was investigated, on June 19, 1804, he was ordered to assume his post on the Council. He served on the Council, except for the interval when the Cortes disbanded it, until his death.

A representative to the Cortes for Seville, he was an ultraconservative member of the Constitutional Commission and highly unpopular with the citizens of Cádiz, both for his political views and his Sevillean origins and because of the yellow fever episode in 1800. The mob's wrath forced him to flee to a warship in the bay for safety. Valiente opposed the "attacks" made in the Cortes on the Crown and Church. As a member of the Council of the Indies in 1809, he criticized the abolition of the Ministry of the Indies in 1787, claiming that subsequently its good work in "taming" colonial elites and bureaucrats had been undone.

Valiente married Tomasa de Hierro. In 1787 she and the children were transported to Havana at royal expense to join Valiente. She went to Spain from Havana in 1798. After Tomasa's death, Valiente married Mariana de León, the daughter of Antonio Manuel León and María Teresa Berjano. In 1814 Valiente was inducted into the Order of Isabel the Catholic.

SOURCES: AGI, Ultramar 400; Santa Fe 548; AGS, 2–66–63, 2–68–203, 13–8–51, 13–9–219; AHN, Cartas de Osuna, 480–82 (*relación*); Trelles, *Bibliografía*, I, 148; Lovett, *Napoleon*, p. 449; Shafer, *Economic Societies*, pp. 182n., 184, 184n., 264n.; Solís, *Cádiz*, pp. 240–241; Alamán, *Historia*, II, 60; Trelles y Govín, *Ensayo*, p. 90; Barbier, "Culmination," pp. 51–52; *Diario curioso*, March 17, 1787 (courtesy of Linda Arnold).

Varas y Valdés, Francisco de (1675–May 29, 1753)

Varas was born in Seville and educated at its university. An attorney of the Audiencia of Seville, on March 20, 1711, he received a *futura* as a judge (*juez letrado*) of the House of Trade in Cádiz, where he served until removed on May 8, 1717. Restored the following January 1, he advanced to president of the body and intendant of the army of Andalusia on August 25, 1721. In 1725 he was returned to his previous post of judge. Later in the year, on July 7, he returned to the presidency and intendancy until replaced on February 27, 1726. Once more, on October 27, 1741, he became president and intendant, serving until 1751 when he gave up the position. He was named to the Council of the Indies in 1731 but never served. After the death of Valdivieso* in 1739, it was rumored he had been appointed but no official documentation was presented in the Ministry of Grace and Justice. Reportedly as well, he was named on February 24, 1739 to replace Contreras,* but the decree was not published. Yet on April 13, 1742, he was ordered to assume his position as soon as his replacement arrived in Cádiz to serve as president of the House of Trade. His name does not appear in the existing attendance records of the Council, however, and he died in Cádiz. Varas held the rank of lieutenant general of the Royal Army.

SOURCES: AGI, Indiferente 844, 898, 899, 1980, 870; AGS, Gracia y Justicia 814; AUSE, Libro 484; Bernard, "Casa," pp. 25, 29; *Gazeta de Madrid*, July 24, 1753.

Vázquez de Agüero, Juan (1688–March 1, 1766)

Vázquez was born in Madrid. His parents were Pedro Vázquez de la Vega and Luisa María de Agüero. He attended the University of Alcalá, but was not a member of its *colegio mayor*. In 1711 the Royal Council admitted him to practice law.

In 1714 Vázquez was sent to Honduras and Caracas on commission. Subsequently appointed an *alcalde del crimen* of the short-lived Audiencia of Sardinia on August 6, 1718, he was briefly to become an *oidor* there. On July 17, 1720 he was named an *alcalde del crimen* of the Chancellery of Granada as one of the former judges in Sardinia to be placed in Spanish tribunals. An appointment as an *alcalde de casa y corte* came in September 1732 along with a commission to visit Buenos Aires and the provinces of the Río de la Plata to investigate defrauding of the royal treasury. His experience was recognized with an appointment of March 19, 1744, as a minister *togado* of the Council of the Indies to replace Martín de Lardizábal.* Vázquez served from March 26, 1744, until his death.

Vázquez married Francisca Maldonado, but had no succession.

SOURCES: AGS, XXIII, 13–8–203; Gracia y Justicia, 138, 141 with *relación* of 1725, 148; AHN, Consejos 13643; AGI, Indiferente 898, 894, 873, *expediente* Vázquez de Agüero; Ballesteros Robles, *Diccionario*, p. 652.

Vega y Guerra Sánchez y Avendaño, Francisco Xavier de la (February 6, 1739–May 16, 1818)

Vega was born in the *villa* of Amusco in the Bishopric of Palencia. His parents were Francisco de la Vega, a city alderman of Amusco, and Mariana Guerra, also from Amusco. His paternal grandparents were Marcos de la Vega of Fuente Andrino, a city alderman of Amusco, and Francisca Sánchez of Lantadilla. His maternal grandparents were Manuel Guerra of Palencia and María Abendaño of the *lugar* of Villamayor de Triviño. Francisco Xavier had five siblings. Matías, who was probably his older brother, was in Panama in 1762 and Cádiz in 1792. Tomás was a cleric. His three sisters were Jacinta, Ignacia, and Sabina.

Vega started his career in 1760 as a clerk (*oficial tercera*) of the notarial office (*escribanía*) of the Cámara of the Indies. In 1767 he advanced as *oficial escribiente* of the archives for the Ministry of the Indies. Nine years later he became the archivist. In 1782 he held the rank of sixth clerk (*oficial sexto*) in the ministry. He subsequently served desks in the Exchequer and War offices. On October 7, 1794, he became the chief clerk (*oficial mayor primero*) of the Secretariat of the Minister of the Exchequer for the Indies. Named a minister *de capa y espada* on January 23, 1803, he remained on the Council of the Indies until his retirement with full salary on April 12, 1818. He probably died a bachelor.

Vega became a pensioned *caballero* of the Order of Charles III in 1792.

SOURCES: AGS, XXIII, 13–9–120; AGI, Indiferente 888, 873, *expediente* Vega; AHN, Estado (Carlos III), *expediente* 647, *pruebas* of Francisco Xavier de la Vega.

Verdes Montenegro y Castro Baamonde, Fernando (April 23, 1682, baptism–August 11, 1741)

Verdes Montenegro was born in the parish of San Juan de Sistallo, Mondoñedo, Galicia. His parents were Francisco Verdes Montenegro and Antonia de Castro Baamonde, both from the Bishopric of Mondoñedo. His paternal grandparents were Bartolomé de Verdes of the parish of Santa María de Villapene and Juana Sanjurjo Montenegro from the *lugar* of Villamartín in the Archbishopric of Santiago de Compostela. His maternal grandparents were Pedro de Castro y Basanta and Ynés Tenrreiro de Lago y Baamonde, both of the Bishopric of Mondoñedo. Verdes had a number of brothers, at least one of whom, Francisco, was older. His brother Miguel was a *letrado* who concluded his career as the senior minister on the Council of Orders.

As a young man Verdes went to Madrid as a retainer of the Conde de Benavente, whom his brother Diego would serve as an accountant. In 1716 he was *tesorero de la guerra* in Valencia. The following year he was an accountant (*contador*) in the chief accounting office (*contaduría mayor*) in Madrid. A knight of Calatrava from 1717, he became the chief treasurer in 1721 and then, on January 14, 1724, secretary of state for the exchequer and the superintendant general of the tax office (*rentas generales*). He was removed from the post of secretary and superintendant general in September 1724 when four million escudos under his control were allegedly missing and exiled to Ciudad Real. In 1728 he was declared innocent of the charges that had led to his removal, given half of his former salary, and, on March 8, named minister *de capa y espada*, a post he held from March 10, 1728, until his death. In 1735 he was also appointed superintendent of the *sisas* of Madrid. Briefly in 1740 and until February 25, 1741, he was again secretary of state for the exchequer. By the latter date his health was shattered.

Verdes married Jacinta Gayoso. Their son José, born in Madrid in 1732, served as a page at court from age eight to seventeen. When still a youth he became a knight of Santiago. At the insistence of his uncle Miguel and against his own preference, he pursued the study of law and was admitted to the *colegio mayor* of Oviedo at the University of Salamanca. Although after many years at Salamanca he was named an *alcalde de hijosdalgo* of the Chancellery of Valladolid and subsequently promoted to *oidor*, his heart was with the court. In 1785 he resigned his post on the Chancellery and accepted an appointment as *mayordomo de la semana*, which he served until his death nearly twenty years later.

SOURCES: AGI, Indiferente 825; AGS, XXIII, 13–9–593; Gracia y Justicia 158, 162, 846, 914; AHN, Estado 2974, 6380 (1); Ordenes Militares (Calatrava), *expediente* 2783, *pruebas* of Fernando Montenegro y Castro; Vignau, *Calatrava*, p. 177; Vignau, *Santiago*, p. 371; Escudero, *Los secretarios*, III, 737; Escudero, *Los orígenes*, I, 107–8.

Viana y Zavala, Francisco Leandro de (March 9, 1730–August 3, 1804)

Viana, a younger son, was born in Lagrán, Alava, to Francisco de Viana and Magdalena Sáenz de Villaverde. His paternal grandparents were José de Viana and

Bartola Pérez, both from Lagrán. Also from there were his maternal grandparents, Francisco Sáenz de Villaverde and Francisca Martínez. His sister María Antonia Viana married Andrés de Aguirre and bore Guillermo Aguirre y Viana, an audiencia minister in Mexico. His brother Felipe followed a career in the Royal Guards. Andrés became a naval captain. Both were knights of Calatrava. Three other brothers, José Francisco, Diego, and Juan Antonio, were clerics.

Viana studied arts in the College of San Buenaventura in Santa Domingo de la Calzada. He received the baccalaureate in civil law from the University of Hirache in 1748 and incorporated it at the University of Valladolid in 1749 and later at Salamanca. From November 1749 to June 1752 he studied law with Baltasar de Lorenzana, an attorney in Valladolid. Entering the *colegio mayor* of San Bartolomé in 1752, he became its rector and received the licentiate in 1755. While at Salamanca he substituted in the chair of *Código* in 1755 for his fellow *colegial* Juan Martín de Azcárate while he was at court securing an appointment to the Council of Navarre.

Viana was named *fiscal* of the Audiencia of Manila on February 21, 1756, and assumed his post on September 20, 1758. He exercised his office energetically, repeatedly proposing schemes to reduce government spending and to increase its revenues. On October 30, 1762, he joined Manuel Galván and Francisco de Enríquez in signing the surrender document for Manila. Like them, he was held in prison for ransom by the British, but, in contrast to them, he was close to Simón de Anda during the conflict. He fled to join him in January 1763, the first judge to do so. The leader of the resistance praised him warmly in 1765 and 1766. Viana's services were rewarded with a welcome promotion to *alcalde del crimen* of Mexico October 26, 1765. The following year he happily left Manila despite the expense the trip entailed. Although he reached Mexico in financial distress, this situation changed soon. Advanced to Mexico's civil chamber on December 5, 1769, he served there until returning to Spain as *ministro togado* of the Council of the Indies with an appointment of May 15, 1776, departing Mexico on April 10, 1777, and entering his new position on October 10, 1777.

Viana was an early opponent of reforms threatening elite interests. He joined Viceroy Antonio de Bucareli in opposing the intendant system and most of José de Gálvez's* innovations. In 1770 Viana became the judge overseer for the Marquesado del Valle, a rich commission. On September 13, 1781, he was given a place on the Cámara, where he served after November 9, 1794, at his pleasure, until he retired with full pay on August 4, 1802. A note of April 26, 1804 revealed that he could live anywhere save Madrid and the royal residences. In 1782 he became the representative for the Council of the Indies on the junta of administration for the Bank of San Carlos in which he held 150 shares (300,000 *reales de vellón*). While on the Council, his advice was influential in reuniting the superintendency with the viceroy in 1787. He also showed himself to be a staunch regalist.

Viana had been refused permission to marry a woman of the district in 1769 but must have gained one later. In 1771 he married María Josefa Rodríguez de Pedroso García y Arellano, born in Mexico in 1755, the daughter of José Julián Rodríguez de Pedroso, a native of Mexico City and knight of Santiago, and María Francisca Pablo Fernández de Tejada. Her maternal grandparents were Francisco Pablo Fernández de Tejada, first Marqués de Prado Alegre, knight of Calatrava, commander of a regiment of artillery, a *familiar* of the Holy Office, and the holder of an entailed estate of the same name, and his wife was Isabel Josefa Luna Sarmiento y Valladares. Viana worked diligently for his wife in a dispute over the sizable Jala estate, securing a settlement of 150,000 pesos. From his wife he gained substantial *pulque* producing properties, and at one time he controlled at least six *pulque* taverns. His official position was advantageous in benefiting from these holdings. Viana's wife inherited the title of Prado Alegre and died in 1814. Their son José Joaquín, who died in 1818, married Josefa Ruiz de Rivera; their daughter María Guadalupe married Luis de Goyeneche, Marqués de Belzunce y de Ugena and Conde de Gausa y de Saceda and relative of Goyeneche.* Daughter Juana de Dios married José María de Allende y Sálazar. Daughter Petra Joaquina married Francisco Crespo y Samaniego.

Viana was admitted to the Order of Charles III in 1780. He became the first Conde de Tepa in 1775 and in 1797 was authorized to found an entailed estate. He was a commissioner for the Basque Economic Society in Mexico.

Viana was a noted critic of the impact of Spain's colonial system on the Philippines. When in Manila he wrote the critical "Miserable and Deplorable State of the Philippine Islands" that lambasted current management. In his celebrated 1765 "Memorial" he called for an end to the Manila galleon monopoly and the islands being opened to free foreign trade with Asia and Europe. The galleon monopoly he considered to be responsible for moral and economic decay. His commercial proposals were influential in the development of the Philippines Company. Alexander von Humboldt considered him a "friend of science." In addition to his work on the Philippines, Viana published *Reglamento para precaver y extinguir en México incendios de sus casas y edificios públicos* (Madrid, 1782).

SOURCES: AGS, 2–42–48, 2–49–181, 2–53–215, 13–9–560, 13–9–545; AGI, Indiferente 894, 892, 885, 872, *relación* of 1775; 1627; Filipinas 273; AHN, Hacienda 5046, *expediente* 31; Estado (Carlos III), *expediente* 75, *pruebas* of Francisco Leandro de Viana; AHPUV, Libro 201; Archer, *Army*, pp. 116–17; Brading, *Miners*, pp. 46–47, 66. Farriss, *Crown and Clergy*, p. 105n.; Fernández de Recas, *Mayorazgos*, pp. 135, 223–25; Hamnett, *Politics*, pp. 18, 42–44; Humboldt, *Ensayo político*, p. 319n.; Calderón Quijano, *Los virreyes . . . Carlos III*, II, 256n.; Bernad, *Christianization*, pp. 301–3; Cushner, *Documents*, VIII, 143, 149–50; Cushner, *Philippine Jesuits*, p. 22; Medina, *Biblioteca*, V, 177–78; Schurz, *Galleon*, pp. 28, 55–57, 411; Tutino, "Creole Mexico," pp. 73–74, 104, 139, 283; *Diario curioso*, April 10, 1777 (courtesy of Linda Arnold).

Viaña, Francisco José (March 3, 1744–July 12, 1826)

Viaña, an eldest son, was born in Cádiz. His parents were Francisco Vitores Viaña, a native of the *barrio* of Fresnada in the Valley of Cabuérniga, Santander, and María Teresa Viaña of Biernoles, also in the Archbishopric of Burgos. His paternal grandparents were Toribio Viaña and Isabel de Terán, both from Fresnada. His maternal grandparents were Francisco Antonio Viaña y Campo and María Fernández Mencadal, both from Biernoles. His brother Lugardo was a Cádiz merchant involved in the Indies trade. He had two other siblings, José and María Teresa.

Viaña attended the University of Seville and received a baccalaureate in canon law in 1766. In 1792 he was the chief clerk (*oficial mayor*) in the Secretariat of State and Ministry of Hacienda for the Indies. On July 19, 1806, he was named chief accountant for South America and given the seat of minister *de capa y espada* on the Council of the Indies attached to that post. He replaced Francisco de Valencia.* Viaña was still on the Council when he died in Madrid.

In 1792 Viaña became a pensioned *caballero* of the Order of Charles III.

SOURCES: AGS, XXIII, 13–9–106; AGI, Indiferente 870A; AHN, Estado (Carlos III), *expediente* 711, *pruebas* of Francisco José de Viaña; AUSE, Libro 598.

Villalengua y Marfil, Juan José de (January 5, 1748–c. 1822)

Villalengua was born in Vélez, Málaga. His parents were Juan Félix de Villalengua, a native of the *villa* of Haro in the Bishopric of Calahorra and a notary (*escribano del número*) in Vélez-Málaga, and Mariana Marfil de Lagos y Rios of the *villa* of Benamocarra, Bishopric of Málaga. His paternal grandparents were Miguel de Villalengua of Haro and María Cruz Villalengua from the *villa* of Foncea in Guipúzcoa. His maternal grandparents were Francisco Marfil de Lagos of Benamocarra and Isabel de los Rios from the *villa* of Yznate in Málaga. He had a half sister, María del Carmen Villalengua y Aguirre born of his father's first wife Ana María Aguirre. In addition, he had a sister named Mariana Villalengua y Marfil.

Villalengua received the baccalaureate in canon law from the University of Alcalá in 1767 and also attended the University of Toledo. In 1763 he entered the Royal Academy of San José for law professors at Alcalá not associated with its *colegio mayor*. In 1767 he took a practicum with Pedro Fernando de Vilches who went on to serve as *fiscal* for the Council of Orders. The Royal Council admitted him as an attorney in 1771.

Villalengua obtained an appointment as protector of the Indians for the Audiencia of Quito on July 24, 1773. Sworn into office on December 2, 1774, he became a *fiscal del crimen* on April 4, 1776, as one of those persons affected by the creation of the new *fiscalía* and the abolition of the former protectorship. Advanced to Lima as *fiscal del crimen* on January 19, 1781, he returned to Quito with an appointment as regent, president, and superintendent general on July 12, 1783, which he served from May 4, 1784, until 1790. As regent he was involved in prosecuting Eugenio de Espejo and saving his relative Ramón García Pizarro from prosecution for his abuses as governor of Guayaquil. Like his father-in-law José García León y Pizarro,* he used the militia of upland Quito for his own benefit rather than for the good of the Crown. Reversing his previous stand, he used his position to attack the subinspector Colonel Anastasio Zejudo when he tried to strengthen the upland militia. He devoted considerable attention to public works in Quito and had the streets paved and public gardens created, and a hospice for orphans and invalids built. González Suárez judged Villalengua wise rather than despotic and one of the best presidents of the late colonial period. On November 18, 1789, he was named regent of the tribunal in Guatemala, and eight days later was given honors of the Council of the Indies. In 1791 he was admitted to the Order of Charles III. On May 11, 1794, Villalengua obtained the ultimate promotion to the Council of the Indies as a *ministro togado*, a promotion encouraged by his father-in-law who himself was then serving on the Council. He reached Cádiz in mid-March 1796 and soon assumed his post, which he occupied until his retirement with two-thirds salary on May 16, 1800.

Villalengua married Josefa Pizarro, daughter of the first regent of Quito, José García León y Pizarro. Villalengua's cousin José Carrión y Marfil served as the first bishop of Cuenca, Quito, in 1787.

SOURCES: AGS, 2–57–153, 2–60–83, 2–65–2, 2–67–68, 2–73–265, 2–73–268, 13–8–44, 15–8–2; AGI, Quito 224 *relación* of 1773, 299, Indiferente 1519, 872, *relación* of 1788, 873, *expediente* Villalengua; Lima 598, AHN, Estado (Carlos III), *expediente* 556, *pruebas* of Juan José Villalengua; Shafer, *Economic Societies*, pp. 170–71; Kuethe, *Military Reform*, pp. 123, 125, 153–54; Astuto, *Espejo*, pp. 60–62; Castillo, *Gobernadores*, pp. 214, 222, 236, 248; González Suárez, *Historia*, V, 324, 331; Rumazo González, *Documentos*, VIII, 229.

Villarrasa Venegas y Anaya, Basilio (June 21, 1724–February 8, 1783)

Villarrasa was born in Granada. His parents were Francisco Villarrasa y Venegas, an hereditary alderman of the *villa* of Alhama, and Josefa Isabela Anaya y Calderón. He had a brother named Juan.

Villarrasa obtained the first of several fellowships in the Imperial College of San Miguel in Granada in 1738. In 1742 he entered the Royal College of Santa Cruz de la Fe in Granada with a fellowship. The University of Granada conferred upon him the baccalaureate in canon law in 1742, the licentiate in 1744, and the doctorate in 1747.

Villarrasa's early career centered on the University of Granada. In 1743 he was named examiner of law students at San Miguel and the College of Santiago, continuing until 1753. In 1746 he represented Santa Cruz at court to congratulate Ferdinand VI on his accession. He served as rector of Santa Cruz in 1748 and 1751, and also served as councilor (*conciliario*) various times. Villarrasa substituted in chairs, was vice-chancellor and vice-rector of the University of Granada in 1745, and became proprietary professor of *Digesto Viejo* in 1751. He competed for canonries of the churches of Cuenca, Murcia, and Jaén. He also practiced law, became a member of the Royal Society of Seville in 1753, and served as counselor (*abogado asesor de cámara*) of the bishop of Jaen.

On January 24, 1758, Villarrasa was named *oidor* of the Audiencia of Guatemala, serving there until advancement to the Mexican audiencia as *alcalde del crimen* on April 13, 1773. Already on his way to Mexico when the earthquake struck Guatemala, he returned to help during the crisis. Villarrasa fed and provided for some nuns, and his wife gave them personal assistance. He risked his life by going into shattered buildings to rescue ill and injured persons. When he learned that some people were refusing to dig graves for the dead as being beneath their status, he grabbed a shovel and gave an example. On September 22, 1774, he became *oidor* in Mexico. Promoted to *fiscal* of the Audiencia of the House of Trade on March 17, 1779, Villarrasa never took up the post, for he was elevated to the Council of the Indies as *ministro togado* the following July 11, a post he assumed on September 15 and served until his death.

Villarrasa married María Teresa Fonseca, the daughter of Fabián de Fonseca Rueda Rico, an alderman of Motril, and Eugenia Luminaty Pérez de Vargas, also of Motril. After Villarrasa's death, his widow complained she lacked the money to bury him.

SOURCES: AGS, 2–43–22, 2–57–43, 2–58–276, 2–63–26, 13–9–422; AGI, Filipinas 273, *relación* of 1753; Ultramar 798, *títulos* of 1756; Indiferente 894, 866, 1981, 873; Pérez Valenzuela, *Nueva Guatemala*, pp. 28–29.

Y

Yopulo y Espadafora, Diego (Variants: Yoppolo, Spatafora) (?–January 19, 1763)

Yopulo was born in Palermo, Sicily. His parents were Pedro Yopulo, Duque de San Blas and Principe de San Antonio, and Agueda de Espadafora, both natives of Sicily. His older brother Luis* also served on the Council of the Indies.

Yopulo was named minister *de capa y espada* of the Council of the Indies on February 8, 1735, for marrying Isabel Piscatori after the death of his brother. His wife had been a handmaiden to the queen and received the post as a dowry. Yopulo retained his appointment until his death. He served in military posts as well, however, and reached the rank of lieutenant general. He died in San Sebastián while serving as commander general of Vizcaya.

Yopulo must have had no children for he left as his heir his nephew Aguislao Bonnano y Yopulo, Duque de Castellana, and the son of his sister Antonia, Duquesa de Castellana.

SOURCES: AGS, XXIII, 13–9–474; AGI, Indiferente 894; Bernard, *Secrétariat*, p. 217.

Yopulo y Espadafora, Luis (?–July 22, 1732)

Yopulo was the brother of Diego.* See the entry on Diego for family information.

An officer in the royal bodyguards, Yopulo received an appointment as minister *de capa y espada* of the Council of the Indies on December 18, 1725. The post was a dowry for his wife Isabel Piscatori, a handmaiden to the queen who was originally to have married Pedro Casado.* Following Yopulo's death, his widow married Diego Yopulo.

Yopulo held the titles Principe de San Antonio and Duque de San Blas.

SOURCES: AGS, XXIII, 13–8–306, AGI, Indiferente 894; AHN, Estado 6380 (1); Bernard, *Secrétariat*, p. 216.

Z

Zúñiga y Guzmán, Baltasar (?–December 26, 1717)

Zúñiga was a gentleman of the royal chamber when named a minister *de capa y espada* of the Council and Cámara of the Indies on June 7, 1700. He assumed his position the following day. Having previously been viceroy of Navarre and Sardinia, from August 16, 1716 to October 15, 1722, he served as viceroy of New Spain. As viceroy he established the *acordada*, a new tribunal designed to administer expeditious criminal justice. Following his tenure as viceroy, he returned to Spain laden with riches, which he used to secure patronage at court. On January 28, 1724, he succeeded Pez* as president of the Council of the Indies. Later in the year he was named *mayordomo mayor* of the queen.

Zúñiga held the titles Marqués de Valero, Duque de Arion, and Marqués de Ayamonte.

SOURCES: AGS, XXIII, 13–9–435; Gracia y Justicia 922; AGI, Indiferente 866; Bernard, *Secrétariat*, p. 211; MacLachlan, *Criminal Justice*, p. 32; Bancroft, *Works*, XI, 290–91; Escudero, *Los orígenes*, I, 69; Coxe, *Memoirs*, II, 299.

Zúñiga y Tovar, Diego de (c. 1665–c. 1738)

Zúñiga was born in Guadalajara, New Castile. After receiving the baccalaureate and licentiate degrees in canon law from the University of Avila, he incorporated them at the University of Alcalá, where he entered the *colegio mayor* of San Ildefonso in 1685.

Named *oidor* of the Audiencia of Chile on March 21, 1690, Zúñiga occupied the post on January 4, 1692. When he arrived he was the single judge in service, a circumstance that convinced him to persuade his colleague Bernardo de Laya y Bolívar to postpone his departure to Lima to join the audiencia there until he had imparted the customs of Santiago's tribunal. From June 1704 to April 1707, Zúñiga held a commission as *corregidor* of Concepción. The *residencia* for his service declared him a "good, clean, and upright judge." After returning to Spain, he was named an *oidor* of the Chancellery of Valladolid in 1709. On October 12, 1712, he became a supernumerary minister of the Council of the Indies, eventually moving into a regular position. When the Council was reorganized in 1717, Zúñiga was named one of the ministers *togados*. On February 18, 1722, Philip V granted him a seat on the Cámara. Zúñiga was allowed to attend Council meetings at his pleasure after November 21, 1735, as a result of his age and infirmities.

SOURCES: AGS, XXIII, 24–171–13; Gracia y Justicia 146; AGI, Indiferente 132, 866, 867, 873; Silva i Molina, *Oidores*, pp. 63–64.

Appendix 1

BRIEF CHRONOLOGY OF SPAIN AND THE SPANISH COLONIES IN THE EIGHTEENTH CENTURY

1700	Death of Charles II; Philip V becomes king
1701	Attempted reform of purchased appointments
1705	Invasion of Spain by Archduke Charles
1711	Battle of Villaviciosa—Bourbon triumph
1713	Peace of Utrecht; British receive the *asiento*
1714	Establishment of the Secretariat of State for the Indies
1717	Reorganization of the Council of the Indies; transfer of the House of Trade from Seville to Cadiz
1717–18	Garzaron *visita* reforms Audiencia of Mexico
1721	Reestablishment of the Cámara of the Indies
1728	Establishment of the Caracas Company
1735–44	Jorge Juan and Antonio de Ulloa visit South America
1737	Expansion of the Council of the Indies ordered
1739	Definitive establishment of the viceroyalty of New Granada
1739–48	War of Jenkins' Ear
1743	Campillo's "Nueva Sistema" written
1746	Ferdinand VI becomes king
1750	Settlement of dispute with Portugal over Brazil's boundary
1751	Suppression of the Audiencia of Panama
1754	Julián de Arriaga becomes secretary of state for the Indies
1759	Charles III becomes king
1761	Third Family Compact

1762 British capture Havana

1763 Peace of Paris ends Seven Years' War; Spain regains Havana, receives Louisiana, loses Florida

1764 Beginning of military reform; first intendant sent to Cuba; improved postal service begins; establishment of tobacco monopoly in New Spain

1765 Beginning of *comercio libre* for the Caribbean

1765–71 Gálvez *visita* to New Spain

1767 Expulsion of the Jesuit order

1771 Initiation of reform of the *colegios mayores* and universities in Spain

1773 Council of the Indies declared equal to the Council of Castile

1774 Intercolonial trade permitted between Guatemala, Peru, New Spain, and New Granada

1776 Expansion of the Council of the Indies; establishment of the viceroyalty of the Río de la Plata, the *provincias internas* in New Spain, and the office of intendant in Caracas; *visitas* authorized for Peru (José Antonio de Areche) and New Granada (Juan Francisco Gutiérrez de Piñeres); expansion of the size of existing audiencias, including one regent per tribunal; José de Gálvez becomes secretary of state for the Indies upon the death of Arriaga

1777 Ruiz and Pavón botanical expedition to Peru begins

1778 Expansion of *comercio libre*

1779–83 Spain at war against England

1780–83 Túpac Amaru Revolt in Peru

1781–82 Comunero Revolt in New Granada

1781 First economic society in the colonies founded (Manila)

1782 Intendant system established in the Río de la Plata

1783 Spain regains Florida in the Peace of Paris; Audiencia of Buenos Aires authorized

1784 Establishment of intendant system in Peru

1785 Creation of *ascenso* that led to the Council of the Indies for *oficiales mayores* of secretariats and expansion of the Council; Caracas Company closed (replaced by Philippines Company); end of the general *visita* in Peru

1786 Establishment of the Audiencia of Caracas and the intendant system in Chile, Central America, and New Spain

1787 Establishment of the Audiencia of Cuzco; Secretariat of State for the Indies divided (Porlier and Valdés named secretaries) following death of Gálvez (Marqués de Sonora); establishment of Junta de Estado

1788 Death of Charles III; ascension of Charles IV

1789 *Comercio libre* extended to New Spain and Venezuela

1790 Separate secretariats for the Indies abolished; affairs united with five Spanish secretariats

1792 Manuel Godoy becomes first minister of Spain; Junta de Estado abolished

1793 *Consulados* created in Caracas and Guatemala

1793–95	War with France
1794	*Consulados* created in Buenos Aires and Havana
1795	Relaxation of trade restrictions due to war; Peace of Basle ended war with France
1796	*Consulados* created in Cartagena de Indias, Veracruz, Guadalajara, and Santiago de Chile; Treaty of San Ildefonso links Spain with France against England; war with England begins
1797–99	Neutral trade allowed in colonies; British blockade Cádiz
1802	Peace of Amiens
1804	Decree of consolidation of royal bonds extended to colonies
1805	Britain destroys combined French and Spanish fleets at Trafalgar
1805–9	Neutral trade allowed in colonies
1806	Miranda's invasion of Venezuela; British invasion of Buenos Aires
1807	Second British invasion of Buenos Aires; French Army enters Spain on way to Portugal
1808	Abdication of Charles IV and Ferdinand VII; constitutional crisis; establishment of juntas and junta control in Spain; Joseph Bonaparte declared king

Appendix 2

NEW MEN NAMED TO THE COUNCIL OF THE INDIES BY POSITION AND DATE, 1717–1808

PRESIDENTS AND GOVERNORS

1. 1717, Jan. 20 D[1] PEZ y MALZARRAGA, Andrés Matías de
2. 1724, Jan. 28 T[2] ZUNIGA y GUZMAN, Baltasar
3. 1737, Jun. 18 T PORTOCARRERO GUZMAN LUNA, Cristóbal Gregorio
4. 1748, Jan. 27 T CARVAJAL y LANCASTER, José de
5. 1763, Feb. 20 T PIZARRO y ARAGON, Juan
6. 1776, Mar. 31 T GALVEZ y GALLARDO, José de
7. 1787, Jul. 15 T MONINO, FRANCISCO
8. 1792, Jul. 28 T PORLIER, ANTONIO de

MINISTROS TOGADOS

1. 1717, Jan. 20 D MIRAVAL y ESPINOLA, Martín de
2. 1717, Jan. 20 D PEDROSA y GUERRERO, Antonio Ignacio de la
3. 1718, Feb. 8 T CEPEDA y ESTRADA de JEREZ, Rodrigo de
4. 1718, Feb. 8 T REMIREZ de BAQUEDANO, Gonzalo
5. 1720, Dec. 12 T SANTOS de SAN PEDRO, Juan Francisco
6. 1724, Feb. 3 T AGUADO FERNANDEZ de CORDOBA, Antonio Francisco
7. 1725, Nov. 20 T MUTILOA y LODOSA, Juan José de
8. 1726, Mar. 28 D SOLA y SOTO, Tomás de

1. D is date of decree.
2. T is date of title.

9. 1731, Jan. 21 T ALVAREZ de ABREU, Antonio José
10. 1731, (?) VARAS y VALDES, Francisco de
11. 1732, Mar. 21 T VALDIVIESO, José de
12. 1733, Jan. 16 T ORUETA y YRUSTA, Andrés de
13. 1734, Jul 24 T PINEDA CAPDEVILA, Antonio José de
14. 1734, Jul. 29 T CORNEJO y IBARRA, José
15. 1734, Sep. 22 T CONTRERAS y ZUNIGA, Pedro Domingo de
16. 1734, Dec. 10 T BAZAN y MELO, Joachin Antonio
17. 1738, Jan. 28 D LAYSEQUILLA y PALACIOS y AGUILAR, José de
18. 1738, Jan. 28 D CARVAJAL y LANCASTER, José de
19. 1738, Aug. 28 T ISLA, Luis Fernando de
20. 1740, May 22 T LARDIZABAL y ELORZA, Martín de
21. 1741, Oct. 28 D SOLA y FUENTE, Gerónimo de
22. 1741, Nov. 4 D PALACIOS, Prudencio Antonio de
23. 1743, Oct. 13 T ROMAY ARMADA y SOTOMAYOR, Antonio Jacinto
24. 1744, Mar. 19 T VAZQUEZ de AGUERO, Juan
25. 1752, Mar. 22 T MORENO HURTADO, José
26. 1752, Mar. 22 T EZPELETA y AMATRIAIN, José de
27. 1752, Mar. 22 T ROJAS y CONTRERAS, José Simeón de
28. 1752, Mar. 22 T LEON y ESCANDON, Pedro de
29. 1760, Jul. 20 D SANTELICES y VENERO, Venturo de
30. 1762, Dec. 22 D TRESPALACIOS y ESCANDON, Domingo de
31. 1764, Feb. 20 T JIMENO RODRIGUEZ, Marcos
32. 1765, Feb. 3 T MOSQUERA y PIMENTEL QUINTANILLA, Luis Francisco
33. 1766, Jun. 22 T BERNARDO de QUIROS, Manuel de
34. 1766, Aug. 23 T CALDERON ENRIQUEZ, Pedro
35. 1767, Mar. 18 T AVILA y SOTO, PEDRO de
36. 1767, Dec. 28 D GALVEZ y GALLARDO, José de
37. 1770, Apr. 4 T ECHAVARRI y UGARTE ELCOROBARRUTIA, Francisco Antonio de
38. 1770, Sep. 27 T CASTRO, Jacinto Miguel de
39. 1773, May 6 D SANTOS DOMINGUEZ, Felipe
40. 1773, May 16 D CARO de BRIONES, Teodomiro
41. 1773, Dec. 5 T AGUERO RIVA, José Pablo
42. 1773, Dec. 12 T LANZ de CASAFONDA, Manuel Miguel
43. 1774, Mar. 16 T DIAZ FREYLE, Manuel
44. 1774, Oct. 10 T CERDA y SOTO, José Antonio de la

45. 1774, Oct. 10 T ORRANTIA, Domingo José de
46. 1776, Mar. 11 D ARECHE y SORNOZA, José Antonio de
47. 1776, Mar. 18 D HUERTA y CIGALA, Jacobo Andrés de
48. 1776, Mar. 18 D MERIDA, Juan de
49. 1776, May 4 T ROMERO y ALESON, Manuel
50. 1776, May 13 T VIANA y ZAVALA, Francisco Leandro de
51. 1776, Jul. 10 T ANTUNEZ y ACEVEDO, Rafael de
52. 1777, Apr. 13 T MUNOZ de la TORRE, Pedro
53. 1778, May 3 T GONZALEZ BUSTILLO y VILLASENOR, Juan Manuel
54. 1779, Jul. 11 T VILLARRASA VENEGAS y ANAYA, Basilio
55. 1782, Feb. 1 T SOLER RUIZ, Gaspar
56. 1783, Mar. 14 T GARCIA LEON y PIZARRO, José
57. 1784, May 24 T GUTIERREZ de PINERES, Juan Francisco
58. 1785, Apr. 27 T ESCOBEDO OCANA y ALARCON, Jorge
59. 1786, Mar. 30 T HERRERA y RIVERO, Vicente de
60. 1787, Feb. 12 D JACOT ORTIZ ROJANO RUIZ de la ESCALERA, Melchor
61. 1788, Oct. 15 T ALVAREZ de ACEVEDO, Tomás Antonio
62. 1789, Jun. 24 T ACEDO y XIMENEZ, Miguel Calixto de
63. 1790, May 24 T MON y VELARDE, Juan Antonio
64. 1790, Aug. 4 T CASTANO, José Agustín
65. 1794, May 11 T VILLALENGUA y MARFIL, Juan José de
66. 1795, Apr. 21 T URIZAR y BOLIVAR, José Antonio de
67. 1798, May 21 T MUZQUIZ y ALDUNATE, Luis Antonio de
68. 1798, Apr. 14 T SOTO, Manuel de
69. 1798, Nov. 27 T VALENZUELA y AGUILAR, Pedro Jacinto de
70. 1799, Mar. 8 D VALIENTE y BRAVO, José Pablo
71. 1800, Dec. 10 T GOMEZ JARA DIOSDADO, García
72. 1803, Feb. 9 T POSADA y SOTO, Ramón de
73. 1803, Mar. 5 T MATA LINARES y VAZQUEZ, Benito María de la
74. 1803, Mar. 5 T SAAVEDRA y CARBAJAL, Francisco de
75. 1804, Jul. 31 T PORTILLA y GALVEZ, José de la
76. 1805, Aug. 13 T LOPEZ QUINTANA, Antonio
77. 1806, Mar. 20 T CORTINES, Francisco Ignacio
78. 1806, Jul. 11 P[1] MARQUEZ de la PLATA y OROZCO, Fernando
79. 1808, Feb. 9 T LOPEZ LISPERGUER, Francisco

MINISTROS DE CAPA Y ESPADA

1. 1717, Feb. 10 T VADILLO ESTRADA y VELASCO, Manuel de

1. P is date of publication.

2. 1721, Jan. 16 T FERNANDEZ DURAN y FERNANDEZ de la CASA, Miguel
3. 1721, Apr. 24 T LUJAN y SILVA, FERNANDO
4. 1723, Apr. 27 T CASADO, Pedro
5. 1724, Mar. 16 T GIRON VENEGAS de CORDOBA, Gaspar Cayetano
6. 1725, Mar. 13 T SILVA RIVERA, Manuel
7. 1725, Dec. 18 T YOPULO y ESPADAFORA, Luis
8. 1726, Feb. 14 T SOPENA y MIONA, Antonio de
9. 1726, Oct. 31 T CASADO y VELASCO, Francisco
10. 1728, Feb. 28 T PIZARRO y ARAGON, Juan
11. 1728, Mar. 8 T VERDES MONTENEGRO y CASTRO BAAMONDE, Fernando
12. 1729, May 4 T CAPECELATRO, Marqués de
13. 1731, Nov. 14 T AGUIRRE y SALCEDO, Francisco Antonio
14. 1735, Feb. 8 T YOPULO y ESPADAFORA, Diego
15. 1735, Feb. 23 T MENDOZA CAAMANO, Mauro Fernando de
16. 1737, Jan. 10 T QUINTANA, Joseph de la
17. 1738, Jul. 15 T ABARIA y YMAZ, Esteban José de
18. 1739, Mar. 14 T DIAZ de LAVANDERO y MARTIN, Mateo Pablo de
19. 1739, Dec. 22 T GERALDINO, Tomás
20. 1740, Oct. 4 T GAUNA y PORTOCARRERO, Juan de
21. 1741, Apr. 18 T OSORIO RUBIN de CELIS, Casimiro
22. 1742, Apr. 23 D FERNANDEZ MOLINILLO, Francisco
23. 1744, Jul. 25 T ARCO RIVA HERRERA, Felipe de
24. 1745, Mar. 14 T TORRES y MORALES, Rodrigo
25. 1745, Jun. 20 T SALCEDO, Manuel Jacinto de
26. 1746, Dec. 4 T TORRERO y MARZO, Joseph
27. 1750, Jul. 5 T MUNIVE y TELLO, Gabriel de
28. 1759, Dec. 20 T PEREZ GAMONEDA CASCO VILLADEMOROS, Juan Antonio
29. 1761, Jul. 5 T BANFI y PARRILLA, José
30. 1767, May 9 T ORTIZ de LANDAZURI, Tomás
31. 1773, Jul. 29 D MAGALLON y ANDRES, Fernando de
32. 1776, Sep. 2 T RADA, Pedro de
33. 1777, Sep. 12 T MACHADO FIESCO, Francisco Xavier
34. 1778, Dec. 24 T MONINO, Francisco
35. 1780, May 14 T IRIARTE y NIEVES-RABELO, Bernardo de
36. 1785, Sep. 1 T HERMOSILLA y SANDOVAL, Ignacio Agustín de
37. 1785, Sep. 1 T FERNANDEZ SARMIENTO y BALLON, Manuel Ignacio
38. 1788, Jan. 16 T MANGINO FERNANDEZ de LIMA, Fernando José

39. 1788, Mar. 11 T AYALA y MEDINA, Manuel José de
40. 1790, Sep. 22 T GOMEZ de GRIJALVA, Francisco
41. 1791, Dec. 18 T URRIZA, Juan Ignacio de
42. 1793, Apr. 22 D FONDEVILA y GUERRA, Francisco Xavier
43. 1793, Nov. 11 T RIVA AGUERO y BASO, Fulgencio de la
44. 1794, Mar. 19 T ESCARANO, Francisco Antonio
45. 1794, Oct. 31 T SALCEDO, José
46. 1794, Dec. 23 ? APARICI ALVAREZ y PEREZ, Pedro
47. 1794, Dec. 23 ? VALENCIA y SAENZ del PONTON, Francisco de
48. 1795, Jun. 26 T HORE DAVILA, Vicente
49. 1798, Jan. 14 T REQUENA y HERRERA, Francisco de
50. 1798, Sep. 15 T OMULRYAN, Ignacio
51. 1799, Feb. 4 D FERNANDEZ de CORDOBA, Francisco
52. 1800, Aug. 4 T ROJAS y HIERRO, José de
53. 1801, Jan. 15 T GAMIZ y ESPINOSA, Antonio de
54. 1802, Aug. 15 D PORCEL, Antonio
55. 1802, Nov. 28 T GALISTEO y MANRIQUE, Tadeo José de
56. 1803, Jan. 23 T VEGA y GUERRA SANCHEZ y AVENDANO, Francisco Xavier de la
57. 1805, Mar. 23 T ALONSO ACOSTA ZORRILLA y DAVILA, Cenon
58. 1806, Jul. 19 D VIANA, Francisco José
59. 1807, Mar. 26 T ALESON, Juan José de
60. 1807, Oct. 27 T URBINA, Cayetano de
61. 1808, Jan. 15 T AMOROS, Francisco

FISCAL DEL PERU

1. 1717, Jan. 20 D CAVALLERO y SOTO, Juan
2. 1720, Oct. 8 T VALCARCEL DATO, Juan de
3. 1721, Jul. 11 T AFAN de RIVERA, Pedro de
4. 1723, Sep. 23 T LAYSEQUILLA y PALACIOS y AGUILAR, José de
5. 1738, Feb. 2 T PALACIOS, Prudencio Antonio de
6. 1744, Mar. 28 T ROJAS, José Manuel de
7. 1749, Feb. 13 T SALCEDO, Manuel Pablo de
8. 1764, Jan. 24 T PATINO, Manuel
9. 1767, Jun. 16 T GONZALEZ de MENA y VILLEGAS, Pedro
10. 1772, Jun. 22 T PINA y MAZO, Pedro de
11. 1777, Oct. 28 T CISTUE y COLL, José de

12. 1803, Mar. 5 T CERDAN y PONTERO, Ambrosio
13. 1804, Mar. 15 T GORVEA y VADILLO, José Lucas de

FISCAL DE NUEVA ESPANA

1. 1718, Jan. 27 T SOLA y SOTO, Tomás de
2. 1726, Mar. 28 T MARTINEZ CARVAJAL, Manuel
3. 1738, Feb. 27 T BORRULL y RAMON, José
4. 1752, Mar. 22 T MALDONADO SANCHEZ ROMERO, Tomás de
5. 1761, Jul. 19 T MOSQUERA y PIMENTEL QUINTANILLA, Luis Francisco
6. 1765, Feb. 14 T CAVALLERO y TINEO, Bernardo
7. 1766, Aug. 23 T LANZ de CASAFONDA, Manuel Miguel
8. 1773, Oct. 8 C[1] PORLIER, Antonio de
9. 1787, Oct. 4 T RIVERA y PENA, Ramón
10. 1789, Nov. 5 T URUNUELA ARANSAY, Juan Antonio
11. 1793, Nov. 7 T POSADA y SOTO, Ramón de
12. 1802, Oct. 17 T HERNANDEZ de ALVA ALONSO, Lorenzo Serapio
13. 1806, Jun. 17 C CASTILLO y NEGRETE, Manuel del

1. C is date of *consulta*.

GLOSSARY

Abogado fiscal Here, a public attorney or prosecutor below audiencia rank.

Abogado general A title employed for the crown attorneys in the ephemeral reorganization of the councils in 1713.

Abogado real A title used for the crown attorney of the *sala de alcaldes de casa y corte* (which see) in the ephemeral reorganization of tribunals at court in 1713.

Acordada A special criminal tribunal and rural law enforcement agency in eighteenth-century New Spain.

Agente fiscal An assistant to a *fiscal* of an audiencia.

Aguardiente Distilled spirits, often from sugar cane.

Alcalde, alcalde ordinario A magistrate and member of a town council.

Alcalde de casa y corte A judge of the tribunal with criminal jurisdiction over Madrid and the royal court, the fifth chamber of the Council of Castile.

Alcalde de hijosdalgo A member of the chamber in the Chancelleries of Granada and Valladolid which dealt with cases involving the status and privileges of the nobility.

Alcalde del crimen A criminal judge on the viceregal tribunals of Mexico and Lima and also in some Spanish tribunals.

Alcalde de la quadra A criminal judge of the Audiencia of Seville; equivalent to an *alcalde del crimen* (which see).

Alcalde mayor A magistrate or officer of a district or provincial government.

Alcaldía mayor The office or jurisdiction of an *alcalde mayor.*

Alférez The official standard bearer of a political entity; also, a subaltern in the navy equivalent to an ensign.

Alguacil mayor The post of high sheriff or chief law officer in a municipality, often largely honorific.

Anteiglesia A parish and municipal unit; the term is employed in the Basque provinces.

Armada de Barlovento The American squadron of the Spanish navy; often referred to as the "windward squadron."

Aposentador mayor The official who oversaw housing and office arrangements for persons living in a royal palace.

Aposento Lodgings provided for retainers and officials at court; here, the tax paid by owners or renters of houses at court.

Arras Sum of money a husband provided to his wife at the time of marriage.

Ascenso The recognized ladder of career advancement through the stages of a bureaucratic hierarchy.

Asesor An adviser or councilor; one who renders legal opinions.

Asesor de marina A legal adviser who works for the navy.

Asesor general An adviser or councilor who renders legal opinions for a viceroy or other senior executive.

Asistente A public official in some municipalities; equivalent to a *corregidor* (which see) in the city of Seville, Spain.

Auditor (of the Rota) A member of the appellate tribunal for ecclesiastical cases created in Spain in 1773.

Auditor de guerra A judge advocate providing legal advice and judicial services to military command.

Ayudante controlor Official involved in overseeing accounts and inventory.

Barrio Usually an urban subdivision; here, a rural settlement dependent upon a village or town.

Caballerizo Equerry. *Primer caballerizo*: immediate subordinate to the *caballerizo mayor*.

Caballerizo mayor Official in charge of the equerries of his master or mistress.

Caballero A gentleman or knight of a military order.

Cámara Chamber or cabinet; The Cámara of the Indies was charged with dispensing patronage.

Cámara de Comptos A tribunal of the Council of Navarre that dealt with treasury matters.

Camarista A member of a cámara.

Canariano, -a A native of the Canary Islands.

Canones The body of laws and rulings delivered by Church councils, a field of ecclesiastical law.

Capa y espada See *ministro de capa y espada*.

Capitan de granaderos A captain of grenadiers.

Caraqueño, -a A native of Caracas, Venezuela.

Carrera de varas The career path of municipal and provincial administration in Spain.

Casa de Contratación The House of Trade, an agency located in Seville and later Cádiz, which oversaw commerce and navigation within the empire and the taxation and regulation thereof.

Cédula, real cédula A communication from the sovereign dispensing some favor or requiring some action. It normally begins with the heading *El Rey* or *La Reina* ("The King" or "The Queen") and is signed by the monarch.

Código The Justinian Code, taught in universities as part of the curriculum of civil law.

Colegial Here, a student at a *colegio mayor* (which see).

Colegio A secondary school.

Colegio mayor A prestigious residence hall and confraternity associated with certain Spanish and Spanish-American universities; the members of such bodies enjoyed elite status within the bureaucracy at certain times. The six most prestigious and in some minds the only "real" *colegios mayores* were at Salamanca (4), Valladolid (1), and Alcalá (1).

Coliseo de comedias Here, a theater in colonial Lima.

Comendador A knight-commander in a military order.

Comisario de guerra An official in charge of fiscal matters relating to the army.

Comisario ordenador de marina An official who served under a naval intendant and had fiscal and accounting responsibilities.
Comisario regio An official royal representative.
Conciliario Counselor.
Consulado A merchant guild and tribunal of commerce.
Consulta A report, brief, or recommendation to the executive-in-council; often a list of candidates proposed by a cámara for a position.
Contador An accountant or auditor in an official agency.
Contador general Chief accountant of an accounting office.
Contador mayor A chief accountant or head of finances.
Contador principal The chief accountant or his immediate subordinate in many government accounting departments.
Contaduría An accounting office.
Contaduría mayor See *Contaduría mayor de cuentas.*
Contaduría mayor de cuentas The central accounting office for the Spanish government.
Corregidor A magistrate and chief administrative officer for district or provincial government.
Correos y caminos Here, the postal service.
Cortes de Cádiz The extraordinary meeting of the parliament in the city of Cádiz during the emergency caused by the Napoleonic invasion and interregnum, 1810–14.
Cruzada (Council of) Body concerned with the tax (*cruzada*) originally conceded by the papacy to help finance war against the Moors.
Decano Senior member of a court or council.
Decretales The collected pontifical decrees and decisions, a part of the curriculum of ecclesiastical law.
Decretales mayores A chair in canon law at certain Spanish universities.
Decretales menores A chair in canon law at certain Spanish universities.
Decreto A chair in canon law at certain Spanish universities.
De paso Here, while passing through; by chance.
Del Despacho The king's private office.
Despacho universal The king's private office.
Despacho universal de lo político Title used in 1714 to describe what was later called the Secretariat of State for Grace and Justice.
Doblon A doubloon, a unit of money that varied over time; here, equal to four pesos (see below).
Encomienda A grant of authority over a group of Indians, carrying the obligation to Christianize and protect them in exchange for labor services or tribute; in Spain, an income received by some knights of military orders.
En gobierno (secretary of state) The single Secretariat of State established in 1706 and lasting until 1714.
Escribanía The office of an *escribano* (which see).
Escribano Here, a notary public.
Expediente A file.
Familiar A representative of the Inquisition, usually lay.
Fiscal The Crown attorney for an audiencia or council.
Fiscal del crimen The Crown attorney attached to the criminal chamber of a court.
Fiscal de hacienda A Crown attorney with special responsibility for treasury matters and cases.
Fiscal de lo civil The Crown attorney attached to the civil chamber of a court.

Fiscalía The office of *fiscal*.

Futura Here, a promise of appointment or succession to a position at some future time.

Gimnasio, Gimnasio de leyes An academy of law with an orientation toward practical experience.

Guardia marina Midshipman.

Hacienda The royal treasury or *exchequeir*; also, a large landed estate.

Informe An official report or brief.

Instituta The compendium of Roman civil law compiled at the order of Justinian; part of the civil curriculum.

Juez A judge.

Juez conservador A judge named to administer and protect a privileged establishment, such as an entail under royal control.

Juez letrado Judge on the House of Trade.

Juez mayor de Vizcaya A member of the Chancellery of Valladolid who heard cases involving Basques.

Juez privativo A judge charged with a specific or one-time function.

Juez superintendente A supervising or executive judge; the judge charged with administering a certain function.

Junta de comercio y moneda Forerunner of the *Junta general de comercio, moneda, y minas* (which see).

Junta de Guerra War committee associated with the Council of the Indies.

Junta general de comercio, moneda y minas The General Committee of Commerce, Currency and Mining established in 1747 when the former *Junta de comercio y moneda* was given responsibilities over mining.

Justicia mayor A high judicial post in Spain, largely honorific by Bourbon times; more generally, a judge in many cities.

Juzgado de obras y bosques Tribunal for criminal and civil cases occurring on property or in palaces belonging to the royal family.

Letrado A university-trained lawyer or holder of a law degree.

Limeño, -a A native of Lima.

Lugar Here, a small town, especially in the north of Spain, with privileges different from those of a *villa* (which see).

Lugarteniente Deputy or substitute; normally limited to a substitute in a high-ranking office.

Madrileño, -a A native of Madrid.

Maestre de campo A high-ranking militia officer; sometimes, an honorific without specific rank.

Manteista Here, a student or graduate from a Spanish university who was not affiliated with a *colegio mayor* (which see).

Marina Navy.

Mariscal de campo Field marshal.

Mayor An adjective denoting primary or senior status.

Mayorazgo An entail.

Mayordomo Majordomo.

Mayordomo mayor Head of the royal household.

Mayordomo de (la) semana Majordomo in the royal household during assigned weeks under the direction of the *mayordomo mayor* (which see).

Media anata A tax collected from certain government officials, consisting of a half year's salary.

Ministro asesor Here, a legal adviser to a body with judicial responsibilities.

Ministro de capa y espada A minister of the "cloak and sword" or "cape and sword"; here a councilor who was named to a position not designated for a *letrado* (which see).

Ministro togado A minister of the robe; one of two kinds of councilor on the Council of the Indies. An official who was also a *letrado* (which see).

Montepío The government-sponsored pension fund for dependents of deceased officials.

Notario Notary; often one who limited his practice to ecclesiastical affairs.

Nueva planta Term often applied to the most recent reorganization of a government body.

Número Here, a "regular" or statutory position on a council or other body.

Oficial Official; equivalent to a clerk in the British usage.

Oficial mayor The chief subordinate officer of a Secretariat of State, or of any agency or tribunal; the chief clerk or administrator; *oficial primero*, *oficial segundo*, and so forth as the rankings continue downward.

Oidor A judge on an audiencia or chancellery; on the viceregal tribunals of America and larger audiencias of Spain possessing civil functions only.

Paisano Countryman; native of the same region as another person.

Peso A silver coin valued at eight reales.

Plaza Here, a garrison.

Preeminencias A privilege or preeminence due to special merit; here the privilege given some Council ministers of attending meetings at their pleasure.

Prima The senior academic chair in a particular faculty; see also *vísperas*.

Primer caballerizo First equerry.

Primer teniente de asistente Here, the senior assistant to an *asistente* (which see).

Procurador general An official designated to defend the interests of a corporate group or institution.

Propios y rentas Here, the tax base for a municipality.

Protector y juez conservador See *juez conservador*.

Provisor A diocesan judge; a person with legal training selected by a bishop to preside over the episcopal court of law.

Pruebas Here, genealogical evidence or proofs required for entrance into a military or civil order.

Pulque A fermented drink in America, made from the juice of the agave or century plant.

Racionero One who held a *ración* or prebend in a Hispanic cathedral.

Real alcaidía del Pardo Territory of the Pardo, a royal property.

Real de vellón A unit of money worth thirty-four maravedis, minted from a mixture of silver and copper. It circulated only in Spain.

Real patronato Royal prerogative that included patronage over ecclesiastical positions; here the staff supporting the use of this prerogative.

Reducción Here, a community of Indians under the control of clerics and in the process of being "civilized."

Regente The regent, presiding officer of an audiencia in America after 1776.

Regidor An alderman or member of a town council.

Regidor perpetuo A lifetime town council member.

Relación de méritos Here, a document attesting to personal qualities and accomplishments presented in support of an appeal for a position or favor; a vita or résumé.

Relator An officer of a tribunal whose task it was to prepare briefs stating the case at hand.

Rentas, Rentas generales General revenues or taxes the Crown collected.

Rentas provinciales Provincial taxes paid to the Crown.

Repartimiento A partition or division, an assessment of taxes, the right to use Indian labor, or the forcing of European goods upon unwilling Indians.

Residencia A formal inquiry conduct at the end of an official's term of office.

Rey intruso The name Spaniards gave José Napoleon I.

Sala de alcaldes de casa y corte The chamber with criminal jurisdiction over Madrid and the royal court; the fifth chamber of the Council of Castile.

Sargento mayor A military officer, equivalent to a major.

Señor Originally one who held jurisdiction over a *señorío*, a gentleman or lord.

Señorío Seigniory; can include properties, titles, and jurisdiction.

Sevillano, -a A native of Seville, Spain.

Sexto Here, a collection of canonical decrees and rulings; a part of the curriculum of ecclesiastical law.

Sisas Excise tax levied on certain foodstuffs.

Suplente A substitute or alternate; substitute deputy at the Cortes of Cádiz.

Temporalidades Properties the Spanish took from the Jesuit order upon its expulsion from Spain and the colonies in 1767.

Teniente asesor This term, *teniente letrado*, *teniente gobernador* and *asesor ordinario* are more or less interchangeable. It describes a deputy and legal adviser to an executive, normally an intendant but often a governor or captain general.

Teniente de ayo Here, aide to the governor of a province.

Teniente de fragata Lieutenant in the navy.

Teniente gobernador A deputy governor.

Teniente gobernador y auditor de guerra A deputy governor and judge advocate for military affairs.

Tercio A military unit equivalent to a regiment; approximately three thousand men.

Tesorería mayor Central treasury.

Títulos y grados The record of one's academic accomplishments.

Togado A *letrado* (which see) or judge of a high court or council.

Ultramar Overseas.

Vallisoletano, -a A native of Valladolid, Spain.

Vecino, -a A property-owning, tax-paying town resident.

Vicario general A bishop's delegate.

Villa A town with privileges that differentiate it from a *lugar* (which see).

Visita An official inspection into the conduct of bureaucrats, usually totally unscheduled and unexpected.

Visitador The person empowered to conduct a *visita*.

Vísperas The junior chair in an academic faculty; see also *prima*.

Volumen A chair in civil law at certain Spanish universities.

BIBLIOGRAPHY

Agúndez Fernández, Antonio. *Juristas extremeños*. Palma de Mallorca, 1962.

Aiton, Arthur S. "Spanish Colonial Reorganization under the Family Compact," *The Hispanic American Historical Review*, Vol. 12 (August 1932), 269–80.

Alamán, Lucas. *Historia de Méjico*. 5 vols. 2nd ed. Mexico, 1968.

Alanis, Boyso, José Luis. *Elecciones de república para los pueblos del corregimiento de Toluca 1729–1811*. Mexico, 1978.

Alcocer Martínez, Mariano. *Historia de la Universidad de Valladolid*. 6 vols. Valladolid, 1918–30.

Alvarez de la Rivera M., Senén. *Biblioteca histórico-genealógica asturiana, "Libro de recepciones del Colegio de San Pelayo de Salamanca" manuscrito inédito*. Vol. 2. Santiago, Chile, 1928.

Alvarez y Baena, Joseph Antonio. *Hijos de Madrid, ilustres en sanidad, dignidades, armas, ciencias y artes. Diccionario histórico por el orden alfabético de sus nombres*. 4 vols. Madrid, 1789. Facsimile edition, Madrid, 1973.

Antón del Olmet, Fernando de. *El cuerpo diplomático español en la guerra de la independencia*. 6 vols. Madrid, 1912?–1914.

Archer, Christon I. *The Army in Bourbon Mexico, 1760–1810*. Albuquerque, N.Mex., 1977.

Arrangoiz, Francisco de Paula de. *México desde 1808 hasta 1867*. 2nd ed. Mexico, 1968.

Arribas Arranz, Filemon. *Relaciones y justificantes de méritos y servicios de catedráticos, profesores y opositores a catedras*. Valladolid, Spain, 1963.

Artola, Miguel. *Los afrancesados*. Madrid, 1953.

Astuto, Philip Louis. *Eugenio Espejo (1747–1795): reformador ecuatoriano de la ilustración*. Mexico, 1969.

Atienza, Julio de. *Nobiliario español. Diccionario heráldico de apellidos españoles y de títulos nobiliarios*. 2nd ed. Madrid, 1954.

Ballesteros Robles, Luis. *Diccionario biográfico matritense*. Madrid, 1912?

Bancroft, Hubert Howe. *The Works of Hubert Howe Bancroft*. Vol. 11. San Francisco, Calif. 1883.

Barbier, Jacques A. "The Culmination of the Bourbon Reforms, 1787–1792." *Hispanic American Historical Review*, Vol. 57, No. 1 (February 1977), 51–68.

Barbier, Jacques A. *Reform and Politics in Bourbon Chile 1755–1796*. Ottawa, 1980.

Baudrillart, Alfred. *Philippe V et la cour de France*. 5 vols. Paris, 1889–1901.

Beristain de Souza, José Mariano. *Biblioteca hispano-americana setentrional*. 3 vols. 2nd ed. Amecameca, Mexico, 1883.

Bernad, Miguel A., S.J. *The Christianization of the Philippines: Problems and Perspectives*. Manila, 1972.

Bernard, Gildas. "La Casa de Contratación de Sevilla, luego en Cádiz en el siglo XVIII." *Anuario de estudios americanos* (Sevilla), Vol 12 (1955), 253–86.

Bernard, Gildas. *Le secrétariat d'état et le conseil espagnol des Indies (1700–1808)*. Geneva, 1972.

Blair, Emma Helen, and James Alexander Robertson (eds.). *The Philippine Islands, 1492–1898*. 55 vols. Cleveland, 1903–9.

Brading, D. A. *Miners and Merchants in Bourbon Mexico 1763–1810*. Cambridge, Mass., 1971.

Burkholder, Mark A. "The Council of the Indies in the Late Eighteenth Century: A New Perspective." *Hispanic American Historical Review*, vol. 56, No. 3 (August 1976), 404–23.

Burkholder, Mark A., and D. S. Chandler. *Biographical Dictionary of Audiencia Ministers in the Americas, 1687–1821*. Westport, Conn., 1982.

Cabeza de León, Salvador, and Enrique Fernández Villamil. *Historia de la Universidad de Santiago de Compostela*. 3 vols. Santiago, Spain, 1945–47.

Cadenas y Vicent, Vicente de. *Caballeros de la orden de Santiago que efectuarón sus pruebas de ingreso durante el siglo XIX*. Madrid, 1958.

Calderón Quijano, José Antonio (ed.). *Los virreyes de Nueva España en el reinado de Carlos III*. 2 vols. Seville, 1967.

Calderón Quijano, José Antonio (ed.). *Los virreyes de Nueva España en el reinado de Carlos IV*. 2 vols. Seville, 1972.

Callahan, W. J. "Don Juan de Goyeneche: Industrialist of Eighteenth-Century Spain." *Business History Review*, Vol. 43 (1969), 152–70.

Campbell, Leon G. *The Military and Society in Colonial Peru 1750–1810*. Philadelphia, 1978.

Canella Secades, Fermín. *Historia de la Universidad de Oviedo y noticias de los establecimientos de enseñanza de su distrito*. Oviedo, 1873.

Carrera Andrade, Jorge. *El camino del sol: historia de un reino desaparecido*. Quito, Ecuador, 1959.

Castillo, Abel-Romeo. *Los gobernadores de Guayaquil del siglo XVIII (Notas para la historia de la ciudad durante los años de 1763 a 1803)*. Madrid, 1931.

Catalina, García, Juan. *Biblioteca de escritores de la provincia de Guadalajara y bibliografía de la misma hasta el siglo XIX*. Madrid, 1899.

Cooper, Donald B. *Epidemic Disease in Mexico City 1761–1813*. Austin, Tex., 1965.

Coxe, William. *Memoirs of the Kings of Spain of the House of Bourbon from the Accession of Philip the Fifth to the Death of Charles the Third: 1700 to 1788*. 3 vols. London, 1813.

Cunningham, Charles Henry. *The Audiencia in the Spanish Colonies as Illustrated by the Audiencia of Manila (1583–1800)*. Berkeley, 1919.

Cushner, Nicholas P. (ed.). *Documents Illustrating the British Conquest of Manila 1762–1763*. Vol. 8, Camden Fourth Series. London, 1971.

Cushner, Nicholas P. *Landed Estates in the Colonial Philippines*. New Haven, Conn., 1976.

Cushner, Nicholas P., S. J. (ed.). *Philippine Jesuits in Exile: The Journals of Francisco Puig, S.J., 1768–1770*. Rome, 1964.

Diario curioso de México de José Gómez, Cabo de Albarderos, in *Documentos para la historia de México.* Vol. 8. Mexico, 1854.

Diccionario de historia de España. 2nd ed. 3 vols. Madrid, 1968.

Enciclopedia universal ilustrado europeo-americana. 70 vols. Madrid, 1907?–1930.

Escudero, José Antonio. *Los orígenes del consejo de ministros en España.* 2 vols. Madrid, 1979.

Escudero, José Antonio. *Los secretarios de estado y del despacho (1474–1724).* 2nd ed. 4 vols. Madrid, 1976.

Espejo, Juan Luis. *Nobiliario de la Capitania General de Chile.* Santiago, Chile, 1967.

Esperabé Arteaga, Enrique. *Historia de la Universidad de Salamanca.* Vol. 2. *Maestros y alumnos más distinguidos.* Salamanca, 1917.

Farriss, N. M. *Crown and Clergy in Colonial Mexico 1759–1821.* London, 1968.

Fayard, Janine. *Les membres du Conseil de Castille a l'époque moderne, 1621–1746.* Geneva, 1979.

Fayard, Janine. *Los miembros del Consejo de Castilla (1621–1746).* Madrid, 1982.

Fernández de Recas, Guillermo S. *Mayorazgos de la Nueva España.* Mexico, 1965.

Fernández-Mensaque, Fernando Casado. "El tribunal de la acordada de Nueva España." *Anuario de estudios americanos,* Vol. 7 (1950), 279–323.

Ferrer Ezquerra, L., and H. Misol García. *Catálogo de colegiales del Colegio Mayor de Santiago del Cebedeo, del Arzobispo de Salamanca.* Salamanca, Spain, 1956.

Figueroa y Melgar, Alfonso de. *Estudio histórico sobre algunas familias españolas.* 5 vols. Madrid, 1965–74.

Fisher, J. R. *Government and Society in Colonial Peru: The Intendant System 1784–1814.* London, 1970.

Fisher, John. "Royalism, Regionalism, and Rebellion in Colonial Peru, 1808–1815." *Hispanic American Historical Review,* Vol. 59, No. 2 (May 1979), 232–57.

Flores y Caamaño, Alfredo. *Don José Mejía Lequerica en las cortes de Cádiz de 1810 a 1813.* Barcelona, n.d.

Gandía, Enrique de. *Orígenes desconocidos del 25 de mayo de 1810.* Buenos Aires, 1960.

García Carraffa, Alberto y Arturo. *Enciclopedia heráldica y genealógica hispano americana.* 88 vols. Madrid, 1919–63.

García Chuecos, Hector. *Estudios de historia colonial Venezolana.* 2 vols. Caracas, Venezuela, 1937–38.

Garrido Conde, María Teresa. "La primera creación del virreinato de Nueva Granada." *Anuario de estudios americanos,* Vol. 21 (1964), 25–144.

Gazeta de Madrid (1751–1808).

González García-Valladolid, Casimiro. *Datos para la historia biográfica de la M.L.M.N.H. y Excma. Ciudad de Valladolid.* 2 vols. Valladolid, 1893–94.

González Suárez, Federico. *Historia general de la República del Ecuador.* 7 vols. Quito, Ecuador, 1890–1903.

Guerra, Juan Primo de la. *Diario.* 2 vols. Tenerife, 1976.

Hamnett, Brian R. "The Mexican Bureaucracy before the Bourbon Reforms, 1700–1770: A Study in the Limitations of Absolutism." University of Glasgow, Institute of Latin American Studies, Occasional Papers No. 26, 1979.

Hamnett, Brian R. *Politics and Trade in Southern Mexico 1750–1821.* Cambridge, Mass., 1971.

Hamnett, Brian R. *Revolución y contrarevolución en México y el Perú (liberalismo, realeza y separatismo 1800–1824).* Mexico, 1978.

Hernández Franco, Juan. *La gestión político y el pensamiento reformista del Conde de Floridablanca.* Murcia, 1984.

Hildner, Ernest G. Jr. "The Role of the South Sea Company in the Diplomacy Leading to the War of Jenkins' Ear, 1729–39." *Hispanic American Historical Review*, Vol. 17, No. 3 (August 1938), 322–41.

Howe, Walter. *The Mining Guild of New Spain and Its Tribunal General 1770–1821*. Cambridge, Mass., 1949.

Hussey, Roland Dennis. *The Caracas Company 1728–1784: A Study in the History of Spanish Monopolistic Trade*. Cambridge, Mass., 1934.

Ibarra, Javier. *Biografías de los ilustres navarros del siglo XVII*. Vols. 2–4. Pamplona, 1951–53.

"Indice de documentos del volumen de 1714." *Boletín del Archivo Nacional de Historia* (Ecuador), Vol. 4, No. 6 (January–December 1956), 33–63.

Instituto Internacional de Genealogia y Heraldica. *Armería y nobiliario de los reinos españoles*. 4 vols. Madrid, 1955–60.

Instituto Panamericano de Geografía e Historia. *Conjuración de 1808 en Caracas para la formación de una junta suprema gobernativa*. Caracas, Venezuela, 1949.

Kamen, Henry. *Spain in the Later Seventeenth Century, 1665–1700*. London and New York, 1980.

Konetzke, Richard (ed.). *Colección de documentos para la historia de la formación social de Hispanoamérica, 1493–1810*. 3 vols. Madrid, 1953–62.

Kuethe, Allan J. *Military Reform and Society in New Granada, 1773–1808*. Gainesville, Fla., 1978.

Ladd, Doris M. *The Mexican Nobility at Independence 1780–1826*. Austin, Tex., 1976.

Lafuente Ferrari, Enrique. *El virrey Iturrigaray y los orígenes de la independencia de Méjico*. Madrid, 1941.

Lanning, John Tate. *The Diplomatic History of Georgia: A Study of the Epoch of Jenkins' Ear*. Chapel Hill, N.C., 1936.

Lanning, John Tate. *The Eighteenth-Century Enlightenment in the University of San Carlos de Guatemala*. Ithaca, N.Y., 1956.

Lanz de Casafonda, Manuel. *Diálogos de Chindulza (sobre el estado de la cultura española en el reinado de Fernando VI)*. Ed. by Francisco Aguilar Piñal. Oviedo, 1972.

Larios Martín, Jesús. *Nobiliario de Segovia*. 5 vols. Segovia, 1956–67.

Leonard, Irvin A. (Trans. and Intro.). *Spanish Approach to Pensacola*, 1689–1693. Albuquerque, N.Mex., 1939.

Levene, Ricardo. *Historia de la nación argentina (desde los orígenes hasta la organización definitiva en 1862)*. 10 vols. Buenos Aires, 1936–42.

Lewis, James A. "Anglo-American entrepreneurs in Havana: the background and significance of the expulsion of 1784–85." In Jacques A. Barbier and Allan J. Kuethe, eds. *The North American role in the Spanish Imperial economy 1760–1819*. Manchester, England, 1984.

Lohmann Villena, Guillermo. *Los americanos en las órdenes nobiliarias* (1529–1900). 2 vols. Madrid, 1947.

Lohmann Villena, Guillermo. *Los ministros de la audiencia de Lima en el reinado de los Borbones (1700–1821)*. Seville, 1974.

Lohmann Villena, Guillermo. *Las relaciones de los virreyes del Perú*. Seville, 1959.

López, Vicente F. *Historia de la República Argentina: su origen su revolución y su desarrollo político hasta 1852*. 10 vols. 4th ed. Buenos Aires, 1926.

López Sarrelangue, Delfina E. *Una villa mexicana en el siglo XVIII*. Mexico, 1957.

Lovett, Gabriel H. *Napoleon and the Birth of Modern Spain*. 2 vols. New York, 1965.

Luque Alcaide, Elisa. *La sociedad económica de amigos del país de Guatemala*. Seville, 1962.

Lynch, John. *Spanish Colonial Administration, 1782–1810: The Intendant System in the Viceroyalty of the Río de la Plata*. New York, 1969.

McLachlan, Jean O. *Trade and Peace with Old Spain, 1667–1750: A Study of the Influence of Commerce on Anglo-Spanish Diplomacy in the First Half of the Eighteenth Century*. Cambridge, Eng., 1940.

MacLachlan, Colin M. *Criminal Justice in Eighteenth Century Mexico: A Study of the Tribunal of the Acordada*. Berkeley, Calif., 1974.

Magdaleno, Ricardo (ed.). *Títulos de Indias: Catálogo XX del Archivo General de Simancas*. Valladolid, 1954.

Mariluz Urquijo, José M. *El virreinato del Río de la Plato en la época del Marqués de Avilés (1799–1801)*. Buenos Aires, 1964.

Markman, Sidney David (ed.). *Colonial Central America: A Bibliography*. Tempe, Ariz., 1977.

Matilla Tascón, Antonio. *Las rentas vitalicias en el siglo XVIII. Inventario*. Madrid, 1980.

Martínez Cosío, Leopoldo. *Los caballeros de las órdenes militares en México*. Mexico, 1946.

Matute y Gaviria, Justin. *Hijos de Sevilla señalados en santidad, letras, armas, artes o dignidad*. 2 vols. Seville, 1886–87.

Medina, José Toribio. *Biblioteca Hispano-americana (1493–1810)*. 7 vols. Edición facsimilar, Santiago, Chile, 1960.

Medina, José Toribio. *Diccionario biográfico colonial de Chile*. Santiago, Chile, 1906.

Medina, José Toribio. *La imprenta en Manila desde su orígenes hasta 1810*. Santiago, Chile, 1896.

Medina, José Toribio. *La imprenta en Quito (1760–1818)*. Santiago, Chile, 1904.

Mejía Ricart, Gustavo Adolfo. *Historia de Santo Domingo*. 8 vols. Ciudad Trujillo, Dominican Republic, 1948–56.

Mendiburu, Manuel de. *Diccionario histórico-biográfico del Perú*. 8 vols. Lima, 1874–90.

Meyer, Harvey K. *Historical Dictionary of Nicaragua*. Latin American Historical Dictionaries, No. 6. Metuchen, N.J., 1976.

Millares Carlo, Agustín. *Ensayo de una bio-bibliografía de escritores naturales de las Islas Canarias (siglos XVI, XVII, y XVIII)*. Madrid, 1932.

Miranda, José. *Humboldt y México*. Mexico, 1962.

Molas Ribalta, Pere. "Magistrados valencianos en el siglo XVIII." In *Mayans y la ilustración*. Oliva, Spain, 1982. Pp. 81–122.

Navarro García, Luis. *Intendencias en Indias*. Seville, 1959.

Navarro García, Luis. "La sublevación Yaqui de 1740." *Anuario de estudios americanos*, Vol. 22 (1965), 373–531.

Nelson, George H. "Contraband Trade under the Asiento, 1730–1739." *American Historical Review*, Vol. 51, No. 1 (October 1945), 55–67.

Nogaledo Alvarez, Santiago. "El Colegio Menor de 'Pan y Carbón,' primero de los colegios universitarios de Salamanca (1386–1780)." *Acta Salamanticensia, Historia de la Universidad*, Vol. 1, No. 4 (1958), 1–181.

Núñez y Domínguez, José de J. *La virreina mexicana: Doña María Francisca de la Gandara de Calleja*. Mexico, 1950.

Ozanam, Didier (ed.). *La diplomacia de Fernando VI. Correspondencia reservada entre D. José de Carvajal y el Duque de Huescar, 1746–1749*. Madrid, 1975.

Palacio Atard, Vicente. "Areche y Guirior. Observaciones sobre el fracaso de una visita al Perú." *Anuario de estudios americanos*, Vol. 3 (1946), 269–376.

Pardo de Tavera, T. H. *Biblioteca Filipinas*. Washington, D.C., 1903.

Pérez Balsera, José. *Los caballeros de Santiago*. 7 Vols. Madrid, 1932–36.

Pérez-Marchand, Monelisa Lina. *Dos etapas ideológicas del siglo XVIII en Mexico a través de los papeles de la Inquisición*. Mexico, 1945.

Pérez Valenzuela, Pedro. *La Nueva Guatemala de la Asunción: terremoto de Santa Marta—fundación en el Llano de la Virgen*. Guatemala, 1934.

Phelan, John Leddy. *The People and the King: The Comunero Revolution in Columbia, 1781*. Madison, Wisc., 1978.

Price, Jacob M. *France and the Chesapeake: A History of the French Tobacco Monopoly, 1674–1791, and Its Relationship to the British and American Tobacco Trades*. 2 vols. Ann Arbor, Mich., 1973.

Priestley, Herbert Ingram. *José de Gálvez: Visitor-General of New Spain (1765–1771)*. Berkeley, Calif., 1916.

Real Academia de la Historia. *Catálogo de la Colección "Pellicer," antes denominada "grandezas de España."* 4 vols. Madrid, 1957–1960.

Restrepo Sáenz, José María. *Biografías de los mandatarios y ministros de la real audiencia (1671 a 1819)*. Bogota, Colombia, 1952.

Rezabal y Ugarte, Josef de. *Biblioteca de los escritores que han sido individuos de los seis colegios mayores*. Madrid, 1805.

Rodríguez García, Vicente. "El fiscal Posada: indice para una biografía." *Anuario de estudios americanos*, Vol. 34 (1977), 187–210.

Roxas y Contreras, Joseph de. *Historia del colegio viejo de San Bartolomé, mayor de la celebre Universidad de Salamanca, vida del excmo. y Rmo. Sr. D. Diego de Anaya y Maldonado . . . Primera parte escrita por D. Francisco Ruiz de Vergara . . . corregida y aumentada . . . por Joseph de Rojas y Contreras, marqués de Alventos*. 3 vols. Madrid, 1766–1770.

Rubio y Borrás, Manuel. *Historia de la Real y Pontificia Universidad de Cervera*. 2 vols. Barcelona, 1915–16.

Rújula y de Ochotorena, José de. *Indice de los colegiales del mayor de San Ildefonso y menores de Alcalá*. Madrid, 1946.

Rumazo González, José. *Documentos para la historia de la audiencia de Quito*. 9 vols. Madrid, 1948–50.

Samayoa Guevara, Hector Humberto. *Los gremios de artesanos en la ciudad de Guatemala (1524–1821)*. Guatemala, 1962.

Sarrailh, Jean. *La España Ilustrada de la segunda mitad del siglo XVIII*. Trans. by Antonio de Alatorre. Mexico, 1957.

Schäfer, Ernesto. *El consejo real y supremo de las Indias*. 2 vols. Seville, 1935–47.

Schurz, William Lytle. *The Manila Galleon*. New York, 1959.

Sempere y Guarinos, Juan. *Ensayo de una biblioteca española de los mejores escritores del reynado de Carlos III*. 6 vols. Madrid, 1785–89. Facsimile edition, Madrid, 1969.

Shafer, Robert Jones. *The Economic Societies in the Spanish World (1763–1821)*. Syracuse, N.Y., 1958.

Silva i Molina, Abraham de. *Oidores de la real audiencia de Chile durante el siglo XVII*. Santiago, Chile, 1903.

Solís, Ramón. *El Cádiz de las Cortes*. Madrid, 1969.

Steele, Arthur Robert. *Flowers for the King: The Expedition of Ruiz and Pavon and the Flora of Peru*. Durham, N.C., 1964.

Stoetzer, O. Carlos. *The Scholastic Roots of the Spanish American Revolution*. New York, 1979.

Tejera y R. de Moncada, José Pío. *Biblioteca del murciano o ensayo de un diccionario biográfico y bibliográfico de la literatura en Murcia*. Madrid, 1922.

Toreno, José María Queipo de Llano, Count. *Historia del levantamiento, guerra y revolución de España. Biblioteca de Autores Espanoles, LXIV.* Madrid, 1953.

Tovar Velarde, Jorge. "La audiencia de Lima 1705–1707: Dos años de gobierno criollo en el Perú." *Revista histórica* (Lima), Vol. 23 (1957–58), 338–453.

Trelles y Govín, Carlos Manuel. *Bibliografía cubana del siglo XIX.* 8 vols. Matanzas, Cuba, 1911–15.

Trelles y Govín, Carlos Manuel. *Ensayo de bibliografía cubana de los siglos XVII y XVIII.* Matanzas, Cuba, 1907.

Tutino, John Mark. "Creole Mexico: Spanish Elites, Haciendas and Indian Towns, 1750–1810." Unpub. Ph.D. thesis, Austin, Tex., 1976.

Twinan, Ann. "Enterprise and Elites in Eighteenth-Century Medellin." *Hispanic American Historical Review*, Vol. 59, No. 3 (August 1979), 444–75.

Udaondo, Enrique. *Diccionario biográfico colonial argentino.* Buenos Aires, 1945.

Valgoma y Díaz-Varela, Dalmiro de la. *La nobleza de León en la Orden de Carlos III.* Madrid, 1946.

Válgoma y Díaz-Varela, Dalmiro de la. *Mecenas de libros su heráldica y nobleza.* Vol. 1. Burgos, 1966.

Vargas Ugarte, Rubén, S. J. *Biblioteca peruano.* Vols. 8–10. *Impresos peruanos.* Lima, 1954–56.

Vargas Ugarte, Rubén, S. J. *Historia General del Perú.* 6 vols. Lima, 1966.

Vargas Ugarte, Rubén, S. J. *Títulos nobiliarios en el Perú.* 4th ed. Lima, 1965.

Vignau, Vicente. *Indice de pruebas de los caballeros de la real y distinguida órden española de Carlos III desde su institución hasta el año 1847.* Madrid, 1904.

Vignau, Vicente, and Francisco R. de Uhagón. *Indice de pruebas de los caballeros que han vestido el hábito de Santiago desde el año 1501 hasta la fecha.* Madrid, 1901.

Vignau y Ballester, Vicente. *Indice de pruebas de los caballeros que han vestido el hábito de Calatrava, Alcántara y Montesa desde el siglo XVI hasta la fecha.* Madrid, 1903.

Weddle, Robert S. *Wilderness Manhunt: The Spanish Search for La Salle.* Austin, Tex., and London, 1973.

Whitaker, Arthur Preston. *The Huancavelica Mercury Mine: A Contribution to the History of the Bourbon Renaissance in the Spanish Empire.* Cambridge, Mass., 1941.

Zilbermann Morales, María Cristina and Jorge Luján Muñoz. "Santiago de Guatemala en víspera de los terremotos de 1773." *Anuario de estudios americanos*, Vol. 32 (1975), 541–71.

Zúñiga, Neptala. *Juan Pío Montúfar y Larrea.* Quito, Ecuador, 1945.

INDEX

Note: An asterisk (*) after a name indicates that there is an entry on that person in this work.

About the Author

MARK A. BURKHOLDER is Professor of History at the University of Missouri-St. Louis. He is the author of *Biographical Dictionary of Audiencia Ministers in the Americas, 1687–1821* (Greenwood Press, 1982), *From Impotence to Authority: The Spanish Crown and the American Audiencias, 1687–1808,* both with D. S. Chandler, and the *Politics of a Colonial Career.* He has contributed articles to the *Hispanic American Historical Review* and the *Journal of Latin American Studies.*